On the Road with Outreach

Mobile Library Services

Jeannie Dilger-Hill and Erica MacCreaigh, Editors

LIBRARIES UNLIMITED
An Imprint of ABC-CLIO, LLC

A B C · C L I O

Santa Barbara, California • Denver, Colorado • Oxford, England

Copyright 2010 by Libraries Unlimited

All rights reserved. No part of this publication may be reproduced,
stored in a retrieval system, or transmitted, in any form or by any means,
electronic, mechanical, photocopying, recording, or otherwise, except for
the inclusion of brief quotations in a review, without prior permission
in writing from the publisher.

Library of Congress Cataloging-in-Publication Data
   On the road with outreach : mobile library services / Jeannie Dilger-Hill
and Erica MacCreaigh, editors.
       p. cm.
   Includes bibliographical references and index.
   ISBN 978-1-59158-678-4 (acid-free paper)   1. Bookmobiles.   2. Library outreach
programs—United States—Case studies.   3. Library outreach programs—Canada—
Case studies.   I. Dilger-Hill, Jeannie.   II. MacCreaigh, Erica.
   Z686.O62   2010
   027.4'2—dc22   2009034430

14   13   12   11   10   1   2   3   4   5

This book is also available on the World Wide Web as an eBook.
Visit www.abc-clio.com for details.

ABC-CLIO, LLC
130 Cremona Drive, P.O. Box 1911
Santa Barbara, California 93116-1911

This book is printed on acid-free paper ∞
Manufactured in the United States of America

Contents

PART II: LIBRARY OUTREACH, A COMMUNITY COMMITMENT

PART III: LIBRARY OUTREACH TO CHILDREN

PART IV: LIBRARY OUTREACH TO SENIORS AND HOMEBOUND

PART V: LIBRARY OUTREACH TO THE INCARCERATED

PART VI: ALL ABOUT OUTREACH VEHICLES

Preface

Welcome to *On the Road with Outreach!* This book promises to be your guide for years to come.

Mobile libraries, appropriately called bookmobiles, are in fact, *libraries on wheels,* available in the United States for over 100 years. And thank goodness, for without them thousands and thousands of families would be without valued access to library services. I often hear, "I remember going on bookmobiles when I was a child!" from those who have experienced the joy of this memorable library service!

Just as public libraries serve local communities of all sizes, so do these libraries reach out to those with travel challenges to the same library locations. Bookmobiles may travel on country roads and highways to schools and day care centers, to senior centers and nursing homes, and to hospitals, jails, and prisons. Their services may include providing access to resources for adults who are new readers or non-readers, to people with low incomes or experiencing homelessness, to people with disabilities, to older adults, to people who speak English as a second language, or those living in rural or small communities where library services are not available.

I first met the editors, Jeannie Dilger-Hill and Erica MacCreaigh, and the many contributing authors of this book, at annual conferences of the Association of Bookmobile and Outreach Services (ABOS) and the American Library Association (ALA). Their dedication to their local library communities and the seriousness of their focus on effective delivery of services impressed and challenged my office to support them with our resources.

What I soon learned was that *they* were the real experts in outreach, and that their experiences and the resources they have developed must be shared with others across the country. In these pages are detailed procedures, tools, and tips that make the wheels go round in a myriad of situations that are routine to most library outreach staff.

Thanks to all of the contributors to this important publication, now these valuable resources are yours to learn and share and utilize in your library communities as well!

Satia Marshall Orange
Director (Retired), Office for Literacy & Outreach Services (OLOS)
American Library Association
www.ala.org/olos

Acknowledgments

We dedicate this book to the memory of Carol Hole and with great appreciation for Bernard Vavrek and John Philip. Their expertise and leadership raised the status of outreach librarianship and laid the foundation for the formation and success of the Association of Bookmobile and Outreach Services. Their contributions to our profession cannot be overstated.

We also want to acknowledge the expertise, gracious sacrifice of time and effort, and patience of the chapter authors. They dealt with many delays ("Is there still going to BE a book?") and last minute deadlines with nary a complaint. This book is truly their work and all the better for it.

And finally, we wish to thank our spouses. Without their support and encouragement, this book would not have been possible.

Introduction

By Jeannie Dilger-Hill and Erica MacCreaigh

It's rare that anyone comes to public library outreach with all the skills and knowledge to provide the full spectrum of possible services. Even those with a library background often find themselves at a loss when changing jobs or expanding services.

On the Road with Outreach editors Jeannie Dilger-Hill and Erica MacCreaigh know exactly what that feels like. When Dilger-Hill took her first job as Outreach Services Manager for Monroe County (IN) Public Library, all her library experience was in Youth Services. She knew a lot about designing programs and selecting books for children, but nothing about programming or collection development on a bookmobile. MacCreaigh came aboard the Arapahoe (CO) Library District bookmobile after several years in adult and correctional library services. She knew a lot about collection development, adult programming, and security, but nothing about children's services or providing service with a collection smaller than 14,000 volumes. And certainly, neither of us knew a thing about roof vents, inverters, generators, and air brakes.

We needed to know how to identify bookmobile service sites (called stops in bookmobile parlance), how to identify community gatekeepers and set up services, how to keep very small but heavily used collections fresh, how to automate our bookmobile and jail libraries, and how to provide public library-style programs on the road.

Literature searches turned up little current information, particularly of the how-to variety. Almost two decades earlier, Scarecrow Press had published *The Book Stops Here: New Directions for Bookmobile Service*, edited by Catherine Suyak Alloway. For years considered the bible of mobile outreach, it had become dated as public libraries embraced new technologies and prioritized more services to underserved populations.

During the earliest years of the new century, annual conferences of the newly formed Association for Bookmobile and Outreach Services pointed to the need for a new bible, a comprehensive how-to-do-it manual of public library outreach services. Like MacCreaigh and Dilger-Hill, public library outreach staff everywhere were clamoring for information about outreach to seniors, childcares, immigrants, urban and rural communities, low-income populations, prisoners, and other groups traditionally underserved by public libraries.

Fortunately, in the absence of such a resource, shortly after beginning her tenure in outreach, Dilger-Hill discovered an electronic mailing list known as the bookmobile listserv. Run by Clarion University's Center for Rural Librarianship at the time when electronic mailing lists were just getting started, the listserv sought to provide networking opportunities for bookmobilers around the country, and soon around the world. This small but dedicated group of people was very generous with their time, answering her most basic questions and welcoming her as a colleague. She began to figure out just exactly what she was supposed to be doing.

A few years later, after she had some experience under her belt, Dilger-Hill began to notice a trend. Those people on the listserv who really knew what they were doing and had all the answers were retiring or moving on to non-outreach library positions. And their wealth of knowledge was going with them. Newcomers to the list (including MacCreaigh, whose outreach supervisor introduced her to the listserv before showing her the bookmobile schedule) began asking the same questions Dilger-Hill had asked not that long ago. Soon (sooner than she would have liked), Dilger-Hill was one of the senior members of the list.

Thus the idea for this book was born. Dilger-Hill wanted to capture the knowledge of those with experience in public library outreach. And she wanted to provide a how-to manual for those just entering outreach for the first time. MacCreaigh, who had recently completed *Library Services to the Incarcerated* and just accepted a consulting position with the Colorado State Library, was eager to learn more about general library outreach and contribute her writing experience to the project.

All we needed now were authors.

On the Road with Outreach assembles a chorus of experts in public library outreach. The authors contributing to this volume represent the best of the best, hailing from across the United States and Canada. Most have years of experience in their field; a few are newer service providers of demonstrated excellence, enthusiasm, and innovation. All belong to a passionate and creative group of librarians and outreach service providers fully committed to making sure no patrons are left behind just because they lack access to a traditional brick-and-mortar library.

On the Road with Outreach focuses on the practicalities of establishing and maintaining mobile library services to various populations. It is divided into six thematic clusters. The first cluster, comprised of Chapters 1–3, covers several aspects of management, including planning and marketing outreach library services, supervising outreach library staff, and managing library collections.

The second cluster, consisting of Chapters 4–6, addresses a variety of general outreach service models for communities comprised of people of all ages, including bookmobile service to rural towns, suburbs and cities, and library programs and services to immigrants and non-English speakers.

Chapters 7 and 8 comprise the third cluster. These chapters cover mobile library services to children, including preschoolers in childcare settings and older children in schools.

The fourth cluster, Chapters 9–11, is all about outreach to seniors. Three service models are featured: books-by-mail, homebound delivery, and lobby stop services.

Chapters 12 and 13 round out the service clusters, spotlighting both on-site and outreach library services to incarcerated adults and juveniles.

The sixth cluster, Chapters 14–16, is all about vehicles, because no outreach service can run without them. Here you learn how to design your vehicle and write your vehicle specifications. You learn about vehicle maintenance and how to automate your vehicle for circulation and Internet access.

Though we've rolled it into the sixth cluster, Chapter 17 actually stands alone. In this chapter, you learn about how the latest mobile communications technologies can be used to fully automate any bookmobile.

Throughout the book and in the appendices, you will find an exhaustive selection of sample forms and information resources most requested on the Association of Bookmobile and Outreach Services listserv. These include bookmobile specifications, sample service agreements, contracts, applications, vehicle checklists, and many, many other working documents.

Because of its broad scope, we expect most readers will find something of interest in this volume. That said, our authors were asked to speak directly to librarians, paraprofessionals, and even volunteers currently working in public library outreach. Our secondary audience is administrators, library directors, and other decision-makers at any level wishing to initiate new outreach services in their community.

With publication slated to coincide with the ninth anniversary of the formation of the Association of Bookmobile and Outreach Services (now an American Library Association affiliate) and freshly revised bookmobile guidelines (see Appendix A), this book stands as a testament to a century of dedicated advocacy and effort by outreach librarians everywhere. We wish you all safe travels and look forward to seeing you out on the road!

Part I

Managing Library Outreach

Supporting Statements

An example of how an outreach mission supports the mission of the library as a whole can be found at Arapahoe (CO) Library District. The District's overarching mission statement is, "We are dedicated to being the best public library for the communities we serve by providing outstanding and personalized service to everyone seeking access to the world of information and ideas" (Arapahoe Library District). The mission of the Outreach department, while informal, addresses its purpose in supporting the mission of the entire District: "We provide regularly scheduled library service to all residents of Arapahoe County whose physical isolation prevents them from independently utilizing the informational and recreational resources of Arapahoe Library District . . . physical isolation refers to people who are either physically limited, such as housebound people or jail inmates, or geographically isolated, whose lack of public transportation or living too far from a library branch would make it difficult, if not impossible, for them to have access to library services" (Walker, 2008).

By specifying its target service population as those who might be left out of the District's mission without help, the Outreach department completes the District's mission to provide service to *everyone*.

the director of the need. Regardless of whether or not your director leads this effort, planning within the outreach department is still essential.

Establishing Your Mission

Claudia Zimmerman, Head of Extension Services at the Holmes County (OH) District Public Library, sums up the importance of planning in this way: "My philosophy has always been that you need to know where you want to go, or you spin your wheels and never grow." You should be able to clearly articulate what you are trying to accomplish by providing outreach services. This is your mission. Your library as a whole should have a mission. If not, make sure you and your director are in agreement about your outreach department's purpose. Everything you plan for and do in outreach should speak to your mission.

Evaluating Your Current Situation

Existing Services

Most of us have inherited an outreach service that already exists, and probably much of it already works well. Still, good planning involves continual evaluation of current services. Here are some questions to ask: How did this service evolve? How did it start? Why do we do it this way? (Beware of the response, "We've always done it this way.")

Look at the level of activity at current bookmobile stops. What are the trends? What do increases or decreases in attendance or circulation say about how well your services are meeting the community's needs?

SWOT Analysis

SWOT analysis is a tool useful in many areas of planning. Essentially, it gives you a snapshot of where you are and any assets and detriments in achieving your objectives:

- *Strengths*: attributes of the organization that are helpful to achieving the objective

- *Weaknesses: attributes of the organization that are harmful to achieving the objective
- *Opportunities: *external* conditions that are helpful to achieving the objective
- *Threats: *external* conditions which could do damage to the business's performance

Determining SWOT for each of your outreach objectives helps you map out your action plan. More on action plans is covered later in this chapter.

Funding

A common complaint is, "We don't have the money to do these things!!" Who does? But that doesn't mean they can't be done. Look at what it will take to accomplish your objectives, both in the short term and over time. If the library doesn't have the money, you will also need to consider outside funding sources, including grants and donors.

When you do apply for funding, many grantors want to know about sustainability—that is, how are you going to keep the program going after the term of the grant expires? You need to plan for this. Too many libraries take on a project for one year, only to abandon it because there is no plan (and no money) to continue it. It's better to start small and sustainably than dive into a big project with no long-term sustainability plan.

Identifying Who Lives in Your Community

You may think you know who is out there, but you might be very, very wrong. Communities change over time, and many communities that have been very stable may change when faced with the challenges of an increasingly aging population, an influx of new Americans, or more young families.

It isn't just about demographics. However, demographics are a good and an important place to start. Even though the full census is only every 10 years, more frequent studies are done in many communities, making more recent information readily available. Some important demographics to consider include social and economic characteristics, and specific information on the population such as age, origin, language, education, and income. The U.S. Census Bureau has an excellent, searchable Web site at http://factfinder.census.gov.

Take a look at the larger community, especially new residential developments. Have new housing developments been built recently? Who is living there? What about assisted living complexes? Go visit these places. Talk to the administrators and the residents. It can also be very helpful to contact the local Board of Education. Local public school boards keep many statistics on their students, including how

Finding Funding

The Arapahoe (CO) Library District started its "Begin with Books" early literacy project with funding from the Friends Foundation. Over time, as the program developed a proven track record of success, more and more of the program was included in the library's operating budget.

because even misinformation can be useful. Remember, it's not the library you want to focus on; it's the needs of the community.

Surveys

Surveys are another way to gather information. You can do paper surveys, or use any number of inexpensive Web-based survey tools, like Survey Monkey. Either way, someone needs to conduct the survey and analyze the results.

Setting Priorities

What you learn from members of the community will help guide your plan. Ask them what they think is most important. While they will not dictate your final plan, any input you get is important. You will then have to decide which services are most desired by your community and most feasible for your library, and the resources you will need in order to provide these services. Once you have collected all your input, it is time to put your plan together.

Writing Goals and Objectives the SMART Way

You have probably heard about goals and objectives, but writing them can be intimidating. The reason it is important to write goals and objectives is that they keep you focused. You know that "to do" list you have at home? While a bit more complex, goals and objectives serve pretty much the same purpose. When you identify your priorities and set specific goals for achieving your objectives, you are more likely to accomplish them. You also provide greater clarity among staff as to what you expect of them. Written goals and objectives help get everyone on the same page.

What's the difference between a goal and an objective? That's a good question and confusing for many people. Usually, a goal is more general, an objective more specific. *Strategic Planning for Results* (Nelson, 2008) defines goals and objectives in this way:

> **Goal:** The benefit your community (or a target population within your community) will receive because the library provides a specific service response.
> **Objective:** The way the library will measure its progress toward reaching a goal.

Another way to think of this is that in the goal, the focus is on the community *impact* of the service. In the objective, the focus is on the library's *actions* toward providing the service.

Objectives are more effective if they are SMART, an acronym that stands for Specific, Measurable, Attainable, Relevant, and Timely. An objective should be as *specific* as possible. It should be very clear what the expectations are and who is responsible for achieving the objective. You also need to know when you have achieved the objective and for this reason an objective needs to be *measurable*. Next, is the objective *attainable?* Is it realistic to expect staff to achieve it or is it impossible? If an objective is not attainable, then it will likely be ignored. A *relevant* objective relates back to the mission of your outreach service. And finally, you must specify the *time* period in which an objective will be accomplished. Saying, "I will begin an exercise program Monday" may be more attainable than "I will begin an exercise program soon." Establishing a timeline for completion of an objective makes it easier for staff to manage their time and ensure success in achieving the objectives.

Developing an Action Plan

This is the nitty-gritty of your plan. An action plan is made up of tactics or strategies, which are what you will actually do to complete each objective. Tactics are about as concrete as you can get; the more specific, the better. It is

---

SMART Action Plan

Objective: The Children's Department under the direction of the department supervisor will implement an Early Literacy Program for babies and parents by July 1, 2010, to include partnerships with other organizations serving the same audience.

Tactics:

- John Q. and Jane D. will research models of early literacy programs and submit recommendations to the department supervisor by April 1, 2010.
- Pat C. will contact community organizations serving babies and parents and submit a partnership proposal to department supervisor by April 1, 2010.
- Mary M. will investigate funding and, upon department supervisor's approval, will secure funding for pilot program by May 1, 2010.
- Children's Department staff will implement pilot program during June 2010.
- Jane D. will compile results of pilot program and submit report to department supervisor by July 7, 2010.
- Department supervisor will evaluate results of pilot program and submit report to Library Director by July 15, 2010.

---

also helpful to include who will be responsible and when each tactic will be accomplished.

This is a merely a broad overview of the planning process, and there are certainly different ways to go about planning for outreach services in your community. But, if you remember nothing else, remember this. The most effective planning is community-based, not library-based. And, if you know what you want to do and you develop SMART goals, objectives, and action steps (tactics), you will be much more successful in getting where you want to be.

MARKETING

It takes much more effort than people realize to get the word out about what's going on in the library. How many times have you said, "Oh, I didn't know about that," only to find out whatever "that" was had been advertised all over the place, but you just didn't see it? And what exactly is marketing, anyway? Is it selling, advertising, public relations, or publicity? Actually, all these terms are related to marketing. Marketing is, according to the *Field Guide to Nonprofit Program Design, Marketing and Evaluation*, "the wide range of activities involved in making sure that you're continuing to meet the needs of your customers and getting value in return" (McNamara, 2003).

So, you have planned wonderful outreach services that meet the needs of your community. Now you need to let people know about them. If you build a great bookmobile, there's no guarantee that patrons will come if you don't market the service. Many of us in library land think that the public *should* know about us, and we are surprised when

One year, we offered interested staff a ride on our mobile library van. It was only around the parking lot, but we gave free popcorn and people had a great time, and it definitely made an impact!

Press Releases

A press release tells the media about news you wish to share. It is very straightforward. An example of a press release appears at the end of this chapter.

In writing a press release, be sure to include all contact information at the top of the release. A catchy headline is important because the media receives many press releases each day and will often select what looks most interesting. Be sure to put what is most important at the beginning of the release. If it sounds very interesting, you may get a call from a reporter who wants to do an article. Most times, though, the newspaper will print the information in your press release in a community calendar. (See Additional Resources at the end of this chapter for a sample press release.)

If you have a communications or marketing department, they will usually work with the media, but you still need to provide the information to them so they can get it out. Often they will be the direct media contact, but will sometimes bring you in for more information.

Working with the Media

Often a press release is not enough, so it is important to develop relationships with the local media. The local newspaper, if you still have one, is a good place to start. Find out who to contact there. Small newspapers often have high turnover, so it does not hurt to call regularly to remind reporters of what's going on in the library. Often, they will agree to print your bookmobile schedule each month at no cost or a reduced rate.

CONCLUSION

This chapter is intended to help get you started, to give you a framework for planning and marketing as a whole, and to get you thinking about how to go about it in your outreach department. Naturally, entire books are devoted to these subjects; see the Resources section at the end of this chapter for some suggestions.

The importance of planning for outreach services cannot be overemphasized, and taking the time to plan will pay off in providing not just appropriate, but customer-focused services. Planning and marketing your services will help you achieve a successful outreach program, of which your library can be proud.

REFERENCES

Carter McNamara, *Field Guide to Nonprofit Program Design, Marketing and Evaluation* (Minneapolis: Authenticity Consulting, 2003).

Jan Meadows, *From Outreach to Equity: Innovative Models of Library Policy and Practice*, ed. Robin Osborne (Chicago: American Library Association, 2004).

Sarah Nelson, *Strategic Planning for Results,* rev. ed. (Chicago: American Library Association, 2008).

"Our Vision, Values and Mission," Arapahoe Library District. Available at: http://www.arapa hoelibraries.org.

"SWOT analysis," http://consulting.about.com/od/glossaryfaq/g/CF_SWOT.htm

Donna Walker, e-mail message to Candice Brown, 2008.

ADDITIONAL RESOURCES

Marketing Samples

Marketing pieces such as these are relatively inexpensive to produce. You have a lot of options in the use of ink colors and the quality of paper or cardstock, which places this kind of print advertising affordable for the most modest budgets.

The Worthington Public Library and Nashua Public Library's homebound services brochures are printed on two sides of 8.5" x 11" paper and simply folded in half. Although reproduced in black-and-white here, in full color Worthington's features an economical grayscale color scheme enhanced with gradations of red; Nashua uses a straight black, white, and red color scheme. These very simple, high-contrast colors not only save you money, but they are easier for patrons with visual impairments to see.

Anaheim Public Library's door hanger is printed on 8.5" x 11" cardstock. In full color, it features an array of bright colors, which are entirely appropriate when marketing to a young audience. Note the area in the center of the door hanger that specifies information about the Guinida Lane service site. This information is actually printed on a label, not the door hanger itself; the space underneath the label is blank. This approach allows you to customize the marketing material for each service location without having to reprint everything when the bookmobile service schedule changes. All you have to do is print new labels.

Note also that the door hanger advises patrons to return the door hanger to the bookmobile for a prize. This allows Anaheim Public Library to gauge how well their marketing material is working.

Nashua Public Library

OUTREACH SERVICES brings books and other library materials to the homebound, the disabled, residents of elderly housing, and others in the community who have difficulty visiting the library on their own.

Outreach Services
Nashua Public Library
2 Court Street
Nashua, NH 03060-3475

Bringing books and more to people who have difficulty visiting the library.

Figure 1.2a and 1.2b: Nashua Public Library homebound services brochure

From *On the Road with Outreach: Mobile Library Services* by Jeannie Dilger-Hill and Erica MacCreaigh, Editors. Santa Barbara, CA: Libraries Unlimited. Copyright © 2010.

Nashua Public Library
Outreach Services

Outreach Services brings books and other library materials to people in the community who have difficulty visiting the library on their own.

Who is eligible for the service?
Outreach is available to those who are:
- confined to their homes for three months or more
- unable to use the library because of illness, physical disability, or age
- residents in nursing homes, assisted living facilities, and senior citizen residences
- teachers at day care centers, family day care centers, Head Start programs, or special at-risk programs

Do I need a library card to use the service?
Yes. Anyone who lives or works in Nashua is eligible for a library card.

What materials can you deliver?
We can bring you hardcover books, paperbacks, large-print books, audio books, magazines, and music CDs. For children, we also offer picture books, board books, puppets, and music tapes.

How long can I keep the materials?
You can keep your materials until our next visit. If the van misses a delivery date, your materials will be automatically renewed.

How will you know what materials I want?
You can request items by contacting the outreach services office at the library at 589-4627 or by sending us email at **outreach@nashua.lib.nh.us.** Or you can request them by using our online catalog at **www.nashua.lib.nh.us.**

In addition, when you sign up for the service, we will have you fill out an interest profile. On this form, you will tell us what type of books you enjoy— for example, biographies, history, romance novels, literary fiction, picture books, and so forth. You can let us know if you want to receive large-print books, hardcovers, paperbacks, books on tape, music CDs, and so forth. Then we will select materials from the library that fit your interests and deliver them to you as well.

What if I can't get to the door?
If you are unable to answer the door when we visit, we can arrange to leave your materials in a safe spot that you designate at your home. You can leave your materials to be returned in the same spot.

Does the service operate on holidays or in bad weather?
The van will not operate on holidays if the library is closed. In addition, it will not operate when driving is hazardous due to inclement weather. Don't worry, your items will automatically renew.

How do I sign up?
For more information, contact Outreach Services at 589-4627 or **outreach@nashua.lib.nh.us.** You can also fill out the form below and we will contact you to arrange service.

Yes, I would like more information on library Outreach Services.
Please contact me to discuss how I would benefit from this program.

Name: _____

Nashua Street Address: _____ Apt. #:_____ Zip:_____

Telephone number: _____ Email address: _____

Do you currently have a Nashua Public Library card? ☐ Yes ☐ No

Type of customer: (check one)

☐ Homebound individual ☐ Teacher/Caregiver at a pre-school, day care, or other facility

☐ Resident of senior housing, nursing home, assisted living, other: _____

Clip and return this form to: Outreach Services, Nashua Public Library, 2 Court Street, Nashua, NH 03060-3475

Figure 1.2a and 1.2b: (continued)

From *On the Road with Outreach: Mobile Library Services* by Jeannie Dilger-Hill and Erica MacCreaigh, Editors. Santa Barbara, CA: Libraries Unlimited. Copyright © 2010.

VISIT THE BOOKMOBILE

We have...
* Books for your reports
* Books to read for fun
* Videos
* Cassettes
* Magazines

We are in your neighborhood

Mondays
Guinida Lane
(behind paul Revere School)
2:30-3:30 pm

Just fill out an application and
have your own library card!
This Program is completely Free!

Bring this Door hanger to the
Bookmobile for a surprise
For more information call us
(714) 765-1738

VISITEN LA BIBLIOTECA RODANTE

Tenemos...
* Libros para reportes
* Libros de diversión
* Libros en español
* Revistas
* Películas

Estamos en su vecindario

Lunes
Guinida Lane
(Detrás La Escuela Paul Revere)
2:30-3:30 pm

Solamente llene una
aplicacion y tenga su propia tarjeta
Este Programa es completamente gratis!

Traiga este cupón y reciba una sorpresa
Para más información llamenos
(714)765-1738

Figure 1.3: Anaheim Public Library bookmobile services door hanger

From *On the Road with Outreach: Mobile Library Services* by Jeannie Dilger-Hill and Erica MacCreaigh, Editors. Santa Barbara, CA: Libraries Unlimited. Copyright © 2010.

Sample Press Release

FOR IMMEDIATE RELEASE

MAY 5, 2009

EHS MUSIC STUDENTS PERFORM AT THE EVERYWHERE PUBLIC LIBRARY

CONTACT: Jane Deaux, Youth Services Supervisor

Everywhere Public Library

555-READ

The Chorus, Band, and String Ensemble of Everywhere High School invites you to a free concert at the Everywhere Public Library on Tuesday, May 5th at 10 A.M.

Everywhere High School in Everywhere, United States, is a public high school dedicated to gifted education. Students in the select band, string ensemble, and choir will perform big band and patriotic music in the Children's library. Children will be able to see and hear band and string instruments played, as well as hear the choir.

The performance will last an hour, and is for people of all ages. There are no reservations required.

The Everywhere Public Library is located at 1234 Street St. Call 555-READ for more information.

2

Managing Outreach Staff

By Amy Varner Stephens

Outreach employees are unique individuals in the library world. Part social worker, part librarian, part delivery person, and part personal (literary) shopper, the job demands staff who are both tough-skinned and appropriately compassionate, as well as possessing the ability to physically handle adverse conditions, including visits to badly run nursing homes and toting boxes or carts loaded with books.

The populations served by an Outreach department will vary by community, but often include low income neighborhoods and schools, senior and disabled housing units or individual homes, nursing homes, jails and prisons, preschools, migrant and immigrant populations, and geographically-isolated communities. It is generally their job to provide library services to the most commonly marginalized and isolated segments of any community. Outreach staff whose job it is to go into people's homes and apartments can easily become emotionally involved with customers' lives, and Outreach may be the only department whose staff regularly attend funerals. Managing staff who spend a great deal of time out of the office and who work with diverse populations can be quite challenging.

Something New Every Day

During my first week with the department, I went on a ride along with the staff, delivering to customers in an assisted living center and nursing home. Our first customer answered our knock with a "come in." Upon entering we discovered her thermostat was spewing some sort of gas, which she had not noticed. I then found myself navigating the labyrinthine hallways of this large facility looking for help while my staff member stayed to attempt to help the customer out of her apartment. Everything turned out just fine, the gas was nothing dangerous, and we went on.

I then took a stack of books to a Mrs. F, who was an extremely frail woman sitting in a low swivel chair with one of our books in her hand. I introduced myself and asked how she was enjoying the book. I realized that she was struggling to speak, and so I first squatted, then leaned forward, balancing my hand on the chair to hear her better. At that point the chair tilted forward, sliding her on top of me! I couldn't get enough leverage to put her back in the chair, and was afraid that if I tried to fall backwards myself I would harm her. I finally reached the nurse button, and help arrived.

On a subsequent day, I helped take books to the county jail across the plaza from the library. Although I had heard the words "into the jail," nothing had really prepared me for the emotional and guttural jolt that comes from hearing solid steel clanging shut behind you and locking you in!

for certain positions. As with all small library departments, there is usually some overlap of duties between all positions.

Library Clerk

Requires a high school degree or GED. Responsible for circulation of items in and out of the department; ordering supplies; finding and processing materials requests; preparing items for delivery by mail; physical delivery of items to senior assisted living facilities and homebound customers; sorting incoming donations for distribution to jail and homeless shelters; processing and repairing library materials; ordering office and operating supplies; other record-keeping as needed.

Bookmobile Driver

Requires a high school degree or GED. May require a special driver's license according to individual state law. Responsible for daily operation and fueling of the bookmobile, working with motor pool department to ensure proper maintenance of bookmobile, and cleaning interior and exterior of vehicle regularly; stocking circulation supplies on the vehicle daily; performing circulation tasks at service sites; assisting customers with reader's advisory and ready reference questions; shelving items on the vehicle; regular shelf reading.

Library Associate

Bachelor's degree preferred. Responsible for developing accurate selection profiles and selecting items for customers living in senior, disabled, or low income sites; coordinating with facility staff to provide services; providing reader's advisory and reference services on the bookmobile; planning and implementing library programming at selected service sites; recruiting, assigning, and monitoring homebound program volunteers; acting as supervisor in absence of Outreach Manager.

Librarian

Master's degree in Library Science preferred. Responsible for managing the Outreach Services department and services; planning and implementing large programming and service efforts; collection development including

---

Delivery Quandary

The circumstances of delivery, specifically of materials to homebound and institutionalized individuals, became a big issue in my department. Associate level staff who were delivering to institutions felt very strongly that they should be the ones to interact with the customers and that the quality of the service would decline if the task of the actual delivery were given to a clerk. Since individual homebound customers received books by mail or had them delivered by a volunteer, it seemed on the surface that face-to-face interaction wasn't always needed. However, there were some locations, especially nursing homes as opposed to assisted living centers, where residents had a hard time connecting with the service without some very personal interaction. While I sympathized with the associates, I realized we were also unable to add more customers unless we could make our service more efficient. In the end, a personable clerk was hired and trained to do the deliveries of items chosen by the associates so that the associates could use their skills and knowledge to help more customers less directly. Another solution might have been to differentiate the locations by communication levels of the residents, and let associates continue to directly serve those at highest need.

selection, organization of materials, and weeding; all duties listed under "Library Associate" as needed.

Outreach Manager

Master's Degree in Library Science preferred. Responsible for hiring, training, monitoring, and motivating Outreach staff; communicating with library administration to ensure that all aspects of the service operate efficiently; serving as the face of the department in the larger community by addressing politicians and community groups about the services Outreach offers; monitoring programs and services for quality and efficiency; assessing customer needs, and responding appropriately; identifying budget needs of the department, preparing budget requests, effectively communicating budget needs to library administration; proposing and implementing new service plans; preparing regular narrative and statistical reports.

SCHEDULING STAFF

Some things that will impact staff need to be considered when scheduling services for your department. For liability and security reasons alone, it is a good idea to have two staff members on a Bookmobile at all times. If your Bookmobile goes to preschools or other institutions, you may be able to require that a member of their staff be present during the entire visit. Two staff members on board protects both you and the customers from intent and ensures a witness in case of accusation.

Physical effort is another factor to consider. You may be surprised at the pure physical challenge presented by serving nursing homes. Books have to be prepared, loaded into tote boxes, then onto carts. Once on the carts, they are pushed outside to the delivery van, the totes are loaded into the van, and finally the cart is loaded also. At each site, the process is repeated. Some sites require pushing a fairly heavy cart through carpeted (and therefore more physically challenging) hallways for what seems like miles. The constant unloading and loading of carts can be physically wearying for staff. The addition of a lift to your delivery vehicle can be a help, but the very nature of what Outreach does means that staff will face more physical wear and tear than the average public library staff member.

This becomes a factor when planning routes for staff. There are many factors to consider when setting up service, including geographic locations, number and type of residents, and the vehicles/resources at your disposal. Included in those factors is the physical impact on your staff and the efficiency of their time. For instance, in the really large institutions, the best choice may be sending two staff at a time, which will mitigate both the time and effort involved. Analyzing the impact on your staff will help prevent burnout and will maximize the efficiency of your service in the long run.

When setting up a bookmobile schedule, be sure to include small breaks for the staff. Check the routes and see if there is a convenience store, fast food restaurant, or similar location between stops where the staff can stop for 10–15 minutes to get a drink and use the bathroom. It can be hard to give up this time, because bookmobile schedules are so pressed for it, but it is essential to maintaining your staff's positive outlook and work efficiency.

If you have a union, of course, be sure to check their requirements as well. A good human resources department will also be a great asset during this process.

SUPERVISORY CHALLENGES

Outreach's special communities and unusual physical challenges require managers to monitor some aspects of the service more closely. Physical stresses among staff who are loading boxes and carts of books should be particularly watched. Require staff to report any injuries or appearance of physical stress right away and work with them to alleviate the pressure. Such a report is a good opportunity to assess the current work load and see if a shift can be made to ease the challenge. Education in ergonomic techniques and proper lifting, or purchasing special equipment such as back braces may be necessary.

The high emotional pressure in Outreach cannot be discounted too quickly. All librarians who work with the public see all sorts of customers, but by definition, Outreach sees the most needy, the least stable, and the saddest segments of the community. Those who work with the elderly, going into their homes on every visit, are often harder hit by their patrons' deaths than staff who work in a branch. Allow staff to attend funerals and seek out the families of their best customers to extend condolences if they wish to do so. In nearly every case, the families will speak gratefully of the joy the service brought to their loved ones' final years. Consequently, this kind of encounter can help ease staff's grief. Be sure to share thank you letters or e-mail from patrons' families with your staff; if you have a staff newsletter that everyone can see, publish those kudos. It helps Outreach staff to be reminded of and commended for their contributions.

Staff can help their own emotional well being by being the agent of change for a customer in especially dire straits. Over the years, we have referred customers to programs that provide assistance with heating bills or an air conditioner in the sweltering Oklahoma summer. Our customers are often underinformed about wonderful programs that can pay for having a bathroom remodeled to ADA standards, or provide in-home respite for a weary caregiver. Find ways to train your staff in the knowledge of these resources. Knowing they can make a difference helps alleviate the emotional stress of seeing customers struggling in these situations.

Also be clear with your staff about their roles and your expectation that they stay within their job description. It is altogether too easy for staff who visit customers in their homes to be tempted to pick up a few groceries, make a phone call to the customer's doctor, or even schedule time outside work to drive the customer to a hairdresser appointment. This kind of overinvolvement in customers' daily lives not only contributes to staff burnout, but could also carry some legal liability. If you know this kind of activity is going on, you have a responsibility to confront the employee about it.

OVERSIGHT AND EVALUATION

There are several tried-and-true techniques to successfully manage staff who spend most of their time out in the field.

Start the process by riding along with them on their routes in all areas, just to get to know the job and the community. Learn how they keep records (or don't!), how they manage their customers' requests, what the communities expect of them, and which issues they run into on a regular basis. The enormity of what they handle on an everyday basis is astonishing!

After learning staff's jobs and the procedures already in place, set up procedures to capture statistics and

In Case of Abduction . . .

During the process of learning how my staff did their jobs, I discovered the haphazardness of their recordkeeping about individual customers. The staff was so experienced that they felt they didn't need to keep detailed records; they knew exactly who they took books to, and what they had read. An amazing feat, but I started to try to convince them to keep records with the abducted by aliens scenario. If staff member A is abducted by aliens tomorrow, how will her sub know what to do? Finally, one of the staff *was* abducted by aliens! Just kidding. Actually, her husband had a life-threatening illness and she was gone for two months. Her husband recovered, and during those two months the rest of the staff realized the importance of recordkeeping.

then use them for benchmarks. For instance, if staff member A is serving 150 people a month, and staff member B is only serving 100 people, try to find out why. There are mitigating circumstances in this scenario—for, instance, the high level of demand and complexity of service for residents in assisted living versus residents of nursing homes—but you'll also find that individual staff have different procedures, some of which are more efficient than others. Standardizing procedures gives staff clear instructions to follow and provides some measure of quantitative benchmarks with which to evaluate.

You should also develop relationships with contacts at the various institutions you deliver materials to on a monthly basis. When scheduled to leave your office for a meeting elsewhere in the service area, check the map and see if there is a suitable bookmobile stop to visit on the way. Call to make an appointment with the activities director or customers if you can. At times, you might just stop in, checking with customers to see if their needs are being met and if their assigned staff member is friendly and professional. Ask them to rate the staff's customer service and professional demeanor. Chances are you'll get less than a handful of negative reviews from these sources. If there is a problem, you will be able to respond effectively.

Neighborhood bookmobile stops are harder to manage and evaluate. Most of those customers are children. You'll often get phone calls directly from customers. Not all of them are happy, but you'll probably discover that this is rarely because of any real issues with staff. Almost always it is either a miscommunication or the customer is insisting on a service or item you cannot provide. You might occasionally cold-call customers who you know are able to communicate well to check on the service they are receiving.

You have no doubt heard this before, but documentation is essential to any supervisor. Keep a file on each

Ongoing Feedback

In our library system, we have a yearly performance review which is supported by the review of monthly reports turned in by the staff. I have found the monthly reports invaluable, and I don't know how I managed without them before they were instituted! It gives not only the statistical reporting that we need to turn in, but also the space for staff to recap any incidents that may have happened, good or bad.

direct report, both in paper form and electronically. Yearly reviews, monthly reports, letters from customers, awards from the system, complaints, summaries of conversations both motivational and disciplinary, all are contained between these two locations. They will prove invaluable both during yearly performance reviews and on occasions when you have to either defend employees or recommend them.

CONCLUSION

When I first became the manager of the Outreach department, my dad asked me what I did. I replied that my staff went out and delivered books to the homebound, provided service on the Bookmobile to low income housing projects, and delivered books to the incarcerated. He then said, "Okay, but what do YOU do?" I said, "Well, I make SURE my staff are delivering books to the homebound, providing service on the Bookmobile, and delivering books to the incarcerated."

Outreach employees are truly special. Their ability to handle the physical and emotional stress that comes with serving special populations sets them apart from other librarians. Staff have told me that the pleasure of being able to make a real difference in the lives of their customers is what keeps them working in the department despite the challenges. I hope you enjoy working with them as much as I have.

3

Mobile Library Collections

By Julie Abbott and Jeannie Dilger-Hill

The small size, high demand, and mobility of bookmobile collections pose many unique collection management challenges. In addition to libraries' typical concerns about selection and acquisition (both of which have particular twists in the mobile library world), there are also issues regarding collection sharing, physical arrangement, and security. This chapter provides an overview of these issues and ideas for responding to them effectively.

INTEGRATED (SHARED) VERSUS DEDICATED (SEPARATE) BOOKMOBILE COLLECTIONS

Pros and Cons

Before making decisions about how to select materials, it's best to determine if your mobile collection will be a dedicated (separate) collection, or if it will be integrated (shared) with a brick-and-mortar library's collection. Traditionally, bookmobiles have been treated like branch libraries, with separate budgets for a separate collection, but sharing a collection with a branch is a viable alternative.

In an integrated bookmobile collection, the majority of the materials on the bookmobile are borrowed from a central library or large branch for a period of a few months, and then returned to the library in exchange for a fresh collection. The bookmobile staff usually have a small budget to purchase new releases, best-sellers, and other items not easily borrowed from the main library. A dedicated bookmobile collection is purchased for and stored by the outreach department with funds specifically earmarked for those materials. It should be noted that in both integrated and separate collections, bookmobile staff will borrow items from a main library or branch to fill specific patron requests.

Before deciding whether to use a dedicated or integrated approach to bookmobile collection development, there are a number of factors to consider.

First, examine your *logistics*. Sometimes, a separate collection is necessary because of where the bookmobile is physically housed. If the bookmobile is not housed near the main library or a large branch, it will be difficult to rotate the collection because materials are not close at hand. On the other hand, a separate collection requires space to house it as materials are rotated on and off the vehicle. With limited shelving space,

long run, many of the requirements are the same, because the overall goal is the same: providing the best possible collection to the bookmobile patrons.

Requirements for a Dedicated (Separate) Collection

- A librarian who knows the bookmobile collection and patronage and has time allotted to select material
- A generous budget to purchase materials, in order to provide a well-rounded collection
- Technical support for acquisitions and processing of materials
- Access to the main library collection for any requests that cannot be filled from the bookmobile collection
- Adequate space to house a wide variety of materials not currently located on the bookmobile

Requirements for an Integrated (Shared) Collection

- A librarian or outreach staff member who knows the bookmobile collection and patronage and has time allotted to select and rotate materials from the main library collection
- A small budget to purchase materials not easily obtained from the main library, such as bestsellers and specialized materials in quantity (i.e., large print, Spanish language)
- Easy access to the main collection supplying the bookmobile
- A computer system that easily allows a change of agency or location
- Access to the main library collection for any requests that cannot be filled from the bookmobile collection
- Selection librarians who are fully aware of the bookmobile collection needs and incorporate them in their selections

COLLECTION DEVELOPMENT POLICY

Before getting into the mechanics of collection development, you need to know what your basic collection development policies are. Chances are your library is going to have an official collection development policy and the outreach collection will fall under that policy. But even if your library does have a written policy, it's worth taking the time to consider outreach's collection development goals and how they fit into the overall goals of the library.

Whether you have a small dedicated collection or a rotating shared collection, you need guiding principles for collection management. The following principles are those most likely to differ between outreach collection development policy and that of the larger library organization:

- Identification of outreach service population
- Purpose of the outreach collection

- Criteria by which materials will be selected for the outreach collection (either purchased or borrowed from main library collection)
- Criteria by which materials will be weeded (or rotated) from the outreach collection

The Utah State Library operates several bookmobiles throughout Utah. Its brief, but thorough, collection development policy for bookmobiles, available online, is a good example for anyone looking to write their own. (Utah State Library, 2006)

SELECTION

The mission of your bookmobile is the first thing to consider when you are deciding what materials to have in your collection. Unless your bookmobile has a primary mission different from circulation of materials, you will want to stock it with the highest-circulating, most popular types of materials you can acquire. Consider what the most popular materials are in your library system, consider the demographics of the people you are serving, and stock your mobile library with materials that match these two criteria.

This varies so greatly among bookmobiles that it is impossible to make generalized statements about what kinds of materials or how much of them you should have. If you are serving only preschools, for example, you would carry all the types of materials that preschoolers and their teachers use, including picture books, some low level nonfiction, teacher support materials, and young children's music and movies. If you are serving only new immigrants with language barriers, you would carry materials in their language(s), English Language Learning materials, and simple nonfiction in English.

A common mistake in bookmobile services is to attempt to do it on the cheap, with older, weeded materials that are not checking out in the library. While a new bookmobile collection can add depth with the inclusion of some older titles, such as classics for children, new and popular materials are essential to the success of the service.

Apply the 80/20 rule. That is, 80 percent of your patrons will be looking for the most in-demand 20 percent of your collection. So, stock as much as you can of that 20 percent, and leave the less-sought titles in a branch library to be retrieved when you have a specific request for them.

For each area of your collection, you will need enough stock to provide critical mass, that is, enough items and variety that most of the patrons browsing your bookmobile will usually be able to find something that appeals to them. But how many volumes do you need to ensure that a particular patron will find a book that appeals to him or her? This amount will vary with the type of collection and the patronage you have using that collection. Often, trial and error will help you answer this question, but the rules of thumb for an overflow collection (below) can help you estimate what you'll need from a shared library collection, too.

In addition to what fits on the bookmobile at any given time, those with a designated collection need an overflow collection so that you can restock when materials on the shelves run low, as well as move seasonal items (particularly picture books) to the shelves during the appropriate seasons and holidays. Bookmobiles with designated collections should plan to own at least twice as many volumes as they can store on the

Picking and Choosing

On our previous bookmobile at Cook Memorial Library, we had room for about three hundred volumes of adult fiction. That allowed us to have a good mix of mysteries, thrillers, chick lit, and so on, so that a patron who read only a narrow range of genre fiction would usually be able to find something new to read. On our new bookmobile, shelf space is more limited and our adult readership is declining, so we now have only about two hundred volumes at any given time. It seems to be enough to allow for the needed variety of genres and authors, but just barely. We can get away with a smaller collection partly because we no longer seem to have western readers or science fiction readers. Not making any attempt to stock those genres leaves us enough room to have the variety we need in the others.

bookmobile at any given time. For your highest-circulating materials, you may need as much as three times the number of volumes you can fit on the bookmobile shelves. For less in-demand areas, you can get by with a much smaller cushion. Look at your turnover rates (how much time items spend off the shelf versus on the shelf) to get a better idea of how many items you will need to keep your shelves stocked.

For the most part, you can follow the acquisitions procedures and collection development policies used by your library. However, there are some things to keep in mind with mobile collections that usually aren't issues for stationary collections. For the most part, these have to do with the size and weight of your items, and durability.

Because you are transporting all of your materials, weight is a serious consideration. You must know the weight-bearing capacity of your vehicle. Don't forget to take the weight of fuel, staff, and any non-fixed equipment into account when figuring the maximum possible weight of your collection. Item for item, paperbacks generally weigh less than hardcovers and media generally weighs less than books of similar size. If your goal is to stock every available inch of shelf space, paperbacks are usually thinner than the same titles in hardcover, so you can fit more titles on your shelves. The flip side of this is that very thin paperbacks (especially children's picture books) are more difficult for patrons to browse and can't match the long-term durability of hardcovers.

You many also be constrained by the height of your shelves. Many vendors include the dimensions of their products in their catalogs; if someone in your outreach department is responsible for selection and acquisition, that person might be able to avoid purchasing materials that are too tall to shelve properly. If you share a collection, you can certainly instruct staff and volunteers to avoid selecting overly tall materials. However, you probably won't be able to avoid having at least a few oversized materials. Displaying these materials on an oversized shelf or in a browsing bin will make them available to your patrons without compromising more compact shelf space for smaller materials.

You must also consider the durability of various formats. Again, what type of items you buy depends on your mission and service priorities. For example, if you want to circulate a high volume of picture books, it may be best to stock large quantities of paperback picture books. These will not survive for long, but they can fill high demand.

On the other hand, you may prefer to retain books as long as possible under conditions of vigorous use. In that case, you should purchase hardcover books with good bindings and quality paper. You pay more for the book at the beginning and it may cost more to process it for circulation, but it should hold up longer. If you expect the books you are acquiring to remain in strong demand for a period of years, more expensive hardcovers can be a bargain in the long run. And, especially with books intended for young children, it is useful to have hardcover books with wash-

> **Costs and Benefits: It Pays to Be Creative**
>
> I once heard of a bookmobile exclusively serving preschools that did not catalog or process their paperback collection in any way. When items were checked out, they just manually recorded the number of items each teacher borrowed and looked for that same number to come back on the next visit. This may go against the grain for librarians accustomed to being able to track who borrowed what, when, where, and how often, but it does work as a low-fuss means of providing service. What was saved in terms of staff time off-set the cost of replacing materials.

able covers. Most paperback books require the extra step of lamination to make their covers washable, and they will never be as durable.

In children's and young adult fiction, popular paperback books are a good buy if the titles will not still be popular a couple of years down the road. For example, Hannah Montana books are hot among the tween girl set right now and paperback copies are perfectly adequate. They may wear out sooner, but in a few years, the next crop of tween girls will have moved on to the next popular series and demand for Hannah will diminish. For more substantial fiction, including perennial classics like *Hatchet* (2007) and contemporary classics like *A Series of Unfortunate Events* (2006), it is better to buy hardcover editions. The higher quality children's books are likely to have a longer shelf life in terms of ongoing readership. So, the better quality material proves more cost-effective in durable hardcover.

Another consideration is wear and tear on your materials from the physical environment of the bookmobile. Whenever possible, covers should be cleanable. All library books get dirty from use, but those shelved on the bookmobile also are regularly exposed to fuel fumes. The combination of sticky children's fingers and the notorious road dust that then clings to the sticky spots on your books can make your materials look dingy and unattractive. And if you can avoid it, don't store materials in your overflow collection in a garage! While it's certainly more efficient to store these materials *near* the garage, dirt, fumes, and even weather elements like blowing rain, snow, and temperature extremes will wear down your materials faster than storing them in a clean, climate-controlled room.

WEEDING

For designated bookmobile collections, constant weeding is a necessity due to limited shelving space. To maintain a continuously refreshed collection in a small space, your weeding criteria for the bookmobile will be stricter than in any other area of the library.

Weeding criteria will vary in different areas of your collection.

> **Not All Weeds Are Created Equal**
>
> On my bookmobile, I weed adult fiction and popular music that hasn't circulated for three months. I give children's books up to six months, depending on how crowded the shelves are. Popular DVDs are old news if they haven't gone out in a month.

> ### Mobile Multitasking
>
> I once heard a bookmobile librarian at a conference humorously describe ripping out barcodes and tossing books out the window while she was driving, using her limited time to get the weeding done. Short of littering, bookmobilers have to squeeze weeding into any free moment we can find!

The goal is to keep the highest-circulating materials in your collection and remove those that are no longer going out. Most brick-and-mortar libraries have some need for materials that never or rarely circulate, such as literary classics and genre series titles. On the bookmobile, every inch counts and there is little room to spare for items that don't go out. You may have a few items you keep for reference (a dictionary and an almanac for example), but the bulk of your space will be designated for circulating materials.

Materials removed from the bookmobile don't necessarily have to be discarded. Some can be rotated to your stored overflow collection and retained for later use. Especially in the children's area, items can be given a rest and put back as much as a year later, when they will be discovered by a whole new crop of young children. Adult fiction from the bookmobile can go into assisted living deposit collections. Sometimes your materials can be moved to another library in your system to refresh their collection, too.

Some bookmobiles also find rental arrangements for their collections to be a useful way to limit the buildup of older materials. Rental services can be an effective means of keeping your collection refreshed and aiding you in your weeding process. The service will provide a list of items to be pulled and all you have to do is get them off the shelf and send them back. Rental agreements usually also allow you to keep some percentage of the books you rent, so you have some flexibility to retain items that continue to be popular among your patrons.

PHYSICAL ARRANGEMENT OF MATERIALS

Space is at a premium on a bookmobile, so every effort should be made to use every available inch. Materials should ideally be arranged so that they are most accessible to the people who are usually looking for them. Optimally, everything is at eye level and within easy reach of anyone who wants to take it off the shelf. Practically, however, something has to be relegated to the top and bottom shelves and the less accessible nooks and crannies of the bookmobile.

There are two typical bookmobile arrangements. Most general-use bookmobiles use some combination of these two techniques.

By Age and Height of Patrons

In this arrangement, picture books and preschool nonfiction are typically shelved on the bottom shelves, readers and elementary-level children's books in the middle, and adult and young adult books on top. An advantage of this method is its eye-level placement. It also works well for stops which have predominantly one type of patron because it spreads patrons along the length of the vehicle, rather than crowding them together in one area. The corresponding disadvantage is at stops with patrons of various ages. Small children may not be able to get to the picture books on the lower shelves with adults standing in front of them browsing the upper levels.

Clustering by Different Groups' Interests

This arrangement involves grouping sections of collection into shelving ranges to create clusters for use by different patrons. This is a good arrangement for bookmobiles that serve age-diverse patrons by allowing adults to browse in their own quiet corner while their children explore their own areas of the bookmobile. It is also makes sense to group materials by format or language, so that patrons who need large print or foreign language materials can go directly to those areas.

Browsing Bins

There is always a temptation to maximize use of space on the vehicle, and when you run out of shelf space, you might consider keeping materials on the floor in some kind of container to facilitate browsing. This arrangement can work well for very limited types of materials, such as board books. But avoid having so many containers sitting on the floor that movement of staff and patrons is impeded and access to materials on the shelves is blocked. Evaluate the pros and cons carefully when you are tempted to set out a box on the floor. Boxes work best for the materials that are needed at some stops and not at others, so that the most in-demand items can be displayed when they are needed and removed when they are not. Containers should be kept small so that they can be moved around easily.

Removable Shelving

Some bookmobiles also have removable shelving in the form of single-sided carts that affix to the wall. If you have distinct groups of patrons at different stops, this can be a useful method of tailoring your collection to their needs. For example, a cart of Spanish materials useful at a neighborhood stop with new immigrants could be swapped out at a school stop with a cart of teacher materials.

Oversized and Delicate Materials

Whenever possible, avoid shelving books on their sides with the spine up. This is a common practice when the shelf height is inadequate. Especially for heavy nonfiction books with poor bindings, such as the Guinness World Records books, this shelving practice puts too much strain on the bindings. With the constant vibration and motion on the bookmobile, bindings break quickly. Your oversize books will last longer if you designate at least one shelf in your bookmobile for them.

> **Go, Speed Racer!**
>
> On one bookmobile, we had heavy adult nonfiction shelved along the back wall over the window. I dumped that whole shelf on to the floor every few years, miscalculating my speed over railroad tracks. Besides creating extra work for me, it didn't do the books much good, either!

4

Rural Bookmobile Service

By Jan Meadows

HISTORY OF AMERICAN BOOKMOBILES

For more than 100 years, public libraries in the United States have provided library services to patrons residing in rural settings such as farms, ranches, and small villages. The first mobile library service to rural areas is considered to have been Maryland's Washington County Free Library book wagon that headed out in 1905 from the county seat of Hagerstown to the small towns and villages in the county. Miss Mary Titcomb, the county's first librarian and the person responsible for sending out the book wagon, wrote in *The Story of the Washington County Free Library*, "No better method has ever been devised for reaching the dweller in the country. The book goes to the man, not waiting for the man to come to the book" (Titcomb, 1951). Libraries across the country today are still holding to that belief, knowing that building a branch in each small town, while the most ideal way to serve them, is not possible or cost effective. However, all citizens deserve access to informational and recreational materials provided by public libraries, and equitable service is only possible through alternate means of delivery. As the decades since 1905 have passed, delivery vehicles have continually improved from that first wagon. Today, bookmobiles, also known as mobile libraries, are truly mobile branch libraries.

PROFILE OF RURAL LIBRARY PATRONS

Who are these rural patrons and why do they choose to live away from the conveniences of the city? As you may surmise, the answers are as varied as the people. Some have lived on family farms and homesteads for many generations and proudly carry on the history and work of their forefathers. Many are members of religious denominations that choose to live without the trappings of modern times, such as the Amish and the Mennonites. Some with young families choose to home school their children and live a simpler lifestyle. Many own and run small businesses in the communities, such as general stores, gas stations, and cafés. Others may work in various governmental jobs in the area such as park rangers, forestry or range management personnel, or in small post offices, to name just a few. In some regions of the country, poverty keeps people in the economically depressed areas in which they were born. The entertainment and information made

- Individual Homes
- Health Care Facility
- Main Street
- Bank
- Correction Camp for Boys
- Rural School
- Main Cross Roads
- Centrally Located Farm/Ranch
- Group of Mail Boxes

Determining Times for Service Delivery

Besides location, timing is crucial. During your road trip and visits with various people, you will have discovered when people already come to town. You need to question further and ask people more in-depth questions. Will it be more convenient if the bookmobile stop is before or after the livestock sale, the mail is dispersed, the farmers' market, and so on? Do afternoons or mornings work better for ranchers and home schoolers? Would the school use the service for their students if you are there during school hours, or would it be better to have the stop when they get out of school? Check with the organizers of the farmers' market; perhaps an arrangement can be made for the bookmobile to park among the vendors and be open during the same hours. It could be a win-win plan for you and the market, with each drawing people for the other. A stop will never succeed if you do not make it available at a time that is convenient to the users. This may mean you need some late afternoon or evening stops, so keep an open mind about what your service hours will be.

In the aforementioned Rural Bookmobile Service survey, libraries responded with wide ranges of time they spent at each individual stop. Some stops were as long as seven and a half hours and a few were only 15 minutes. The two most common stop lengths were one hour and two hours. This is not an exact science, so you need to consider several factors. Short stops are not recommended unless you have a very remote stop at a crossroads or a farm where you know there will only be a few people in the area who have the potential to come and who are fully prepared to be there at the appointed time, such as the lady with the wheelbarrow previously mentioned.

When establishing a new stop in an area that has had no previous service, you should schedule enough time to catch the attention of and be available to the people just passing by. If it is in a town you should stay no less than two hours, and more if possible. It takes time for people to realize you are going to be there every week or month, at the same time, on the same day. It also takes time for people to establish a routine that involves coming to the bookmobile. If the vehi-

If You Feed Them, They Will Come

In one of the small towns in our service area, Tuesday is homemade donut day at one of the rural cafés, and the café can count on a lot of traffic that day!

cle is only there for a short time, only the few people who happen by will know you are there. Advertising and posting of schedules will help raise public awareness, but the actual bookmobile parked and open is your best way to let them know you are there and ready to serve them.

You should also consider the number of people who live in the town or area. Your pre-

Building Community

While developing your stop locations and times, you will be building community with your rural patrons. This is crucial! Rural communities are generally very close-knit and like to have a relationship with the people they interact with in business and services. Having the relationship builds trust, and they want to know that you are as good as your word. Most folks like to have a conversation with the staff, not just get their materials and run. Once a relationship is built, you have a friend for the library, and for the staff, for life. Patrons will share produce from their fields and goodies from their kitchens. If you bring them books to help them build a barn or make a quilt they will give you credit over and over again for making the project possible. They will take you into their fold, care if you have been sick, and miss you when you are on vacation. Not all, but many will consider you extended family. This is one of the bonuses of the job!

vious visits and research for the area should give you some information with which to project usage. If you have the potential for a lot of patrons, establish the schedule to fit that potential. If you only give the stop a short amount of time because beginning use is not very high, you are not allowing for growth. When use builds and you have another stop in a neighboring community right after this stop, you will be unable to expand the stop time without disturbing the open time and patron use at the following stop. It often takes a good year or more to really get a patron base established.

Rural Schools

Because many rural bookmobiles provide a stop for rural schools, we should spend some time discussing this service. These schools often do not have any funds for their own library, or if they do have one, it is not extensive. There is always a political debate about whether public libraries should or should not provide this service or if the schools should use their own tax dollars for their own library, but that is something that your library officials will have to decide. It is often the case that the bookmobile is the only exposure to a library that a child in the rural community will have. Going to the school is, of course, the best place to reach the children.

If you decide to work with a school to set up a stop that will be open to the public as well as used by students during school hours, there are several steps that need to be taken at the very start. You need to meet with the school superintendent, principal, or other decision-making authority to let them know how a public library operates. You need to let the school officials (and parents) know that as a public library you do not censor materials that are checked out by anyone, regardless of age. It is up to the school staff to do that. When a parent comes to them complaining about something the child has checked out, they need to know that as public library employees, bookmobile staff will not stop a child from checking out anything.

Letters to school staff and a parent letter sent home with the registration slip should clearly state the no-censoring policy. The school can avoid problems as a result of this policy by requiring that the teacher or an adult aide accompany the class to the

Constantly working on a rural bookmobile can be physically taxing. If you have a small staff and switching routes is not possible, some days off the road should be a part of the scheduling. On these days the collection can be refreshed, office tasks can be completed, flyers can be created to advertise new or faltering stops, and so forth. This gives the staff a breather from the long routes and normal routine, and will help to keep morale up and fatigue at bay. Plus, all those things that never get done can finally be accomplished!

Most of all, the bookmobile staff always need to remember they are more than library employees; they are goodwill ambassadors! Rural people are quite accustomed to waving to passing vehicles on country roads, while driving or while working in their yards and fields. The bookmobile staff needs to return the wave with a smile. When children are out playing at home or a school, they should honk and wave; they will hear a chorus of "It's the bookmobile!!" ringing in their wake. Anywhere they go, after they have worked at the rural stops, the staff will be recognized and spoken to, so they need to respond in a friendly, genuine fashion. All of these seemingly small gestures go a long way in making your rural bookmobile stops a successful venture.

TYPES OF VEHICLES

Many styles of vehicles are used for rural mobile library services. Bookmobiles can range in size from 26 feet to 40 feet long and can be built on a school bus chassis or a transit bus chassis. Other truck chassis are used for smaller vehicles ranging from 15 feet to 20 feet long. Some libraries use tractor-trailer units. A few libraries have converted RVs or vans to provide service to their rural patrons at a cost they can afford. However, a vehicle built by a specialty vehicle vendor to carry the heavy load of library materials is safest and will last the longest.

The size of vehicle you need for your service depends on several factors. Be sure you know the answers to the following questions:

- What are the roads in your rural areas like? Narrow and twisting, mountainous or flat, gravel, dirt, or paved?
- How many people will you potentially be serving? Busy towns, small farms, crossroads, schools?
- How many materials and what formats will you need to carry? Books, VHS/DVD, compact discs, kits, board books?
- What types of terrain will you be covering? Interstates, dirt roads, winding highways?

If your roads are narrow, twisting, or mountainous you will most likely need a smaller vehicle to maneuver them. If you expect to serve a lot of people you will want a larger vehicle to give people room to browse the collection. If you are only going to very rural places where only a few people at a time will be on board, a smaller vehicle or even a raised roof van should suffice. The more materials you plan to carry, the bigger your Gross Vehicle Weight Rating (GVWR) needs to be.

Money, of course, is always a big factor for libraries, but it is recommended that you buy the best built vehicle on the best chassis you can afford. It will pay off in the long run by lasting longer, requiring less maintenance, and being safer on the road.

MAINTENANCE

Routine Upkeep and Repair

Life on country roads takes a toll on a vehicle. There are several ways to plan for maintenance:

- A week of down time every quarter so the mechanics can perform all engine, body, and generator maintenance as well as the facilities staff doing repairs to shelving, lighting fixtures, desks, and more
- Scheduled maintenance day each month for routine maintenance and needed repairs
- A method to address maintenance needs as they arise

There doesn't seem to be a perfect way to plan for routine maintenance. One tried-and-true method is scheduling one day a month for maintenance, but not publishing it on the printed schedule. Before you go to the stops that will be affected, check with your maintenance staff to see if they will need the vehicle for any work. If not, proceed as usual. But if they do, be sure to post signs and tell patrons as they check out that you will be skipping our next scheduled visit. This method eliminates having down days published and then finding you do not need them, causing service suspension when it is not necessary. Depending on who does your maintenance, whether the county garage, in-house mechanics, or the local garage, you may have to devise a totally different system. The important part is that preventive and routine maintenance must be attended to religiously. More information about bookmobile maintenance is presented in Chapter 16.

Breakdowns

Of course, you will have breakdowns that are completely unpredictable. *Before* the situation arises, you should have some procedures in place to alert patrons of service interruption, as well as procedures for your staff to follow during breakdowns on the road.

The following are some ways to alert other library staff and patrons that you are unavoidably off the road:

- A message posted on your library Web site
- A message recorded on the voice mail on the bookmobile staff phone
- Inform the library's phone operator
- Alert prearranged stop contacts by phone or e-mail so they can inform patrons, such as the postmaster, school secretary, grocer, or a local patron

library system. If the staff at your library don't know about it, they are not going to spread the word when someone comes into the building or calls in search of library service near his or her rural home. Host an open house in your bookmobile at a general all-staff meeting, get on the agendas for department and committee meetings, and tell staff what you are doing out there on the mobile library in the country. Volunteer on library committees so other staff members get to know you. Use e-mail to keep everyone updated on new schedules, special programs, and when you will not be at stops because of maintenance. Send out the printed schedules to every public service department and all the branches. Invite library staff to spend a day cross-training on the bookmobile. Keep your service in the limelight at the library so everyone gets used to seeing it, becomes familiar with it, and can be your advocate with rural patrons.

External Marketing

There are many ways to get the information about your service out to rural patrons. If your library can afford a mass mailing to the zip codes involved, print up a flyer, brochure, postcard, or whatever you can manage with the bookmobile's picture on it, in color if possible. Keep the text short and to the point; very few people will take the time to read long, involved mail. The picture will be the key to them recognizing you at the stop.

You have already been out and met storeowners, the postmaster, and other local key contacts. Go back to these people and ask them if they will post a flyer featuring the bookmobile's picture and/or your schedule on a public bulletin board, in a window, or someplace in their facility. Ask the grocer if he will put a schedule in every order of groceries. Ask the café if they will keep a stack of schedules on the counter where the people pay their bill. While you are there, offer to bring out books or media for them. If you get them using the bookmobile, they will tell more people about the service than you could ever personally reach.

If there is a local newspaper or newsletter in the area, invite the reporter/editor to the bookmobile and tell them all about your service. Ask the schools to put the stop times and locations in their monthly newsletters to parents. They can urge parents to keep their children reading during the summer and you can make it fun with a summer reading club. When the parents bring their children, you can inform them of all the services and materials you offer for adults.

Marketing doesn't stop once you have the people using the bookmobile. Display new books face out on some shelves or on the desks and benches. Decorate the bookmobile's small bulletin boards with beautiful or fun pictures from old calendars or discarded book covers from Technical Services to make it interesting and inviting. (Make sure they are appealing to all ages, not just children.) Keep the interior neat and clean so it is pleasing to enter. Offer occasional programs to entertain or provide information for the patrons. For example, have the bloodmobile accompany you to stops to take blood pressures, do cholesterol checks, and collect blood donations. Programs do not have to be long and involved or mean a lot of extra work for you. Programming, like marketing, is only as limited as your imagination.

CONCLUSION

This chapter only outlines the highlights of conducting a rural mobile library service. You will learn something new every day. You will experience something unexpected every day. You will help someone more than you will ever know every day. You are off on a wonderful adventure every day. Never forget how valuable your service is or how important it is to provide it. Be proud! You are carrying on a long and excellent tradition.

REFERENCES

Jan Meadows, "United States Rural Bookmobile Service in the Year 2000," *Bookmobile and Outreach Services* 4, no. 1 (2001): 47–63.

Mary L. Titcomb, *The Washington County Free Library: 1901–1951* (Hagerstown, MD: Press of Hagerstown Bookbinding & Printing, 1951).

Bookmobiles are useful for some of these types of outreach. With bold graphics and the name of the library emblazoned across its body, a bookmobile can be described as a travelling billboard. A bookmobile can also be a hit in a parade or a community event.

Community Building

A natural secondary role for bookmobile service, particularly service to neighborhoods, is community building. Modern neighborhoods, whether because of poverty or poor planning on the part of developers, often lack gathering zones where neighbors meet naturally. The best bookmobile service sites give neighbors a chance to visit with each other and develop a sense of community Since a bookmobile is such an intimate space, it lends itself to striking up conversations with others. This kind of social networking happens naturally, more so than in the larger environment of a library building, and bookmobilers should strive to create an atmosphere that supports this friendly interaction.

In the neighborhoods where a bookmobile works best, friendships form between parents, children make playdates, people gossip, joke, talk about the books they've read, and the community becomes more fundamentally connected. In other neighborhoods, once the patrons show off their jewelry to their neighbors, brag on their children and other possessions, they've said all they have to say to each other, and disappear back into the woodwork. You can't tell which kind of neighborhood one might turn out to be until you try it.

Service Delivery

Bookmobiles can effectively accomplish all three styles of outreach. But the specialty of bookmobiles is delivery of services. Nothing can make library services more accessible than a mobile microcosm of the library itself.

A bookmobile can be adapted to provide just about any type of library service. The Public Library Association's latest edition of *Public Library Services Responses* (Garcia and Nelson, 2007) lists 18 roles for the public library. Any of these roles can be performed by a bookmobile and every bookmobile performs some of them. The role in which bookmobiles traditionally excel, however, is the collection. Since collection is a primary role for most public libraries, mobile service via a large vehicle that can carry as many materials as possible is the best means to extend that primary role into your community.

You can easily deliver most other library services outside the library by other means. Information is provided via online catalogs, subscription databases, and links to recommended Web sites. Programs can be delivered by transporting performers and their supplies, renting space in other facilities, and striking deals with your local park service for outside activities. You can provide delivery services to homebound patrons, or teachers, or other agencies, with smaller vehicles or even staff members' own vehicles. But if you wish to provide access to the stuff of library service out in your community, there is no better method than having a browsing collection on wheels ready to go where needed.

TYPES OF BOOKMOBILE STOPS

Different libraries have different criteria for determining how to deploy their bookmobile services. Bookmobilers call their service points stops, and they will be referred to as such from here on.

In general, there are three different types of stops in bookmobile outreach:

- Institutional
- Need-based
- Convenience-based

Institutional Stops

These types of stops are dealt with more fully in other chapters. Institutions include schools, preschools, senior facilities, treatment centers, correctional facilities, and any other place that requires you to work with an intermediary to your individual patrons. For example, you might work with an activity director of a senior facility regarding scheduling your stop, and advertising and promoting your service. In some cases, the specific needs of another institution may affect your circulation rules, for example, what types of materials you may circulate at a school, or how many items each student may borrow. In most communities, this type of stop is best scheduled in the morning or early afternoon.

Need-Based Stops

Your demographic analysis will show pockets of underserved populations within your service area. These are people who need library service but don't have the resources to access them or the knowledge that they can. Neighborhoods with a *need for service* tend to encompass:

- Low income people
- New immigrants from another country or newcomers to the service area
- People with language barriers
- People with literacy barriers
- People with lack of access to transportation
- People who are not highly educated, but have high hopes and expectations for their children's educations

A library considering using bookmobile outreach can prioritize its service targets however it determines it should. However, since the primary mission of bookmobile service is usually to serve the underserved, populations who *need* mobile outreach to access their library should have priority for the service as you set your bookmobile stop schedule. Those who have little or no access to fixed library facilities in your community have the greatest need for library services to be delivered to them. The bookmobile circumvents transportation and geographic barriers to access by bringing materials directly to their neighborhoods. The small, welcoming, and friendly bookmobile environment can also overcome more subtle reluctance to use the library among those who may find larger library facilities intimidating. This process of developing the library habit among newcomers benefits both the library users themselves and the community as a whole.

Convenience-Based Stops

Neighborhoods that can benefit from *convenience service* tend to encompass:

- Professional, sometimes dual income families
- Highly educated people who have high hopes and expectations for their children's educations
- Children who are very heavily scheduled with other activities
- Library devotees, such as people who appreciate and use their library services regularly

Convenience service sounds like a frill, but is it? Ranganathan, the father of modern cataloging, posed as his fourth law of library science: "Save the reader's time" (Gorman, 1998). We use classification systems to shelve like material together for efficient browsing; we make displays of popular materials; we allow holds on materials. We make databases and catalogs accessible to remote users. Even due date stamps or receipts at checkout could be considered convenience services for library patrons. Where does bookmobile service fit into that model? It goes beyond bringing information to the remote user. Bookmobiles bring actual materials to the patrons.

Convenience stops can be a bargain for both libraries and the patrons they serve because they can serve as filler in a route schedule. For libraries, after the fixed costs of operation are tallied, such as maintenance, collection, staff training, and mobile communications fees, the costs of providing services are only staff salaries and fuel. These combined can run as little as $50 an hour. The more your bookmobile is open to patrons, the more people will use it, and the less it costs per capita to operate.

A well-used convenience stop also saves patrons time, money, and energy. Even a large low-mileage bookmobile reduces overall emissions by reducing the number of other vehicles driving to the library. Consider an hour-long bookmobile stop 10 miles from the library, served by a bookmobile that uses one gallon per 10 driving miles and one gallon per hour to run its generator. The vehicle will use up to three gallons of fuel serving the stop. If the stop serves at least three individuals or families who might otherwise drive themselves to the library, the stop breaks even on fuel use for the community as a whole, assuming their cars run about 20 miles per gallon on the 20-mile round trip to the library. Obviously, the more patrons served, the more savings on fuel (and emissions) for the community as a whole.

IDENTIFYING SERVICE NEEDS

Who Qualifies for Bookmobile Service?

The public library has an obligation to make its services available to everyone in its service area. Most public libraries define their community of service geographically, by county, township, city, village, or district. If there are unserved or underserved people within your community who cannot or do not use your library buildings, you need some form of mobile outreach.

Providing access to your collection or any of your other services and programs outside the library via bookmobile is called for when you have population groups in your service area that meet these two criteria:

They lack access to your fixed facilities (stationary libraries)
They are geographically clustered

Some people meet one criterion, but not both, such as homebound people with disabilities. These individuals are unable to access the library, due to lack of transportation or general poor health, but may not be geographically clustered. (Group homes are the exception.) Because it is usually inefficient to serve individual patrons via bookmobile, a smaller form of mobile outreach to reach them is called for, such as books-by-mail or homebound delivery. (These methods are discussed in Chapters 9 and 10.)

So who does meet both criteria? As we have seen, bookmobile patrons tend to fall into at least one of the following categories:

- Institutionalized people: seniors in assisted living or nursing homes; teens and adults in residential treatment facilities; people in group homes; prisoners

- Nontraditional library users: low-income families; non-English speakers; immigrants

- Time-poor people: two-income families; busy professionals

Identifying Potential Bookmobile Patrons

One simple method to determine whether you have people in your community who meet your service criteria is to compare demographic information about your community against your library use data. Are people who live within a mile of your building more likely to borrow materials than people who live farther away? Do you have ethnic or language groups underrepresented among your users? Do children of working parents attend your children's programs? Do teens use your reference service? For every type of service, especially circulation of materials, check your usage patterns against your demographics.

Changes in your community may happen faster than demographic reports can keep up with, so in addition to looking at demographic statistics, you can rely on your own observations within your community. Is there a new neighborhood being built on the edge of your service area? Do you notice people speaking a different language in your grocery store, one that you don't hear spoken in your library? Keep your ear to the ground; read the local paper; keep the lines of communication open with other service agencies; go outside the library regularly to stay in touch with what is happening in your larger community. If there is a disconnect between your community of library users and the larger community you serve, it should become apparent to you.

Numbers Never Lie, but Do They Matter?

Not every variation in your data will call for mobile outreach. I recently analyzed the gender and age data in my district's patron records. From census data, I know that the community's population of males and females is roughly equal. Our library's registered children are about 50 percent male, 50 percent female and our registered teens are about 52 percent female, 48 percent male, indicating that we are missing a few teenage boys in the district, but we are not far off the mark. For adults, the ratio shifts to about 67 percent registered females, 33 percent registered males. This gender gap is even more pronounced among our homebound patrons, although this may be attributable to life expectancy. Does my district's gender gap in patron registrations call for mobile outreach? Possibly. However, it might also call for some kind of publicity designed to reach men, or a shift in programs or collections to appeal to them. But men as a group probably do not need a bookmobile stop because as a group they don't meet the criteria of being geographically clustered or lacking transportation to the library building.

IDENTIFYING SERVICE SITES

Identifying potential service sites involves knowing the geographic layout of your community and knowing the likeliest places where people congregate. Once you've established the existence of target groups in your community, you'll need to figure out where and when to best serve them.

If you have lived and worked in your community for a long time before planning for outreach, you have a distinct advantage over a newcomer. Whether you are a newcomer or an experienced veteran at your library, you can use the following techniques to learn your service area on a more detailed level, neighborhood by neighborhood. This detail will help you determine if you need a bookmobile and, when you are ready to deploy it, it will help you to decide where to deploy it.

Maps and Satellite Images

Maps and satellite images will give you a visual overview of your community. Good sources of these are MapQuest and Google Maps. (Just keep in mind that satellite images available online are out-of-date. You will need to confirm the information on the ground.) Examine them for the big picture. Where is your housing most dense? Where are your major thoroughfares and what are your traffic patterns? How does your library fit in? Are there walking paths or biking paths that connect to it? Are there neighborhoods cut off from walking or biking access to your library by highways or train tracks? Which neighborhoods have cul-de-sacs, big houses on small lots, and only one way in and out of the subdivision? Which have apartment buildings or condos, townhouses or duplexes, square city blocks with narrow streets, or winding suburban lanes with no sidewalks?

Densely populated neighborhoods are often a good fit for bookmobile service because most of your bookmobile users will come from the immediate area around the stop. The more people within the immediate area, the larger a potential market you have for your service. Neighborhoods that are geographically isolated, even when they are close to a fixed facility, may also be successful stop locations. If people, especially children, are unable to get to a library due to a barrier such as a major road between their neighborhood and the building, that may be a good stop. Neighborhoods with no sidewalks or walking/biking paths are often isolated and without community gathering places. Look for places that are cut off from easy access to your library facilities and then examine them for evidence of the type of population groups you are trying to reach.

A densely populated apartment building a mile away from the library and across a river from your library might or might not be a good bookmobile service location. If it is populated by working young adults who all have cars and are rarely home, a bookmobile stop probably won't work. But, if it is populated by young families who are frequently home with little or no transportation, a bookmobile stop would be a great success.

Exploration

Drive Arounds

Spend some time exploring your territory. Use your map to learn what is where. If your service area has easily available public transportation, learn how your patrons use it to get to your library building. How much does it cost and how long does it take? If most people drive to your library, chart how long it takes to get there. How much different is it at rush hour? When you set your criteria for bookmobile service, you may want to use distance or time away from the library as one criterion. You may give priority to stops two or more miles away, or 15 or more minutes away. You can plot this information with concentric circles around your library location on your map.

Look at your neighborhoods. For each, consider who lives there. Are there families with young children, teenagers, retirees, or a mix? Is there a gathering place such as a playground in the neighborhood? Are there people of mostly one ethnicity or a mix? Is it a newer or an older neighborhood? (Note the size of the trees.)

Go back to your demographic and geographic analysis. Where are the dense neighborhoods? The low-income or otherwise needy neighborhoods? Where are the neighborhoods farthest from the library or otherwise isolated by geographical obstacles? (A geographic obstacle could be a river, a highway or major thoroughfare, an industrial area between a neighborhood and the library location, anything that despite proximity limits people's ability to get to the library.) Are there places where a lot of newcomers tend to live, such as new housing developments and apartment complexes with high rates of turnover?

For many bookmobile operations, serving children and families is a priority. Unless you are targeting singles or older adults without children, you will find it useful to look for what we at Cook Memorial Library traditionally call kidsign. Think of yourself as a hunter scanning for evidence of your quarry. You are looking for concentrations of families in the neighborhoods you are evaluating for service. Look for backyard play equipment, basketball hoops in driveways, or signs of affiliation with the local schools. Car seats, bicycles, skateboard, bumper stickers reading "my child is an honor student at . . ." will give you a sense of the concentration of children in a neighborhood as well as their ages. (It can be useful to have some library identification on your car when you do this, so you don't look like you are casing the neighborhood for less public-spirited reasons.)

Bathroom Breaks and Meal Breaks

Sufficient driving time and bathroom break times need to be built into the schedule, observing labor law requirements for break times and dinner times. Staff cannot reasonably go longer than three hours without an opportunity to use a comfort station. Try not to create shifts longer than three hours, or when you must, allow time between some stops to get to a public restroom without throwing the schedule off.

If your bookmobile is out over the lunch hour or from afternoon to evening, depending on the length of your shifts, staff may need a meal time. A five-hour shift is too long with just short bathroom breaks for most people, especially since bookmobile work can be so intensive.

Memorable Stop Schedule

Prime time for neighborhood bookmobile stops is similar to the concept of prime time in television programming. More people are home and available for leisure activities in the early evening. In the Cook Memorial Library district, prime time is roughly from 6:00–8:00 P.M. Afternoons from the time school lets out until about 5:00 P.M. are also good for bookmobile stops. Your service area may differ, but this is a typical pattern for most suburban neighborhoods.

Stops should start at memorable times, on the hour or half hour if possible. If your start times are easy for patrons to remember, you'll see the patrons more regularly.

Routes

Consider geographic proximity and driving times between stops. Try to cluster stops together. You should also consider traffic patterns. It might be more efficient for the vehicle to stay out, rather than return to the library, during your rush hour and dinner hour. Right around five P.M. can be a tricky time for bookmobile stops, but depending on your local conditions, it may not be a good time to travel much distance, either.

Parking

Where you park your bookmobile is as important as when it's open for business. The best parking places are natural gathering spots in a neighborhood. If there is a centrally located playground or park and there is a nearby place suitable for parking a large vehicle, it could be a perfect stop location.

Timing Is Everything

In the communities I have served, each of which covers about 48 square miles, 15 minutes is generally sufficient time to get from one stop to another. Your service area may be larger or you may have other obstacles to work around. For example, at one stop we needed to make a left turn out of a subdivision. We found that we had to allow more travel time at that time of day, just to allow time waiting for the opportunity to turn!

If there is no park, or there is no nearby large vehicle parking, or the park does not appear to be well-used, look for a busy intersection. If a neighborhood has one main road, with a series of cul-de-sacs off of it, a good stop location would be just off the main road at its intersection with the first cul-de-sac street. Your bookmobile will be off the main street but visible to everyone entering and leaving the subdivision.

Typically your bookmobile entrance will be located on the passenger side of the vehicle, so that patrons enter from the side of the road on which the bookmobile is parked. Situate your vehicle so that most of your patrons will enter from the same side of the street so that they don't have to cross the street. At institutional stops, parking close to the door of the building is advisable. Try to avoid leaving a passageway between the door of the building and the bookmobile so that other vehicles don't come through.

Some bookmobile operations use traffic cones or signs outside the vehicle to make approaching traffic aware of pedestrian traffic around the vehicle. A well-lit vehicle (inside and out) is also an asset in making drivers aware of activity around your parked vehicle. Before deciding to use extra signage outside the vehicle, consult your library administration, as insurance or legal liability issues may affect what type of warnings it is advisable to use. If you have a stop in a high-traffic area where this is a significant concern, consider moving the stop to a nearby side street to reduce the risk to your patrons.

If there is no viable intersection near the entrance to a subdivision, try a location deeper in the subdivision that is close to a cluster of families you have identified as potential users.

The closer you can get to your patrons, the more likely they are to use your services. Everybody would love to have a bookmobile stop right outside their front door. The further you are from your patrons, the less likely they are to come, especially younger patrons who are not allowed to venture far from home. In the typical suburban neighborhood, only older children, teenagers, and motivated parents of young children will walk more than a couple of blocks.

Duration

On rare occasions, you might have a small institutional stop, such as a day care or elder care, for which a half-hour stop is perfect. If you have only one or two people picking material for a larger group, or a single scheduled visit by a small organized group of 12 or fewer people, a half-hour stop can work.

No, Wait . . . Location Is Everything

A few years ago, the last large tract of land in the district I serve was slated for development. Gradually, over a period of years, several hundred new single family homes were built. The development is about three miles from both our main library and the nearest small branch library. The people who moved in were mobile, and therefore not in need of bookmobile services to have any access to the library at all, but they were far away enough from the nearest fixed service points to benefit from convenience stops.

Over the years, as each subdivision was completed and more houses were occupied, we tried various permutations of stop schedules. We usually used our summer schedules for this experimentation. In some subdivisions they worked and the service continues to be well-used. In others, once the novelty of bookmobile wore off, people stopped coming. Some of these stops are right across the road from each other, and I would be hard-pressed to identify the differences between them.

For neighborhoods, however, at least 45 minutes has been established as an optimal minimum bookmobile stop time.

Stop times should be adjusted to reflect their level of use. The following is an example of how two one-hour stops in an evening might work:

5:30 P.M.: Depart from library
5:45–6:45 P.M.: First stop
6:45–7:00 P.M.: Travel time between stops
7:00–8:00 P.M.: Second stop
8:00–8:15 P.M.: Return to library

Now, let's assume that over time the use of the first stop lessens and use of the second stop grows. In the next version of the schedule you might choose to shorten the first stop to 45 minutes and lengthen the second stop to an 75 minutes.

Patron Lifestyles

The more you know about your patrons' schedules, the better you can provide them with bookmobile service. In the summer, do the kids go to camp? If it's a day camp, when do they get home? Likewise, during the school year, how and when do kids get home? There is no point in having a bookmobile stop from 3:00–3:45 in a neighborhood where the kids get off the bus at 3:40.

Continuity

Continuity is important when considering schedule changes. If you have a successful stop that has been at 7 P.M. Thursday nights for 20 years, think twice before moving it. That said, if you need to free up a prime time slot for a new stop, a successful stop that can stand the strain of a schedule shift is a better candidate for rescheduling than a struggling stop. If you change a stop time, expect the use of the stop to diminish temporarily.

Seasonal Scheduling

Most bookmobile operations set an annual timetable for adjusting their schedules. You might choose to do it by the local schools' schedules, by Daylight Savings Time, or by other local criteria. Most bookmobiles adjust their schedules two or three times a year. At Cook Memorial Library, we change our schedule at the beginning of June, at the end of August, and sometimes at the beginning of January.

Know Thy Stops

I made a mistake with one stop early in my career by not being familiar enough with one of my neighborhoods. I made what I thought was a modest change to a stop, switching it from a Thursday to a Tuesday afternoon. It was a moderately busy stop before the switch. After the switch, a local parent told me that many of the children attended CCD (religious instruction) on Tuesday afternoons. The switch was a disaster; most of my regulars were not at home when I was at their corner. In the next round of schedule revisions, I moved the stop back, but it never completely regained the previous level of activity during my time at that library.

Other Considerations

When you have selected your stops and established your schedule, don't be afraid to change or adjust as you learn what works and what doesn't in your library territory. Neighborhoods that appear to be virtually identical demographically may have subtly different qualities that affect people's use of your bookmobile service.

Give need-based stops longer to gel than convenience stops. Before cancelling, look at factors that may be affecting use of the service. It might be a bad time for many of the residents or you may be parked in a place they don't see. Try moving the stop a block over or giving it a different time slot. If you are trying to reach people who are culturally unfamiliar with library use, are new to this county and culture, or have low literacy, do some marketing and give the community adequate time to discover the bookmobile before you cancel.

In convenience-based service neighborhoods, if bookmobile service is not working after a few months and you have made a reasonable effort to promote it, move on. The ability to move your library service to where it is most needed and most used is the greatest strength of mobile service. Mobility and the willingness to use it is key to the effectiveness of the service.

Measuring Impact

Forty to 50 checkouts per hour constitute a successful bookmobile stop. This number can be an average over time, especially for seasonal stops. In calculating circulation per hour, for stops that are longer or shorter than one hour, remember to use the correct multiplier to get the correct per hour figure. (Example: a 45-minute stop with an average of 30 checkouts per stop has an average of 40 checkouts per hour.)

Some bookmobiles also measure attendance to evaluate their stop usage. Most rely on manual methods such as using a hand-clicker each time someone comes through the door. Electronic door counters used in stationary libraries are not usually effective on a bookmobile.

When considering both circulation and attendance types of measurements for statistical purposes, keep in mind the type of stop and the style of use. For school stops, for instance, you may have high attendance but each student may only be allowed one item at a time. For neighborhood stops, families may use your service sending only one person or using only one library card for the whole family. Either method used consistently will give you a good idea of how much your service is used. If you do not measure attendance, note anecdotal reports by your bookmobile staff indicating that a stop is minimally used. In densely populated suburban and urban areas, a stop that is frequented by only one individual or family is not generally a good use of resources, even if your single user checks out enough items each time to meet your usage criteria.

Need-based stops tend to be higher circulating than institutional and convenience-based stops. At Cook Memorial Library, busy need-based stops show from 90 to 200 circulations per hour on average. At peak times, the bookmobile is packed with people wall-to-wall, front-to-back. Checking out stacks of materials to each patron or family group, our intrepid bookmobiler strives to devote his attention to fully serving each person, but time is limited and it is not usually possible to do more than take a few reserve requests, offer a few suggestions for reader or viewer guidance, and do his best to briefly address (and note for follow up) any more intricate reference or reader's advisory needs.

At the less time-pressed convenience neighborhood stops, circulation averages from about the 40 per hour minimum to about 80 per hour. At this speed of service, it is possible to devote more in-depth attention to each patron's needs. We can field typical questions like suggested reading for a second grade boy reluctant reader or why fairy tales and poetry are a good addition to picture books for your preschooler. We've even steered the Guinness World Records devotee to other types of nonfiction!

The bookmobile can be a circulation machine. Going into high-need and high-interest neighborhoods, equipped with the right kind of materials, circulation per hour is limited in practice only by the speed at which your circulation system can operate. But, having an aim and expectation of 60 to 80 circulations per hour may be more effective for providing a broader spectrum of library services. You can tweak the length and timing of your stops until you find the right mix of services for the type of bookmobile service you wish to provide.

DAMAGE CONTROL: WHAT TO DO WHEN YOUR BOOKMOBILE BREAKS DOWN

Just as library branches sometimes deal with faulty plumbing, cut power lines, and interrupted phone service, bookmobiles sometimes suffer from engine trouble, flat tires, and aging generators. Bookmobile services are also vulnerable to major road construction barriers and extreme weather.

If your bookmobile is grounded for scheduled repairs or unexpected mechanical problems, or because extreme weather makes it unsafe to travel, it's important to communicate with patrons and provide as much service as you can. Patrons must be contacted, and it's a good idea to use as many communications methods as possible to reach everyone. If you have an on-site contact at a stop, you may provide them with signs that notify or remind patrons of changes to the bookmobile schedule. You may employ radio announcements or a voicemail bookmobile hotline. At small stops, you may have the option of calling individual patrons to keep them informed.

If weather is not the reason for cancelling service, you may have the option of offering some form of substitute service in another vehicle. Try to use a vehicle with your library's logo or identifying marks. If your staff can deliver materials in their own cars or in library vehicles without logos, consider investing in large sheet magnets that can be attached to a car door. Large freestanding signs that can be placed around the neighborhood help raise awareness that bookmobile service is here, even though the bookmobile isn't.

Bring whatever rudiments of service you can provide, including reserved materials, bags for collecting returns, paper and pen or laptop for doing circulation, and some small smattering of a browsing collection. Your patrons will understand your limitations, be amazed at your dedication, and appreciate your efforts to go the extra mile.

Whenever you miss a scheduled stop, for whatever reason, waive fines on your next visit.

CONCLUSION

Mobile outreach is one of the best means to bring the benefits of library service to all our patrons. A bookmobile—properly stocked, staffed, and scheduled—can mean the difference between alienation and indifference, and full engagement in all the enrichment possibilities public libraries have to offer . . . right at patrons' front doors. Best of luck to you as you develop your mobile outreach program.

REFERENCES

June Garcia and Sandra Nelson, *Public Library Services Responses 2007* (Chicago: American Library Association, 2007).

Michael Gorman, "The Five Laws of Library Science Then & Now," *School Library Journal*, July 1998.

6

Library Services to Immigrants and English Language Learners

By Emily Klopstein, Becky Russell, Pilar Castro-Reino, Lisa Murillo, and Lou Petterchak

United States immigration policy has a history of welcoming workers for their labor. Naturally, then, our nation's public libraries have a corresponding history of serving immigrant populations. According to the 2000 census, 12.5 percent of the U.S. population were foreign-born and more than half (54%, or about 20 million people) come from Latin America (National Council of La Raza [NCLR], 2008). A 2007 American Library Association study notes that "about 21 million people in the United States speak limited or no English—*50 percent more than a decade ago.* Staff is faced daily with someone who needs services and does not speak English" (American Library Association [ALA], 2007).

This chapter focuses on library services targeting English language learners and immigrants. Common needs of these populations are addressed, followed by discussion about how libraries can meet those needs by tailoring traditional library services and implementing innovative service concepts.

COMMON CHARACTERISTICS OF ENGLISH LANGUAGE LEARNERS AND IMMIGRANTS

English language learners, immigrants, and refugees approach the library for help in making connections with appropriate social service programs, education and training opportunities, and community resources like recreation centers and day cares. The library's role is to be a warm welcoming place where they can get valuable connections to information, technology, and services.

Successful services and outreach to immigrant populations and English language learners respond to the following common factors:

A Service Tradition

Denver Public Library (DPL) began serving English language learners nearly a century ago. Its first bilingual neighborhood branch library collection appeared in 1913 when the Decker Branch opened with half its books in English and the rest in Dutch! Since the early 1990s, DPL has initiated programs and services targeting the city's growing number of Latino residents. Additionally, Denver is home to a significant population of Vietnamese people, serves a wide range of immigrants working in local industry, and is a refugee resettlement location. By providing a welcoming space, friendly staff, empowering programs, popular collections, and technology to stay in touch with family abroad, DPL helps new Americans participate in and enjoy not just the library, but also life in the city in general.

- Distrust of government entities
- Lack of understanding that public libraries are free and public
- Strong family orientation
- Potentially low literacy skills in the native language
- A wide range of cultural norms and expectations

The family bond is often stressed in immigrant situations—for example, when a child is called upon to translate for his or her parent at their own parent/teacher conference. The library can offer parents the tools and information they need to restore a healthy family balance. The library's authority in promoting study habits and healthy family communication can support and strengthen the family structure. In a new country and in situations when children often know more than the parent, the library can support and advocate for parents by supplying them with knowledge and times for family learning. It's important to do what you can to preserve the parent's position as head of the family. When a child is translating for a parent, be sure to respond to the parent, not the child. In DPL's intergenerational programs, we try to avoid doing anything that might undermine a parent's authority in his or her family, focusing our attentions on supporting parents' efforts in helping their children learn.

IDENTIFYING SERVICE NEEDS

The U.S. Census Bureau reported in 2007 that 16 states across the nation have at least half a million Hispanic residents (United States Census Bureau, 2007). The American Library Association states that smaller communities are serving ever-larger populations of English language learners and that the majority of libraries serving English language learners are in communities with fewer than 100,000 residents (ALA, 2007).

One recent publication reports that 54 percent of Latinos have visited a library in the past year and that most Latinos appreciate spending time in the library's relaxing and friendly atmosphere. Additionally, Latinos expressed appreciation for programs such as English language instruction, and the library's computer/Internet access (Flores and Pachon, 2008).

Studies such as these can inspire baselines to guide new projects and assist libraries or groups attempting outreach activities by providing background information. However, data alone should not limit or dictate your activities. In working with immigrant populations in the library, it is crucial to employ your own observations, the experience of library staff, and the input of your community to determine your direction.

An organization first needs to assess its role as information provider and its commitment to outreach. An obvious place to start is filling the gaps in the areas of materials resources, services, and programs, but much hinges on the organization's determination to include diversity, inclusivity, and logical prioritization in their planning.

Your service experience can begin when you simply make room for solutions as newcomers ask questions. Match your understanding of their expressed needs with a drive-around, census data, plus any other ways to gather community information about your area, and even include some sophisticated marketing program if you can. Presto! You've got a community analysis!

To identify the service populations beyond statistics, use your powers of observation! Who lives in your neighborhood? Who uses your library? For what purposes do they use it? Is local business signage in English, or perhaps Spanish, or Vietnamese? Drive around your community looking for these markers.

Budget will probably be your greatest determining factor in planning for additional services. Be strategic and start with the easiest: who is coming in today to your branch who could be served better? Do you have any contacts in the community who could give you ideas? Would your customers be open to sharing their ideas with you? If so, consider starting a neighborhood advisory committee that could meet monthly or bimonthly.

Services are determined by the needs of the population. If computer usage is extremely popular, find ways to better serve your community by expanding computer services. Adding additional computer stations is one way to expand, but an expansion can also be achieved by limiting the time each customer is allowed per day on your existing computer stations. Researching why the computers are in such high demand will assist you on how to expand this type of service appropriately. If computers are utilized much more by a particular age group, then make a plan for how to serve them better.

Due to budgetary constraints, it makes sense to focus on the immigrant populations that are the largest. (For example, Denver Public Library's largest immigrant groups are Spanish speakers and Vietnamese.) And even though you won't be able to provide full bilingual services in all languages, remember that if one type of service does not meet a need of a particular group, another one could. For instance, if Chinese customers are not able to locate books in their language, it's quite possible that another type of media such as CDs or DVDs will meet their needs. Since arts-and-crafts is mainly a visual activity, it transcends any language barriers; therefore, children and families from any background could participate and have an enjoyable library experience.

REACHING IMMIGRANT AND ENGLISH LANGUAGE LEARNING POPULATIONS

Engaging the Community

Following your community analysis, you will have identified key stakeholders in the community. If time and resources allow you to organize meetings of a neighborhood advisory committee, that is a great start. But equally productive relationships are easy to start with more one-on-one approaches.

DPL's Language & Learning Libraries

In 2004, seven of DPL's branches were identified as part of a market segmentation approach often practiced in the business sector. These branches, now known as the "Language and Learning" libraries, were selected based on analysis of library usage patterns, the city's changing demographics, and geographic considerations. In addition to providing standard or traditional library services, they focus on immigrants and Spanish-speaking adults seeking adult learning programs to improve their quality of life. Staff members enjoy providing a welcoming place where immigrants can keep in touch with friends and family, follow the news, apply for jobs, do homework, and learn.

Once you start programming, see who you're attracting and build relationships from there. A valuable level of trust can be gained through the organic process of getting to know your community through your programming attempts and asking for their honest feedback in developing future programs or services.

Promoting Library Services

Marketing is discussed in-depth in Chapter 1. However, some promotional techniques for reaching immigrant and non-English speaking populations bear mention here.

To promote programs to immigrant families, go where the kids are. Visit schools, early childhood education centers, and daycares and send translated fliers home with students. Attending parent night events at schools is a great way to get information directly into parents' hands. Your library can also choose to attend community festivals, neighborhood events, or any other opportunity where the community gets together and you can have a booth, a read-aloud session, or other presentation of your services.

Partnerships are mutually beneficial in reaching out to families who frequent other cultural, educational, and recreational facilities across the city. When promoting library services, make certain you are not in competition with other local agencies. If you position your services to complement those of other local agencies, you'll have much more success with partnerships. Organizations and agencies you might consider include:

- Consulates of major immigrant groups
- Catholic charities and other religious charitable organizations
- Immigrant organizations, such as the Immigrant Solidarity Network, the Immigration Voice, and the like
- Churches, mosques, synagogues, and other places of worship
- Cultural interest groups
- Social service agencies that specialize in immigrants
- Boys and Girls Clubs
- Local school districts and colleges

Foreign-language media outlets, such as radio, television, and newspapers, should figure into your marketing strategy, and it's easy to contact them because they usually have English-speaking staff to help you. Radio is one of the most far-reaching and effective means of marketing library programs and, compared to television, is a less costly way to advertise.

Don't forget to employ frontline library staff when promoting new services and programs. Be sure they understand the program and its goals and are able to communicate that clearly to customers. Supply them with flyers or bookmarks to insert with each check-out, or to refer to when customers inquire.

Translation

Translation is a major challenge of promoting library programs and services to immigrant groups. It's advisable to employ a combination of means to effectively translate library promotional materials and signage: utilizing your staff's own language abilities; contracting translation services outside of the library; even hiring a foreign language Web librarian to create and maintain foreign-language content on your Web site.

PROGRAMS AND SERVICES

Providing library services to immigrant populations in addition to your traditional base requires dedication, determination, creativity, and flexibility. Time and resources are limited, so to be strategic about what you offer special populations of any kind, especially in the beginning. Seek programs that are efficient and effective, and lend themselves to interagency partnership. The following programs are especially relevant to immigrants and English language learners and will probably be the most successful as you're starting out.

- Beginning (and/or intermediate) English language learning programs
- Computer classes
- Children's activities that run concurrent with adult programs, such as bilingual citizenship workshops

Libraries with solid funding, strong community partnerships, and/or staff with ample experience serving this population should also consider offering GED, Life Skills, Citizenship, Intergenerational programs, English level 2, and/or English conversation classes. Bear in mind, though, that your emphasis should always be focused on the needs of the user. Be open to the demands of your community—what do they need or want? Start by offering English, computer instruction, bilingual kids' programming and see what your audience suggests for the future.

Through these programs, you have the potential to reach:

- Self-directed learners
- Working adults whose schedules conflict with a more formal class
- Students already participating in traditional language acquisition classes, but needing practice in conversation skills
- Students supplementing formal learning opportunities
- Students with little or no classroom experience, or those who have long been absent from classrooms
- Illiterate students who may not qualify for more structured language acquisition programs

- Parents and caregivers without other childcare options
- People with transportation challenges
- Learners intimidated by more formal learning environments

An essential part of adult educational programs is an introduction to the library and its services, including how to acquire a library card; how to check out materials; the fact that library materials are free and must be returned; why late fines are charged; and an introduction to other library use practices and policies.

English Language Learning Programs

English language learning programs are more than an introduction to American culture and the English language; they also serve as the human connection to the world of libraries and learning. Even illiterate students who might not qualify for more structured language acquisition programs can participate in basic language learning programs at the library. Such programs should allow participants to relax and build their confidence with each class or activity.

Ideally, each language learning lesson should be stand-alone in format. By stand-alone, we mean that lessons at specific skill levels should not be progressive, or build on previous lessons. At first glance, this might seem counterproductive. However, for a variety of reasons, individual attendance in language learning classes is usually sporadic. Each lesson should feature a distinct topic, like transportation or grocery shopping, at exactly the same skill level as the previous lesson. This allows learners to pick up wherever they left off. At any time, learners may feel they are ready to move on to the intermediate level, or to a more formal learning environment beyond what the library can offer. Network with local institutions providing English Language Acquisition courses. Inform your immigrant community of locations where they can continue their English studies.

Additional English learning opportunities can be offered through language-learning software like Rosetta Stone, the Mango online language-learning program, or free online via USA Learns (from the

Tu Biblioteca Hoy

In 2006, the Denver Public Library received an Institute of Museum and Library Services (IMLS) grant we called *Tu Biblioteca Hoy/Your Library Today*, the primary purpose of which is to serve a growing demographic of Spanish-speaking adults with limited English language skills. The grant was sought to meet the needs of a growing demographic of library customers and Denver residents—a need identified by the library, but for which funds were not available through the Library's regular budget. In the grant proposal and in planning a new generation of library services to newcomers, DPL staff built on its history of serving immigrants in Denver.

Today's library programs for adults include practical English language learning programs, GED support, computer instruction, and topical seminars on lifestyle issues. In partnership with the local Museo de las Americas and the Denver Art Museum, children's enrichment programs promoting literacy, art, and culture are offered at the same times and locations as adult programs. In this way, DPL strives to make it convenient for immigrant families use the library together. The weekly impact of 7 locations offering 6–7 programs per week is an average of 45 *Tu Biblioteca Hoy* programs serving newcomers and language learners in the city of Denver!

U.S. Department of Education). CD-ROMs can be circulated, but bear in mind that they won't serve those without home access to computers very well. Library access significantly improves the usability of these kinds of programs.

Service Begets Service

DPL's Hampden Branch holds English programs once a week. One group of students consisted of many women from the Middle East and Korea. Some were particularly diligent and successful and still come back to say hello and keep in touch with their teacher. One former attendee has even established a charity to help build schools in Pakistan and rescue camel boys from their dangerous jobs in Dubai and Saudi Arabia.

With proper licensing, you can make language-learning software programs available on library computers for in-library use or your library's Web site for remote access at any time. For in-library use, you should provide headphones. Another innovative concept is the Language Learning Lab, where a library meeting room or cybermobile is equipped with computers (often laptops), headphones, and a trained assistant to get learners started.

English programs offered at the library should serve as a complement to other options already existing in the community. English at the library can be a springboard to more formal learning environments. As with every other topic of study, the library is a good place to start. Once customers acquire some basic skills or knowledge, it is the strength of the library to refer them to where they might be able to learn more. Your goal should be to understand the network of English learning options available in the community and prepare learners to attend those other agencies' programs by making them aware of their next step and giving them the confidence to progress.

Computer Instruction

New immigrants and English-language learners are among those most impacted by the digital divide. Computer classes aimed at beginners are particularly relevant for that reason, and also attractive for the population as a means of staying in touch with friends and family abroad. Topics can include:

- Using computers, including basics like using a mouse and navigating Windows
- Creating simple text documents
- Setting up and using e-mail accounts
- Using the Internet to find housing and jobs
- Applying for jobs online

Like language-learning programs, weekly computer instruction should follow a stand-alone format. Most people will pick and choose which classes to attend, anyway. One might need Internet instruction, but already has an e-mail account. Another might like to register for e-mail, but already has basic skills. Others need to start from the beginning, while still others take a course over and over again until they feel comfortable with their abilities.

Laptop Computer Classes

Courses in computer instruction were added to the TBH roster in the fall of 2007 with the installation of wireless Internet at our locations and the purchase of 15 laptops per location. A curriculum of practical computer skills was developed, resulting in a series of six computer classes. The series is continuous: after the sixth week of computer instruction, the series begins anew. The six classes cover the following basic syllabus: Beginners, Documents, E-mail I & II, and Internet I & II.

You may discover that computer classes are the only programs for immigrants and English language learners for which you have to register participants. Often, it is the most popular program you can offer these customers. You'll also be limited by the number of computer stations in your lab. Be sure to keep the registration process is as minimal as possible to avoid giving the impression that you're monitoring attendance. (Remember that many immigrants, in particular, do not associate good intentions with government agencies.) A simple sign-up sheet should require first name only. It also always helps to assign a welcoming staff member to greet learners, help them sign in, and answer any questions they may have.

Many options exist to provide computer instruction to immigrants, language learners, or any other members of your community. Do you have a bank of two or three computers in one relatively isolated area of the library? You could begin by offering small group instruction scheduled during a quiet time for your location, or even before the library opens to the public.

If your facility is near a high school or college, you might explore the option of using scholars in need of volunteer hours. It is often easy to find first- or second-generation representatives of the immigrant community at the local high school, able to communicate bilingually. They may be able to sit one-on-one with customers for one or two hours a week after school to assist with computer learning. That would be a very simple way to start, but might make a nice impact or inroad as you explore this new program.

Life Skills Workshops

In addition to learning the English language, immigrants and others may appreciate some introduction to American culture and institutions. This may translate into any number of workshop topics, such as:

- Purchasing a house
- Planning healthy meals
- Starting a business
- Resume-writing, job searching, and other job and career skills
- Helping children succeed in school
- Maintaining personal safety
- Managing money

Library staff can present life skills workshops, but ideally, you should enlist business owners and other professionals to act as partners in providing these programs.

Courses in life skills can greatly supplement English language programs by offering information on American culture, beyond speaking the language. The format should be informal—like sitting around a table together talking through concerns. Presentations can blend lecture and participation, leaving plenty of room for questions.

Your library can often make contact with potential life skills presenters through networking with local business groups such as the chamber of commerce, the Hispanic and women's chambers of commerce, or other small business groups in your area. Emphasize the benefits of informing immigrant groups about their consumer options. While we cannot promote brands or products, knowledge alone will maximize the number of people looking into their business resources. Once other businesses in your community hear that the library is offering this type of programming, they'll soon contact you to see how they can partner as well.

Intergenerational Programs

Immigrant parents may lack the confidence or knowledge to help their children with homework. Intergenerational programs are an opportunity for the library to show all family members about resources that can help with homework. Both parents and children appreciate activities they can do together as a family. Storytimes and other fun family activities are an opportunity to introduce fun books, reading and prereading skills, and encourage families to check materials out and take them home to enjoy together.

Family literacy and education are among the most important factors in determining a child's academic success. Parents who bring their children to the library demonstrate that education and learning is valuable. When parents attend educational programs in the library, their children are exposed to books, to reading, and to experiencing the public library as a fun, educational, and interactive environment. This creates a connection between these families and the library. They may discover not only a resource for books and materials, but also the potential to enhance their lives through human connections and the power of literacy.

Since family is culturally important to many of the largest and newest immigrant groups, particularly Latinos, Asians, and Middle Easterners, you'll experience more success when you welcome participants of all ages to your programs. Making families feel comfortable instead of limiting or separating family members leads to successful participation.

If you have the space and staffing to provide a children's program while the adult program is also going on, it can make parent-learners feel relaxed to know their child is nearby but productively occupied. That's the concept of concurrence—separate, but simultaneous. Offering children's activities concurrently with adult programming makes participation easier for some parents. Bilingual craft and literacy activities occupy children productively for the programming hour, thereby allowing families to enjoy the library together. In this way, you can reduce the childcare barrier so that parents can study while their child attends a storytime or craft activity.

If you need to have children and adults share the same place, try to carve out a children's area and have at least one staff member dedicated to providing the children

> ## Museum Partnerships
>
> DPL's children's programs are offered in partnership with two local museums: the Denver Art Museum and the Museo de las Americas. The programs are scheduled simultaneously with our English language learning, GED, and computer instruction programs. In this way, DPL strives to reduce the childcare barrier for our learners so parents can study while their children attend bilingual craft and literacy activities.
>
> The emphasis for every concurrent children's program is a literacy tie-in that connects books to an interactive craft that follows each storytime. Enriched Arts and Crafts programs introduce local artists who focus on culturally connected crafts such as piñatas, Guatemalan worry dolls, Mexican *papel picado,* or Chinese New Year dragons.

with a library activity of their own—perhaps a storytime, or even just the chance to select and read their own books quietly while their parents are working. Puzzles or coloring are other quiet alternatives.

Part of programming for nontraditional learners or in a nonformal environment is being open to whatever comes your way. What would traditionally be viewed as an effective learning environment is not practical for many immigrant families. By letting go of traditional American assumptions about learning and definitions of things like class and teaching, you'll open the door to a more practical and valuable learning environment for the families you serve.

The principle is that learning will happen one way or another, but only if immigrant customers feel able to be themselves.

Go with the flow, be accommodating, and let your focus be to build confidence and provide a welcome space. Be as free as possible in allowing access to learning regardless of circumstances. Be prepared for babes in arms at the English program, and breast-feeding during computer class. Smile! Relax! Let go! Be open to the variety of learning styles and needs you'll encounter when serving immigrants, refugees, and English language learners. It's about them! Support their choice to come to the library and make that effort to help learners feel comfortable and welcome.

Managing Multiple Languages

Even when your programs focus on a specific language group, they can be appreciated by newcomers from around the globe seeking to improve their status and comfort in living in this country, state, and city. The goal is to have everybody feel welcome in the library, so programs should have universal appeal and be offered to customers of all backgrounds. In the case of a multitude of languages, English tends to be the most universal and so students of all backgrounds can learn English together.

The bilingual or trilingual facet can be incorporated via assistants. Even if you are unable to find an instructor who is bilingual, by pairing the instructor with a bilingual youth volunteer as an assistant, you can double your language capacity.

TBH programs are not formal pedagogical classes, but opportunities to learn some new vocabulary and grammar and practice skills in a nonthreatening environment. At one of DPL's branches the students in the beginning English classes often represent two or three or more native languages. The instructor is patient and creative and ends up relying on English and body language for teaching. The students in these classes express satisfaction with what they learn and say that they are gaining confidence in using English.

COLLECTIONS

Census data can be used to determine if you should serve your population with a foreign-language collection. Research your service area and neighborhoods for immigrant groups and languages spoken. Also, look around to see what is happening, as not all immigrant groups cluster in neighborhoods. The size of the population, cost of obtaining the collection, and the availability from the publishers will be major factors in your acquisitions.

Pay attention to what customers are demanding. Circulation statistics and your observations of in-house use will help inform you. Obviously, you'll have to balance what customers want with what you have space for (or are willing to make space for.)

Employ resources like Criticas and WebJunction for information on vendors and materials. Keep in mind though that your target community will also know where to acquire the materials to serve them. These are questions you could bring up at a community advisory committee meeting.

Customer demand should dictate your format choices. Spanish language materials are now widely available, but you'll be challenged to locate materials for some of your other language groups.

If you don't have a bilingual collection development librarian, utilize staff or a trusted member of the community. Find an experienced staff or community member involved in this area, or one that keeps up-to-date with this type of collection.

Keep foreign-language and bilingual materials separate from the English language collection. Particularly for new library users a separate section is less intimidating and less confusing.

For service to Spanish speakers, magazines and movies should be an integral part of any Spanish-language collection. These popular materials attract not only Latino women, but also men who may not otherwise enter a library. You should also purchase materials to support any programs you are offering, and these can be specially showcased during each program. Consider books, databases, DVDs, and audio on subjects such as English Learning, GED, computer skills, and citizenship, in addition to general reference information in the native language.

CREATING DIVERSITY-FRIENDLY LIBRARY SPACES

Ideally, a diversity-friendly space would be arranged intuitively along common lines of understanding and inclusion. Always be sensitive to the possibility of stereotyping. This may be another topic to discuss with your community advisory team.

Diversity-friendly spaces demonstrate an understanding of family dynamics and composition. One idea to try is the Comfy Corner (DPL features these in our Community Learning Plazas; see sidebar). In the Comfy Corner, small children can entertain themselves, play with each other or their siblings, or watch an educational DVD while the rest of their family do homework, work on resumes, practice English, and more. In this way, the children are near and also engaged.

> ## Community Learning Plazas: Where Families Come Together
>
> In the fall of 2008, Language & Learning branches began experimenting with the intergenerational literacy concept through a program format we named the Community Learning Plaza. The Plaza is a space in a library community room in which all members of the family can learn together on a variety of topics including English, computer skills, homework, citizenship, and GED through online resources and with the assistance of library staff, volunteers, and TBH instructors. They also feature Comfy Corners, with child-size seating, pillows, bean bag chairs, and oversized stuffed animals, as well as board books, simple puzzles, other toddler and prekindergarten toys, and sometimes even a DVD player.
>
> Community Learning Plazas provide a flexible learning experience by connecting the entire family with technology for learning. This pilot has proven popular and plans are underway to expand the number of hours per week that the library can offer Community Learning Plazas in 2010.

Bilingual signage may be ideal, but can be costly. Additionally, it may not be a wise investment if the community is undergoing dramatic change. Instead, explore ways to communicate signage universally through symbols or pictures.

Above all, making the environment as safe and welcoming as possible is what helps make parents feel more comfortable having their children in the library. And again, hiring friendly staff is crucial to your success. A warm smile trumps any outdated space.

STAFFING

Library Staff

Frontline staff are the most critical component of providing services and programming to immigrant populations. Dedicated and friendly service staff are key, especially when serving those who value interpersonal connections, such as Spanish speakers .

Start by recruiting staff who can sincerely relate to the community with personable and welcoming qualities a non-English speaking newcomer would appreciate. It can take many years to build up this staff. If your library is just beginning to head in this direction, you might begin by hiring someone who has lived or can relate to the immigrant experience. When your veteran staff get to know an immigrant on a personal level, they will be much more empathetic in working with the population. Not only do your immigrant customers see themselves then reflected in your staff, but your staff begin to understand the profound undertaking these groups go through trying to adjust to life in a new country.

When making new hires to serve a non-English speaking population, advertise for the diversity-friendly qualities you want this individual to possess. These might include:

- Bilingualism
- Extensive knowledge of the countries of origin and cultural norms of the groups you wish to target
- Experience working with customers who speak the language
- Positive attitude
- Excellent interpersonal and problem-solving skills.

Incorporating inclusivity via hiring even at the paraprofessional level can offer insider knowledge and lead to greater identification between the library and the community. Staff may uncover their own coping skills as their thinking shifts—just as new Americans find themselves coping as they adjust and use your institution!

Recruiting bilingual staff and developing foreign-language skills in veteran staff enhances service capacity and improves the library experience for the target audience. The same tools that customers use to learn English can also be utilized by library staff to build or practice their foreign-language skills.

In addition to foreign-language training, cultural competency training improves our ability to serve immigrant and non-English speaking populations. Participants learn about communication styles and strategize how to apply them in customer interactions. Staff are also given time to explore behaviors and attitudes that enable them to work effectively in cross-cultural situations. This training helps staff understand the community being served, plan outreach activities, and capitalize on their own strengths to benefit customers.

More than anything, the support and enthusiasm of frontline staff is fundamental to the success of any outreach and services to immigrants and English language learners. Programming and collections bring new people into the building, but friendly service keeps them coming back and encourages them to tell friends and their community about the library. Even more important than language skills is that staff display an open-minded willingness to help people who might not be familiar with the institution of the public library. As reported in *Latinos and Public Library Perceptions*, "Latinos are more concerned with friendly staff service than Spanish language access" (Flores and Pachon, 2008). It is probably safe to assume a similar opinion of most non-English speaking customers.

Staff should take whatever steps are needed in creating a warm welcoming atmosphere where immigrants and language learners feel comfortable. It can be time-intensive to assist someone unfamiliar with computers fill out an online form to apply for jobs or government services, but the investment is worth it. Give tours of the library to adults in your language learning and computer instruction programs to show them the library's materials and explain about library cards, borrowing privileges, and even the different machines they might encounter in the library. It's important to take the time to dispel mysteries so that newcomers do not feel intimidated or embarrassed by unfamiliar self-check machines or a computer reservation station.

There are big rewards when staff members make an effort to get to know customers and their families. The family bond is very

Bilingual Staffing

In addition to increased programming targeting Spanish-speaking adults in Denver, the Language & Learning libraries also feature enhanced bilingual service staff and resources. As part of the *Tu Biblioteca Hoy* grant, staff involved in providing expanded services to immigrants and Spanish speakers have the chance to learn Spanish and be trained in cultural competencies to better serve immigrant populations. Bilingual staff receive bonus-pay for their skills and when we recruit new staff members, language skills are a priority. DPL's seven Language & Learning branch libraries also feature sizeable Spanish language collections for adults and children.

strong in many immigrant communities and adults are delighted when a staff member can greet their children and offer to help them find a book to read or some paper and pencil to scribble with while the parents use a computer. We hope to serve more families in this way in our Community Learning Plazas, flexible spaces for different kinds of projects where families can work together to improve their language skills and pursue other learning activities.

Teachers

Selecting the right teachers is vital. The teachers set the tone and make the bilingual setting work. For these reasons, hiring flexible and creative teachers is essential. Instructors should be selected according to their experience, interpersonal skills, flexibility, and overall willingness to work closely with the team toward the goal of building participant confidence in a warm, comfortable environment.

Post "now hiring" flyers in your branch of course, but also think of other viable outlets—we've even used Craigslist at times! Computer, English, and other instructors can be found at local institutions such as elementary schools, high schools, and community colleges. Word-of-mouth advertising works, too. Teachers are especially good at spreading the word to other teachers, so be sure to keep the local schools informed of your need for instructors. You should also consider partnering with agencies specializing in adult ESL. These agencies are sometimes for-profit businesses, although many non-profit organizations exist, and these organizations are often more than willing to partner with libraries to provide their services.

Compensation of instructors varies widely. Some may even volunteer. If your library is partnering with another agency, you should have a contractual agreement that specifies which agency will pay the instructors' fees. If the library is responsible for compensating instructors, funds can come from the library's budget or via grant funds.

Retired teachers are also make reliable instructors; if there is a college in the area where students are in training to teach, they may be open to helping the library in this endeavor. Also try making use of local library schools if applicable. Library school students often need volunteer hours, or wish to develop their resume with practical experience providing programming. High school honor students who need to complete volunteer hours are another valuable resource for their technology skills and sometimes bilingual skills as well.

Consider hiring volunteer assistants as well for your programs. Here again, teen volunteers are a great resource. Having assistants on hand can bridge some of the challenges to conducting a program for participants with a wide range of educational experience and backgrounds. Youth who are the children of immigrants can also provide support for the bilingual environment. To top it off, your high school volunteers have the potential to become your future instructors!

If you do attempt to recruit teachers from other local area institutions, be certain you are not seen as competing. Be clear in communicating how your programs complement others being offered in the area, and that by employing teachers from local institutions, you are doing so in partnership, not in competition.

EVALUATION

Being responsive to the service needs of immigrants and English language learners does not always reflect success in same way library programs are traditionally measured. Typically, the success of library programs are measured by statistics and, most often, high attendance numbers equal success. However, where programs for immigrants and language learners are concerned, program quality can conflict with high attendance.

One challenge of serving immigrant populations is retaining participants in ongoing programs, like language learning classes. Most often their ability to participate is contingent on basic survival needs, especially financial ones. Immigrants can be itinerant, so someone at your library this week may be absent for the next several weeks, only to show up again. Childcare is another costly and complicated obstacle for many immigrant families.

In responding to the changing needs of these customers, you need to redefine the meaning of success. High attendance is not the best measure of success, for two reasons. First, attendance numbers alone tell you nothing about the quality of the experience for participants. Second, the diversity of educational backgrounds and financial needs of program participants calls for an optimum attendance of about eight people per program.

If the goal is *quality*, instead of *quantity*, the focus shifts to what immigrants and language learners need most of all if there's any chance of keeping them as regular library customers: a feeling of safety, confidence, and welcome. Viewing success as a quality experience for the individual all but guarantees a more relaxed atmosphere for hosting programs. This conveys to our participants that the library is exactly what we wanted most for it to be: a welcoming place! People can't learn if they're afraid, so more intimate, informal programs foster comfort in the learner and relationship-building between the learner and the library, both of which contribute to a welcoming learning environment.

Some library-provided English programs across the country use testing as a metric, but for the reasons stated above, DPL has chosen not to test. We've found it difficult to get exact measures when implementing English learning for groups with such varied educational backgrounds and in stand-alone units that allow for sporadic attendance. Instead of attempting to assess academic progress, we ask our program participants if they enjoyed the programs, feel they learned something they can use in daily life, and feel more confident about their skills. A standard survey is administered for each type of program at least twice each semester to get participant feedback.

English proficiency testing requires knowledge, skill, and academic qualifications beyond those of most public library staff. Some libraries contract with program providers for more formal academic classes. These providers may be qualified to do more proficiency testing. Rates of class completion or the ability to demonstrate an increase in skill level can be influential in seeking funding for this type of program. Weigh the benefits of each approach and decide which might work best for your situation.

SPECIAL SERVICE CHALLENGES

A changing population and one that is increasingly more diverse is a challenge to providing consistent programs. It will be nearly impossible to target every language and/or immigrant group in your service area. However, many cities have networks of agencies, like the Denver Coalition for Integration, that provide services and support to new immigrants and refugees. The public library should be an active participant in networks of this kind.

Another obstacle in serving immigrants is their suspicion or distrust of government services and buildings. Being asked for documentation, recent raids of work-sites suspected of employing illegal immigrants, or past experience living under corrupt, violent, or fascist regimes, all contribute to this uneasiness. To counteract this feeling, service staff should be friendly, flexible, and understanding in order to gain the customers' trust. Library rules can be particularly confusing and off-putting to customers to whom public libraries are completely alien. Staff need to be particularly accommodating regarding library card sign-up, empathizing and informative about fines, and sensitive to customers' learning curve. In order for immigrants to fully enjoy your library system, you will need to explain library policies and procedures repeatedly.

At times, the very success of the library's programs presents a challenge. With an increase in attendance, space limitations and outdated designs can make it difficult to accommodate growing numbers of participants. Be thoughtful and creative to strategize solutions. Consider varying the times classes are offered: If your programs are overly successful, you might have to move them to a time that is less overwhelming, or when fewer people can attend. Explore your options. Could another time be offered? Are neighborhood partners willing to host additional programs at their location?

If program popularity or branch layout are challenging, try having a traffic director at the front door to greet attendees and help get children to the children's activity, if there is one. Offering Family Literacy activities at busy times is another strategy. The busy evenings are often times when families come to the library together anyway, and offering an activity that engages everyone to work together means parents will be there not only to help and learn with their children, but also to provide supervision.

Other obstacles are the misconceptions that arise from the public and even from library staff about services to immigrant and English language learners. As the economy constricts, residents find themselves competing for the same resources, and backlash against serving immigrant communities often intensifies. Sometimes community members have concerns about serving undocumented immigrants, who are often incorrectly characterized as not paying taxes and therefore undeserving of special allocations of library resources. The political climate is a factor that impacts immigrant and non-English speaking communities, but over which the library has little influence.

The most common extreme fear expressed by members of the general public is that the library plans to replace English-speaking staff and English-language services and materials with Spanish-only services. While this can be a highly charged, hot-button topic for a lot of people, there are some basic customer service approaches with which to respond.

Prepare your staff for challenges. Brainstorm some reactions and have your staff build scripts around how they might best address them. Make your stance simple, positive, and fundamental. It is not wise to engage in debate or confrontation. Be sure that individual staff members know your library's brief and official response to concerns expressed by officials or the public. Also be sure that they know to refer questions they do not feel comfortable with to their supervisors.

Prepared sets of "Frequently Asked Questions" with responses are very helpful for staff to refer to when facing challenges. FAQs can even be made available online for the staff and the public. This is a good and accessible way to explain the library's official policy and the principles that guide its services to immigrants and non-English speakers.

Another resource is your organization's Community Relations department. They can be instrumental in preparing scripts, and having FAQs posted on the Web site, but also are available to respond to questions from the media. Make certain your staff knows the organizational structure and feels confident about when, where, and how to refer inquiries. You might also consider putting in place a policy about this so that your library has a consistent message when handling an individual or group that might like to create an issue out of library services to immigrants or non-English speakers.

It is possible to turn many of these hostile discussions around by focusing on how services for non-English speakers can also positively impact the English-speaking community; for example, computer classes and GED are available to benefit everyone in the community and online language-learning tools can be used by English-speaking customers to learn a new language for their upcoming vacation. Reiterate the fact that library programs and services are not exclusive.

You can attempt to build understanding based on common ground, but you will not win all these discussions. It can take a long time for your community to accept or adjust to their new neighbors. In conversations with both the established community and Denver's newcomers, we consistently hear from customers who appreciate these services and looked forward to expanding language programs to eventually include opportunities for English-speakers to learn Spanish.

Library ethics dictate that we serve everyone. American public libraries have a tradition of service to the residents of their communities, regardless of citizenship. Our professionalism and ethics can be tested when implementing services to groups often the focus of scrutiny, politics, or controversy. Ethics of confidentiality, access, and equality of service are especially crucial when embarking on outreach to an under-served population.

CONCLUSION

It can seem like a huge undertaking to begin outreach and programming for immigrants and English language learners, but if you look within your organization there may already be projects you can build on. Many front line public service staff people are creative, observant, and great sources for ideas about what your immigrant customers want and need. Try to take advantage of expertise and ideas imbedded at every level of your organization.

An important aspect of providing any new service is a willingness to try, experiment, fail, and ultimately succeed. Be open to input and feedback, understanding that you might not get it right on the first try! Patience, flexibility, and creativity are characteristics to cultivate when providing library services to immigrants, refugees, and English language learners.

It is only after 15 years of serving Spanish-speaking customers that DPL has taken on such an ambitious level of programming. We've built up this capacity over years and years of experimentation, hiring the right team, thinking creatively, and being open to all the possibilities of service.

Getting your staff and organization accustomed to the idea of serving diverse populations right now is the way to go! Even if you don't currently serve immigrants and non-English speakers or if the immigrants residing in your service area disperse, serving linguistically and culturally diverse customers is only going to become more and more a part of the work libraries do. Making it systemic and normal within your organization will pave the way for smooth service in the future.

REFERENCES

American Library Association. "Serving Non-English Speakers in U.S. Public Libraries: 2007. Analysis of Library Demographics, Services and Programs" (Chicago, IL: American Library Association Office of Research and Statistics, 2008). Available at: http://www.ala.org/ala/aboutala/offices/olos/nonenglishspeakers/docs/Linguistic_Isolation_Report-2007.pdf.

Edward Flores and Harry Pachon, "Latinos and Public Library Perceptions" (Dublin, OH: OCLC Online Computer Library Center, 2008). Available at: http://www.trpi.org/PDFs/Latinos_&_Public_Library_Perceptions_Final.pdf.

National Council of La Raza. "Five Facts about Undocumented Workers in the United States" (Washington, D.C.: National Council of La Raza, 2008). Available at: http://www.nclr.org/content/publications/download/50720.

United States Census Bureau, "Resident Population by Race, Hispanic Origin, and State: 2007," 2009 Statistical Abstract. Available at: http://www.census.gov/compendia/statab/tables/09s001s8.pdf.

Part III

Library Outreach to Children

7

Serving Preschool Children and Childcare Providers

By Theresa Gemmer and Ruth Pettibone

The problem is that we have concentrated exclusively on teaching the child how to read, and we have forgotten to teach him to want to read. . . . There is the key: desire. It is the prime mover, the magic ingredient.

—Jim Trelease

LITERACY RISKS IN AMERICA

Today in the United States, 60 percent of children under the age of five are in some form of out-of-home care on a weekly basis (Iruka and Carver, 2005). It is often difficult for childcare or preschool providers to take children to the library, either because they don't have transportation or because of the difficulty of managing a flock of preschoolers outside the controlled environment of their center. Also, busy families today often do not make taking their children to the library a priority. All of these factors combined set the stage for a literacy crisis.

Reading books and interacting with books is essential to learning to read. Our primary aim in providing bookmobile service to preschool and childcare centers is to make a child's first contact with books thrilling. It has been demonstrated that children are more likely to choose looking at books or being read to as an activity when an attractive variety of books is presented, but strong classroom collections may be the exception rather than the rule. Susan B. Neuman's 2001 study of books in childcare centers concluded, "Book collections in early childhood classrooms averaged from mediocre to poor. Without efforts to reverse this trend, early childhood programs will not close the book gap for children of low-income families" (Neuman et al., 2001).

Compounding the problem, in many states the qualifications for teachers in preschool and childcare settings is minimal, although the early childhood profession is working hard to upgrade this. Affordability of childcare is the main issue here. Someone who has put the time and money into a college degree usually expects to work for more than minimum wage. Higher teachers' wages mean higher childcare costs to

Dream Come True

"Books!" screamed a four-year-old on her first visit to the bookmobile. She narrowed her eyes. Turning to me, she added, "This better not be a dream." She had never been to the library and her delight in discovering that such a place, full of books, existed in the world still makes me smile. (TG)

Book Worms?

Caregivers in childcare centers are increasingly called upon to run their facilities like preschools, a task for which they may have little or no training. A student at one preschool chose a book about worms, and his teacher said, "That's good because we are going to be studying insects next week." I tactfully informed her that worms are not insects, but she rallied with caterpillars as an example and wanted to know if worms were not insects, then what were they? "They are worms," I answered. She did not appear convinced. (TG)

parents who may themselves be working for minimum wage! And higher wages for teachers mean less money for other resources (books, for example) in the classes.

SETTING UP SERVICES

Identifying Needs and Advocating for Services

The additional resources listed at the end of this chapter are a starting point for learning about your service area's preschool population and making contact with the childcare/preschool community. You will find that these sites tend to be gateways with interconnected references; we have listed sites separately to highlight their unique importance in doing your community scan and developing local contacts. Once you've identified your contacts, conduct a community analysis using demographic data, interviews with teachers, suggestions from branch library staff, and input from professionals working with at-risk communities. Survey other libraries to determine relative costs of different library services. Don't forget to consider what services you would be willing to sacrifice in order to implement a new service. Unless you will be getting more staff and a larger budget, some services you currently offer may have to be retired.

Once you identify the user needs in your service area, you need to determine what kind of services you will provide and make your case for those services. Part of the start up process is taking risks and advocating for your cause. You must let your library leadership see your enthusiasm and the impact library services to childcares will have on the community. Consider creating a mission statement. This does not have to be long, but it does need to be understandable and demonstrate a passion for the service. Above all, take time to plan. Initiating outreach services is a big undertaking and trying to plan it while you simultaneously try to provide it is extremely difficult and prone to fail.

Before contacting sites about providing bookmobile service, establish parameters for your service. What will you offer? What are the expectations of the childcare center? What are the consequences if certain obligations are not meet? For example, if an integral part of the service is children taking books home to share with their families and the center refuses, you might choose to discontinue service. But if you request they sweep the leaves off the sidewalk and they do not, you might simply remind them. It is important to establish these guidelines before approaching a site so you can be clear from the beginning.

Negotiating Services with Childcare Providers and Facilities

When a new site contacts you for bookmobile service or if you identify a potential service site, in addition to being able to have time available to add them to your routes, they must meet your criteria for service. These might include:

- Childcare licensing by the state
- Critical mass of children, for example, at least five preschool-age children in the childcare
- Geographic proximity to a branch library
- Facility or childcare provider receives local or state subsidies for serving a certain percentage of low-income families
- Written agreement to take responsibility for borrowed library materials
- Adequate parking
- Teacher/childcare provider presence aboard the bookmobile when children are aboard or in the classroom during library storytimes

Outreach services to preschools and childcare providers are a partnership between the library and the childcare facility. You should provide new sites with a letter outlining your service criteria and expectations. Sample letters to providers and parents can be found at the end of this chapter.

Scheduling, Routing, and Parking

There is narrow window of opportunity for scheduling storytimes in childcare centers. Before 8:30 A.M., children are still arriving and getting settled. After 11:45 A.M., they are

---

Energy Conservation

You have to consider your own energy reserves when planning your routes and storytime schedules. I have found that my storytime limit is four per day. It is simply too much of an energy drain to do more. I do have a single Head Start site with three morning and afternoon classrooms that I visit in one day. I abbreviate the storytime slightly and am still worn out by it! (TG)

Flexible Scheduling

I have a preschool site with 80 to 100 children in four morning and four afternoon classes. Two classes join for storytime, so I do two storytimes in the morning. With checkout time, I am there for 90 minutes. At another site with four classrooms and a similar numbers of preschoolers, I can only do one storytime and it takes them closer to two-and-a-half hours to organize their children to all come out to the bookmobile. When I did two storytimes there, they ran out of time before lunch! Although this example is the extreme, you have to make allowances for both where you can park safely in relation to classroom doors, and the teachers' organizational abilities when developing the schedule. In one situation where I gave the longer-standing customer their ideal time (everyone seems to want 10:00 A.M.), I was chronically late. We switched to an earlier time for her and she is happy because I arrive on time. The slowpokes that formerly had the earlier time are now motivated to better organization by running up against their lunch breaks if they dawdle too much and they are happy because they got the favored 10:00 A.M. spot. Now that I know my customers, accept that one size doesn't fit all, and accommodate their individuality in the schedule, I seldom run late. (TG)

eating lunch, and after noon they are napping. Three storytime visits with bookmobile selection time is maximum in the morning. Preschools and Head Start programs often have morning and afternoon sessions, so they are an option for afternoon visits.

Typically, you can reasonably visit two sites with two or three classrooms each morning. It works out generally to about 45 minutes to perform a 15-minute storytime, allow the children and caregivers time to select their books afterwards, and travel to the next site. Whenever possible, routes should cluster sites together so that travel time between sites is minimized.

Once you have a tentative schedule, begin recruiting customers. Contact the daycare director whenever possible. Be enthusiastic about what you are offering. Sell the customer on what you will provide. For example:

"Hello, I'm Jane Doe from the Neighborhood Library Bookmobile. We have an opening in our schedule and like to offer bookmobile service to you and your children. We will visit regularly and give the children the opportunity to visit the bookmobile, touch books, and checkout books to share with their families. We will also provide a literature-based, age-appropriate, exciting storytime in addition to the storytimes you provide. May we plan to visit you the first Wednesday of every month at 9:00 A.M.?"

At this point you can negotiate. Be prepared to explain the reasons for any issues which are a given. In the example above, the reason could be the intrinsic value of a positive experience with parents and how that trains children to love reading. Once you have established service and agreed upon what you will offer and what you ask of them, be consistent. If one site is confronted for breach of contract all sites must be confronted in the same way. First, it is equitable. Second, the providers talk with each other and they will know if the rules change from site to site.

The final issue is a safe place to park the

bookmobile. Unless you are already familiar with a service site (sometimes it is a former center reopening), you should check out the location before bringing the bookmobile there. This is especially important at childcare homes where there is no parking lot. Busy streets and cul-de-sacs can be particularly treacherous.

> ### Helpful Hint
>
> If you will be managing circulation with an agency card, you should include an application to be completed by a person in authority. These cards are similar to the cards any patron receives, except that instead of a personal photo, there is a picture of the library on the front. I keep a notebook with a list of my customers and their card numbers both in script and in a barcode font that allows me to read them with a scanner. I give them their actual card so that they can use it at the library in between my visits. By keeping my paper copy, we don't have preschoolers jostling for their book checkout while teachers search frantically for their library card. While the centers rarely take the card to the library, one center does use theirs to look up books online and reserve them for me to bring, a practice I encourage. (TG)

Managing Circulation

Outreach to childcare facilities and preschools is more than traditional bookmobile service. It is a pre-literacy program. All of the components must work together to encourage reading and a love of books early in life.

Agency Cards

Even if you don't have a bookmobile, there are a variety of ways that you can help childcare providers get books into their classrooms. First, you need to provide a way to check out materials to the facilities rather than to the caregivers themselves. One option is to issue agency cards which require someone with authority to authorize payment for lost or damaged materials. You should also identify a contact person for the organization. If the executive director or owner signs the form, they may wish to assign one of the classroom teachers to be responsible for interaction with the library.

Personal Cards

Another approach is to issue cards to the children. In some libraries, each child is given an application for a standard card to be used in a branch and an application for a bookmobile card which is kept on the vehicle so children do not have to carry the card from home. You can also issue a single card and keep a duplicate (or a list of card numbers) aboard the bookmobile, for the same reason. Issuing cards directly to the children requires you to get parental permission;

> ### Keep Books in the Center
>
> We encourage centers not to take the books home. One center that really thought this was a good idea found that they had a difficult time getting the books back on bookmobile day and had a high loss rate. Also, we are trying to get books into the classroom for daily use. I would rather partner with one of the programs that give books to at-risk kids so that they can keep books in their home. (TG)

a sample letter to parents is featured at the end of this chapter. This approach also raises the question about whether or not children will be allowed to take bookmobile books home. If this will not be allowed, you will have to make sure teachers and childcare providers will enforce this.

MODELS OF SERVICE

Delivery Methods

The ideal service to preschoolers provides trained library staff demonstrating reading aloud and introducing the teachers to good books, and gives children and caregivers the opportunity to choose from a bookmobile to fit their interests. The children love the experience of a library that is just their size and it is inside a truck! Teachers tell us over and over again how important the opportunity to select their own book is to the children. They report that the children bring their special book to them and ask to be read to throughout the time between visits. This print motivation and desire to engage with books is a critical piece in developing literacy skills.

If a bookmobile isn't feasible for your library service area, van service can be an effective alternative in getting books to children in centers. Sno-Isle Libraries covers two counties, one of which is comprised of two islands. Because their territory is huge and includes both densely populated urban areas and large distances between smaller towns, they incorporate their childcare routes with deliveries to senior facilities. Each childcare facility on the route has a storytime with a trained librarian or paraprofessional on a bimonthly basis. Each month the center receives a mixed box of books which includes any special requests from that center. Kansas City Public Library engages an outside delivery service to supply their preschool customers with book kits. You can arrange books on rolling carts and use a van with a lift to roll book carts into the center for children to choose from.

Whatever delivery method you choose, your collection and staff are key to a successful service.

Classroom Support for Teachers

Kits

Enlist the children's staff in the library building to encourage childcare providers to come to the library to pick up books for their classroom. Do a mailing and invite caregivers to call you to choose books on their classroom themes and to read aloud. Provide themed kits or preselected collections of materials that busy caregivers can pick up at a local branch.

Many libraries have developed theme kits so that a caregiver can ask for books on particular subjects and have a kit to pick up at the library branch most convenient for them. Once kits are assembled, it is quick and easy for staff to satisfy the requests for common themes. Music and teacher resource books are excellent additions to picture books in the kits. Some libraries have a supply of duplicate copies to replace worn, missing, or damaged items. Others do not catalog the exact contents and just switch out materials as needed. If you have to wait for all the items to be returned, or to order replacement copies in order to recirculate the kits, you soon need a large separate area and organizational system for incomplete kits, awaiting lost pieces.

Storytelling Kits

Columbus Metropolitan Library's Storytelling Kits enable teachers to present storytimes in between Bookmobile visits. Each prepackaged Kit includes 12 books, 4 storytelling aids, 4 songs, 2–4 fingerplays, 2–4 crafts, 2 activities such as games, and 2 community activities related to the central theme. (RP)

Many centers follow a fairly predictable pattern of themes, following the seasons. Remember, too, that books about seasons themselves are always popular. The annual cycle of themes includes:

- *Winter.* Holidays, snow, community helpers, families, boxes, indoor warmth, hockey, eating, birthdays (i.e., Martin Luther King, Jr.), patriotism (President's Day), grandparents
- *Spring.* Baby animals, farm animals, frogs, gardens, insects, baseball, birds, new babies
- *Summer.* Sea life, oceans, camping, swimming, bike riding, soccer, skating, picnics, Fourth of July, parades, carnivals, fairs, vacation, back-to-school
- *Fall.* Pumpkins, harvest, apples, holidays, spiders, scarecrows, football, clothing, circus, fire safety, "about me"

Multiple copies of titles for these subjects are needed and used. On your bookmobile or van, place these near the teacher resource books, with labels indicating the topics so that teachers can quickly pick from commonly used themes.

Classroom Collections

Another approach is to have a variety of book and music collections available to check out by the box. Again, this is easier to manage if you have a system that allows you to replace lost or worn copies to recirculate them promptly on return. Resource books for teachers and music CDs are important additions to classroom collections.

You might also consider a giveaway books program. Through outside funding the Columbus Metropolitan Library Bookmobile provides a collection of paperback books for each classroom in the fall. These become the property of the classroom and stay in the building. Classrooms might also be good recipients of discarded library books in good condition or book sale leftovers.

STORYTIMES

The fire of literacy is created by the emotional sparks between a child, a book, and the person reading. . . . The aim should be to make reading seem as fabulous as it is for most of us: fun, hilarious, thrilling, useful, interesting, amazing, essential, and desirable.

—Mem Fox

Silly Themes

Children won't always notice that your storytimes follow themes. Once when I told the children I had chosen "silly books" as my theme, one child said "you always choose silly books." I had to admit that silly books are my storytime favorites.

Teachers also don't always clue in. I have to chuckle when I choose apple stories in September or farm stories in spring and caregivers say with surprise, "That's what we are studying this month!" An amazing coincidence. (TG)

An essential part of bookmobile service to daycares is providing an exciting storytime experience. Each storytime should center on a specific theme to build context and hold children's attention. This also helps you focus your selection process. Theme-based storytimes are a great way to support teachers' curricula, so see if you can get their lesson plans and try to plan your storytimes around them. You'll figure out the annual curriculum schedule after awhile.

Due to the influence of multimedia in many children's lives, books can seem too sedentary at first. So, a variety of books, flannel stories, prop stories, songs, and fingerplays should be included to capture their interest. Generally, three or four storytelling aids are sufficient per storytime. Tactile elements are truly a plus for building both excitement and trust. They help create a high stimulus environment, which helps children build a positive connection with books and stories.

Selecting Books

One essential factor of a successful storytime is that you choose books *you* like, especially when you will be reading them many times in one month. Your obvious enjoyment of a book stimulates children's interest and makes the reading more fun for all. Besides that, here are more points to consider.

Length and Size

If you are reading all of the words, keep the book short at first. For a group setting, the longest books should rarely be beyond three to four sentences per page and only if the children are used to group storytime. Balance books this long with books one or two words per page. Balance length per page with the number of pages. The more you read to them, the longer their attention span will become and you can gradually introduce them to longer books. For preschoolers today, a storytime book is long if it exceeds 30 words per page maximum.

For group storytimes, don't use very small books. Use at least standard size books and only use big books if you can handle them smoothly. Their focus on the story will be much improved if they don't have to struggle to see the pictures or be distracted by your difficulty manipulating the book.

Illustrations

You should look for illustrations that are colorful, artistic, funny, bold, and active. Beware of highly detailed illustrations, especially if you've got a big group. The more detailed a picture is, the closer the audience needs to be to see it and generally, the audience will need more time to look at it. Overly detailed pictures can be real detriments in a storytime setting.

Consider the following questions. Can you easily identify what's going on in the pictures? Can a four-year-old? Are the pictures realistic? Do they support the story? If you can answer yes to these questions, chances are the book will be more successful with your storytime groups.

Characters

Characters should be likable and should share some strong similarities with the children in your audience. Characters should be developmentally recognizable to children, even if the characters themselves aren't the same age as they are. For example, Rosemary Wells's Ruby, as the classic fussy big sister, is instantly recognizable to younger siblings. What about cultural similarities? Your selections should reflect the ethnic and cultural diversity of your audience. Get specific. Don't assume that just because several children speak Spanish that they all come from Mexico, or if several are Native American that they all have experience living on rural reservations.

Characters should also reflect variances in family structure, including single parent families and households in which extended family members live. Different economic situations should be presented. Also consider cultural norms particular to your geographic locale. For example, children in Cincinnati may have never ridden a horse, but they know about it from television. On the other hand, it's unlikely they know anything about lobstering. Unless they are learning about something like this in preschool, it's better to stick with familiar subjects for storytime.

Theme, Age Appropriateness, and Scope

Consider what the story is about. Do the children in your audience relate to the concerns facing the characters? Children must also be able to understand the concepts in the book. For example, preschoolers don't get held back a year in school, so this concept will be foreign to them. Five-year-olds have very different concerns about bedwetting than three-year-olds.

Do the children know their letters? If not, do not try an alphabet book. Avoid abstract concepts with preliterate children, because that skill comes after letters. For example, Amelia Bedelia books are too advanced for preschool children. They do not understand the puns, so it is not fun. You can try books like these one-on-one, but they're not good preschool storytimes. (That said, children love books like *Dogzilla*, which is a spin off Godzilla, although the play on Scarlett O'Hairy's name goes over their heads entirely.)

Cumulative tales like *The House That Jack Built* can be problematic at this age because very young children often struggle to remember the parts that are repeated. Repetition is a good learning too, though. Books like *Silly Sally, The Old Lady who Swallowed a Fly*, and *The Little Old Lady who was not Afraid of Anything* are worth a try with very young audiences, but you may find them more effective with somewhat older children.

If the children cannot tell the difference between a rhino and an elephant, plots relying on distinguishing elephants from rhinos, cheetahs from leopards, and so forth will

Judging a Book by Its Cover?

Initially, I thought storytime was primarily to entertain and engage children, but I have learned that it is valuable to teachers as training as well. They learn different finger plays and songs, and see new books. One teacher said to me, "The director told me to watch what you do in storytime because the children never want to listen to me. I notice that you hold the books like this." She demonstrated how I hold the books with the pictures facing the children. She had been reading them with only the cover for the children to see!

go over their heads. If they can not tell a tiger from a lion, assume they only know how to distinguish basic, broad animal groups like cats and dogs.

The success of stories using various fruits and vegetables depends on how many different types the children know and how many they can remember once you tell them. All of this is not to say you shouldn't give children a little challenge on occasion. For example, if they know basics like apples, oranges, bananas, grapes, show them apricots or raspberries. If they know apricots or raspberries, take in pomegranates. If they struggle with apples and oranges, though, do not push beyond that in a story. Also assume they will be still struggling with lettuce, beans, and corn and do not challenge them with okra, parsnips, and turnips.

COLLECTIONS

Wear and Tear

The books that go into a center are generally more heavily used than those in a home setting. A popular book about sharks or dinosaurs may be enjoyed by up to 20 children a day for 25 days, getting 500 uses before its return. As heartbreaking as it may be to see the latest book about Tyrannosaurus Rex discarded within a year, after only five checkouts it may have had the equivalent of 10 years of circulation to individuals! A budget sufficient to cover replacement of standards and to add new books regularly is essential.

Encourage caregivers to keep library books in a special spot and bring them out to look at together. Caregivers with the lowest loss rate are those who supervise the children using the books. Some put all of the books out on shelves for the children to select from freely. One envisions happy children sitting with their books in peace, which is what you see sometimes. At other times, you might see two children fighting for the tiger book, each with a firm hold and no giving way. (The book, of course, does give way.) Even the best caregivers cannot be on top of everything children are up to at every second. The point is, you must not expect pristine books to return from your customers, and you cannot charge them for the inevitable little rips or barcodes and labels that have been peeled

To Fine or Not to Fine

I would not charge for the aforementioned tiger book, unless it is a first circulation or if heavily damaged books are becoming a chronic problem at a particular facility. While Everett Public Library's outreach circulation policies allow us to waive charges for lost or damaged materials, we also have the option to charge customers as appropriate. (TG)

off or you will lose your customers.

Children over-whelmingly choose books with a shining plastic cover on the out-side. They reject even perennial favorite titles like *Patrick's Dinosaurs* or *Cinderella* when pre-

> **Teaching Responsibility**
>
> Most of my board books are picture books in that format. A consequence of too many books ripped willfully at one center was that the children were limited to choosing from that section. They knew of the wonders of the rest of the bookmobile and it was hard for them to be so limited in their choices. I also brought a pile of discarded *Zoobooks* magazines for them to practice turning pages with. The situation has really improved at that site. (TG)

sented in a buckram cover. While you have the choice of paying more for a sturdy library binding, it is the pages that almost always give out first. Consider stretching your budget by buying more copies in the less expensive binding, which also allows you to buy additional titles as well as baby and toddler books in board format. Board books are less expensive than the paper picture book versions and sturdier than paperbacks.

Some centers will return every book, every time, in pretty much the same condition they went out in. Unfortunately, that is not the norm. Whoever shelves your materials should inspect them and mend the little rips so they don't become enormous tears and lost pages. Set aside any that need more than minimal repair for more serious mending or discard. If a center is returning many severely damaged books, talk to your contact person and tell her that she has returned books beyond normal wear and tear damage. Suggest she keep the library books in a place where she can supervise their use. Then if it doesn't get better, start charging for the damaged books. Also bring the ruined books for show and tell at the next storytime. Use all of your thespian skills with a very sad face and tell the children how sad you are that no other child will get to look at this beautiful book because it was ruined at their center. Talk about how to take care of books and ask them to tell you they will do their best to take care of the books. Then, brighten up and go to the fun of stories.

Nonfiction

Preschoolers are particularly interested in nonfiction books with real pictures. Forty-six percent of Everett Public Library's preschool circulation is nonfiction. Teachers choose more storybooks, so we estimate the children probably select 75 percent nonfiction.

There is a growing number of series books that are particularly good for preschoolers. Capstone Press Pebble Plus books have a range of seasonal nonfiction, including titles on spring, summer, fall, and winter. They also cover a wide variety of other high interest topics such as dinosaurs, vehicles, plants, animals, stars and planets, and have an excellent ABC and Counting series. The illustrations are clear and vivid, and the text short enough for teachers to read at circle time. The text does not have the flow of storybook language, but it is very readable. They also include bilingual (English/Spanish) editions of many of their titles. Recently, a four-year-old asked Theresa for a star book. He didn't want the books about stars that she showed him. What he wanted, as he showed her on his selection, was a book with the Capstone Press logo which features a star!

Harper Children's "Let's-read-and-find-out" science series is written to read aloud with the text reading as a narrative. The newer entries in the series feature colorful attention-getting illustrations. Some of the older entries have been updated with more exciting illustrations and have been republished in recent years.

Eye Wonder books are published by Dorling Kindersley on many preschool topics of interest. Dinosaurs, space, volcanoes, big cats, are some of the topics covered. Gail Gibbons, Seymour Simon, Cathryn Sill, and Darlene Stille have written many excellent preschool nonfiction titles.

For materials of all kinds, determine the racial/ethnic/cultural background of the children you will be serving. It is important they see themselves as people who read. If every book and every poster reflects people who don't look or dress like them, children will come to understand reading is not for them.

Board Books

Your collection should have a large collection of board books for babies and toddlers, but also titles for preschoolers. Paperbacks don't hold up very long in preschool use, so board books are a less expensive alternative to hardbound picture books for some titles. Babies love to look at books with pictures of baby faces and bright colors and clear shapes. For three-year-olds, they are still a good size and shape to allow them to manipulate them on their own without damage to the book. Books with cutout pages like *The Very Hungry Caterpillar* and *Color Zoo* hold up much better in the board book format. You can keep larger picture book versions in the collection as additional copies.

Picture Books

The picture book collection needs a selection of both classic titles and new books. Look for titles that will appeal to preschoolers as read-alouds. If a book has more than a minute of text per picture, or pictures that are detailed when viewed closely but not clear from 10 feet away, it is not a good fit for storytime use.

Children want scary stories, stories about ballerinas, trains, and dinosaurs. Because of the unpredictability of the children's book publishing market, if you order something that turns out to be more popular than you expected, order more copies as soon as possible so that they don't go out of print before they're inevitably loved to death. Be sure to order the award-winning books (Caldecott, Coretta Scott King, Children's Choice, and so on) each year.

Early Readers

The early reader collection should be maintained separately from the other picture storybooks to help caregivers to choose books for children who are learning to read.

Publishers reading levels are generally noted on the spine or face of these titles; however, the formulas used to determine those levels can vary widely from publisher to publisher. Some reading series are phonics-based, while others focus on sight reading. When you look inside you will quickly see how much they vary. My best advice is to encourage the caregivers to choose a variety of levels of readers and topics so that the children can find their level, rather than going strictly by the publishers' indicated grade level.

Teacher Resources

Teacher resource books are an essential part of the collection. You could provide books about ages and stages, Piaget, and other theory-oriented materials, but what is most useful to caregivers are books that have theme units with suggested activities and art projects. Caregivers often don't have enough scheduled planning time, so easy-to-follow books with curriculum ideas that utilize readily available materials make their jobs much easier and offer more interesting experiences for the children. Mary Ann Kohl publishes excellent preschool art books. Pamela Schiller, Gayle Bittinger, Kathryn Totten, and Jean Warren are other authors to look for. Gryphon House and Williamson Books (an imprint of Ideals Books) publish curriculum idea books for preschoolers.

Media

At this writing, most centers are using the compact disc format for music. CDs make it easy to start at exactly the track you want. Lullabies, dance, and activity CDs are especially popular. Raffi, Greg and Steve, Nancy Stewart, Ella Jenkins, Pete Seeger, and Georgianna Stewart are some classic and modern children's musicians.

As with music CDs, most centers now have CD players for the children to sit and listen to books with the text read aloud to them. Teachers report that it is a favorite activity and you can feel good about providing books-on-CD because it encourages literacy development.

Movies, however, are another matter. The ECEAP (Washington state preschool equivalent of Head Start) and Head Start classrooms do not have televisions for video. Neither do high quality childcare centers and preschools, whereas childcare centers that serve low-income children are much more likely to have a television than a library corner or area (Neuman et al., 2001).

Because of compelling studies on the negative effects of too much screen time on preschoolers (MacBeth, 1996; Wright et al., 2001) the authors do not recommend actively supporting video usage in preschool classrooms.

ORGANIZATION OF MATERIALS

Does it need to be said that the books need to be on low shelves for the preschoolers to reach them? Use the higher shelves for chapter books which are used by the grade school children in summer and after school childcare. You might also pull out the drawing and crafts books for older children and put them on higher shelves because the covers often attract preschoolers who will be disappointed by not having a story or interesting pictures to look at.

Everett Public Library's bookmobile is shelved by the Dewey system with a few exceptions. The picture books are grouped by authors' last names, but not alphabetized past the first letter. So, you might see Child, Carlson, Cline, Carle, and Child, and so on in any order on up to "D." This makes shelving faster and because even the "S" section takes up less than one shelf, specific requests aren't too time-consuming to locate. Spreading out popular authors or titles also gives more than one child at a time an opportunity to spot their books. It makes the shelves look more interesting since some authors' books have a very similar look on the spines.

The nonfiction is filed in conventional fashion to a degree. Most of the nonfiction titles are too slim for the call number to fit on the spine, so the books are organized to the point where likes are kept together, but it does not matter if one tiger book was written by an author starting with A and others by C or D. The folktales and nursery rhymes are separated just to give them a better location, and not organized past 398. The dinosaurs are only organized to the 567.9 field. This choice is personal, based on our circulation volume and to keep our library page from going insane trying to maintain perfect order. The children are asked not to reshelve books (both for order and to avoid damaging them when they try to shove them in without making a spot for them), but they still do creative shelving. As with any bookmobile, workable shelves must be slanted to keep books from falling off in route. Having shelves full also helps prevent book spills, but remember to keep them loose enough that little preschool hands can pull them off the shelves.

On our 24-foot long bookmobile, the teachers station themselves near the door by the checkout desk to keep the children from escaping, making the shelves near the door the ideal place for music and teacher resource and theme books. Bright tabs point out the topics on the current theme shelf within easy reach. The teachers are encouraged to choose more books for their classrooms, especially storybooks, since the children select so heavily from nonfiction.

STAFF

As in any outreach library position, staff providing services to preschools need to be adaptable and outgoing. If they are choosing books for preschoolers, their training needs to include familiarity with classic titles for preschoolers as well as keeping up to date on new books. If they will be performing library storytimes, they need to be able to read with expression and be fairly unflappable.

Staff need to be able to lift heavy loads and have training in lifting properly. Especially if you are doing deliveries with a van, the job will involve

Extreme Storytime

I was engaged in a storytime where I faced the windows in a preschool classroom. As I was reading, I saw the ground begin to roll, and the trees begin to sway madly. While I wanted to run out of the building, screaming "Earthquake! Run for your lives!", I instead calmly shut the book and said "Children, I believe we are having an earthquake." At that point the teachers snapped to and got the children under the tables. That was the most dramatic storytime interruption I've ever experienced, but I've also had children wipe their noses on my skirt and blurt out that 'so and so had worms on their privacy.' I've even seen Santa Claus arrive on a fire truck! Regardless, everyone lives happily ever after. (TG)

a great deal of lifting and toting boxes. Check library supply catalogues for sturdy folding hand trucks to alleviate some of the physical stress. A colleague whose library made a decision to change from bookmobile service to deposit collections bemoaned the amount of lifting and carrying she is now required to do. With the bookmobile, the books were transported by the children with small or occasional transfers of materials to and from the office. Now, instead of delivering storytimes, she spends time sorting books into boxes and lugging them about.

CONCLUSION

Any children we inspire to read or listen to books are a success story. We inspire children who can then inspire families to be lifelong learners and library users. We strive to place books in as many children's hands as possible. We wish you the very best of luck as you reach out to our future.

REFERENCES

Eric Carle, *The Very Hungry Caterpillar* (New York: Philomel Books, 1987).

Carol Carrick, *Patrick's Dinosaurs* (New York: Clarion Books, 1983).

Lois Ehlert, *Color Zoo* (New York: Lippincott, 1989).

I. U. Iruka and P. R. Carver, "Initial Results from the 2005 NHES Early Childhood Program" (NCES 2006-075). National Education Household Surveys Program of 2005. Available at: http://nces.ed.gov/pubs2006/2006075.pdf.

Tannis MacBeth, ed. *Tuning Into Young Viewers* (Newbury Park, CA: SAGE Publications, 1996).

Multiple authors. *Cinderella.*

Multiple authors. *The House that Jack Built.*

Multiple authors. *There was an Old Lady who Swallowed a Fly.*

Susan B. Neuman, et al. eds. *Access for All: Closing the Book Gap for Children in Early Education* (Newark, DE: International Reading Association, 2001).

Peggy Parish, *Amelia Bedelia* series (New York: HarperFestival, 1999).

Dav Pilkey, *Dogzilla* (San Diego: Harcourt Brace Jovanovich, 1993).

Linda D. Williams, *The Little Old Lady who was not Afraid of Anything* (New York: Crowell, 1986).

Audrey Wood, *Silly Sally* (San Diego: Harcourt Brace Jovanovich, 1992).

J. C. Wright, A. C. Huston, K. C. Murphy, M. St. Peters, M. Piñon, R. Scantlin, and J. Kotler. "The Relations of Early Television Viewing to School Readiness and Vocabulary of Children from Low-Income Families: The Early Window Project," *Child Development*, no. 72 (October 2001): 1347–1366.

SAMPLE LETTERS TO PROVIDERS AND PARENTS

Letter of Introduction to Facility #1

Dear <<Childcare Provider>>,

I am pleased to be able to extend Everywhere Library's bookmobile service to your center. An application for a library card is enclosed. Please return completed application to Everywhere Library Outreach Services, 1234 Street St, Anywhere, USA, 56789.

The bookmobile visit will include a storytime for the children, and time for them to select books from the bookmobile. Generally it works best to have storytime first followed by a visit to the bookmobile. It is helpful to me to have the storytime area ready before I arrive (that is, toys picked up). Although I can't promise to always arrive exactly on time, I will call if I will be more than 5–10 minutes late. Our first visit will be <<day and date>>, beginning at <<time>>. I will bring a calendar showing your schedule for the school year.

The bookmobile carries a variety of books and music CDs for children and resource books for caregivers, but it is still only a small selection of what is available at Everett Public Library. If you are hoping to find certain titles or books on a specific subject, you may call and leave a message at <<phone number>>, contact me through e-mail at myemailaddress@work, or give me a written list in advance. I will make every attempt to have them for your next bookmobile visit.

Approximately two weeks ahead of your scheduled visit, we will send a list of items currently checked out on your card. Although we like to recirculate materials each month, it isn't generally a problem to renew those you can't find immediately or wish to keep longer.

I look forward to seeing you and your children during the upcoming year. If you have suggestions for improvements in our library bookmobile service, please pass them on to me or to my supervisor, Ms. M. at <<phone number>>

Sincerely,

Letter of Introduction to Facility #2

Dear Educator,

The Bookmobile is a preliteracy program. All of the parts have been designed together to encourage reading and a love of books early in life. Each visit gives the children an opportunity to handle and checkout books on the vehicle and provides an exciting storytime experience. It is important that the teachers actively support the Bookmobile staff to make our visit a positive experience for the children.

Teacher collections and Teacher Storytelling kits enable teachers to present storytimes when the Bookmobile is not there and enhance your lesson plans with delightful books. We suggest the teachers get an Educator Card, a card that gives teachers special privileges for fines and lost materials. Check with our staff on the Bookmobile for more details.

Enclosed, please find calendars that you can hang in your rooms as a reminder. We have also enclosed library card applications. Please ask your parents to sign the applications. Parents do not need to remember to send the library card each time we visit. Instead, your students will check out on a special bookmobile card. All we ask is that you remind your students to return the books they checked out each time we visit. Finally, the bookmobile is on a tight schedule. Please be expecting us and do not schedule other activities during these periods. If cancellation is absolutely necessary, contact Outreach Services at <<phone number>> as soon as possible.

We also request that children not be restricted from going on the bookmobile because of bad behavior at another time. We view reading as essential. Just as a child would not be kept from brushing his/her teeth, we ask that they not be kept from finding books on the bookmobile or enjoying storytime.

Our cooperative effort to help youngsters develop a vital relationship with books, reading, and libraries is so important. We appreciate your willingness in opening doors to their futures through reading.

Sincerely,

Letter of Introduction to Parents

Dear Parents and Guardians,

The Outreach Services Division of the Library will be bringing the colorful Children's Bookmobile to your child's daycare. The daycare teachers, along with our dedicated staff, want to work with you to promote reading and a love of books with your child. The vehicle will visit your child's daycare center every other week. Your child will check out books on a library card and take them home to enjoy with you.

We ask that you:

- Comjplete 2 library card applications
- Take responsibility for the books your son or daughter checks out
- Ask your child about storytimes and read books with them
- Help remind your child about returning books to the Bookmobile on library day
- Call the Outreach Division to report missing library cards or any books that are lost or damaged

The Library will provide:

- Library cards
- Great books and book cassette kits
- A fun and exciting library visit
- Exciting story programs just for youngsters
- Workshops for parents about reading with children
- A workshop for teachers about giving book programs
- Storytelling kits for teachers

We are excited about providing daycare centers and youngsters with books, and helping your child develop a love for reading.

Great reading,

ADDITIONAL RESOURCES

Literacy, Learning Gap, and Childcare Web Sites

American Library Association. Every Child Ready to Read @ Your Library. Available at: http://www.ala.org/ala/mgrps/divs/alsc/ecrr/ecrrhomepage.cfm. Homepage for the Public Library Association Every Child Ready to Read campaign. Check out the research links.

Federal Interagency Forum on Child and Family Statistics. ChildStats. Available at: http://www.childstats.gov. This site offers easy access to statistics and reports on children and families, including population and family characteristics, economic security, health, behavior, social environment, and education.

U.S. Department of Health and Human Services. National Child Care Information and Technical Assistance Center. Available at: http://www.nccic.org. State by state data collected about children in childcare. Especially look at links for Kids Count Data Book, and the "state contacts" link which serves as a gateway to your state agencies involved in early learning.

National Association for the Education of Young Children. Available at: http://www.naeyc.org. The professional organization for preschool and childcare professionals; provides links to your local affiliates.

National Association of Child Care Resource and Referral Agencies. Available at: http://www.naccrra.org. Provides link to your local CCRRA, which can provide you with contact information for local childcare centers and preschools.

Susan B. Neuman, University of Michigan, School of Education. Available at: http://www-personal.umich.edu/~sbneuman/index.html (accessed November 15, 2008). Research and publications by Susan B. Neuman. Many of the journal articles are available for free in PDF format.

Susan B. Neuman, Donna C. Celano, Albert N. Greco, and Pamela Shue, eds. *Access for All: Closing the Book Gap for Children in Early Education.* (Newark, DE: International Reading Association, 2001). Neuman's study of books in childcare centers is essential reading (and less than 100 pages including tables and graphs) for data to support outreach to childcare centers.

U.S. Census Bureau. "Population and Household Economic Topics." U.S. Census Bureau. Available at: http://www.census.gov/population/www/index.html. Official United States Census Bureau site. Here you can find age, languages spoken at home, income data, and more.

U.S. Department of Agriculture. Healthy Meals Resource System (HMRS): Providing Information to Persons Working in the USDA's Child Nutrition Programs. Available at: http://healthymeals.nal.usda.gov. The U.S. Department of Agriculture provides food to childcares serving low-income families. Click "Locate My State Agency" to find local contacts to help you determine which centers in your service area qualify for the USDA's program.

U.S. Department of Health and Human Services. "Early Childhood Learning and Knowledge Center." Administration for Children and Families. Available at: http://eclkc.ohs.acf.hhs.gov/hslc. Includes links to your local Head Start programs.

Publishers of Preschool-Level Books

Capstone Press. http://www.capstonepress.com.
Dorling Kindersley. http://us.dk.com/static/cs/us/11/childrens/intro.html.
Gryphon House. http://www.gryphonhouse.com.
Harper Childrens. http://www.harperchildrens.com/teacher/K-3/science.asp.
Williamson Books. http://www.idealsbooks.com.
Zoobooks. http://www.zoobooks.com.

8

Serving School-Age Children

By Mary Anne Marjamaa

Serving children has always been a priority for the public library. Public libraries dedicate time, space, and money to attract children into special areas devoted to their needs. Bookmobile service is no different. Depending on the library system where the bookmobile unit is located, there are several service models from which to select.

Most libraries with community units serve customers ranging in age from infants to seniors. A bookmobile that serves this broad population will have a full range of resources and will include a section devoted to the needs of children. Customers can expect a small collection of core books plus highly popular children's books and media when they visit a bookmobile. Most services can request materials for special projects either in person, by phone, or by Internet and bring them during the next visit. Additionally, there may be a public access computer on board that is available to the customer to do quick reference research.

The St. Louis County Library has a long tradition of bookmobile service to children. It is a relatively new library system, starting in 1947 in what was, at the time, a rural county. Not having buildings or branches, the County Library founders decided the fastest way to get the library services to the people was through a mobile service. At its high point, the St. Louis County Library had 26 units and most of them went to schools. Over time, branches were built and many bookmobiles were retired. Today, there are 10 mobile units, 7 dedicated to schools and preschools, 2 serving nursing homes and senior residents, and 1 community bookmobile.

It is important to look past the idea of a bookmobile as a delivery vehicle and expand its purpose to a library outreach vehicle. The bookmobile is taking the services to children where they are. Every time a child comes on the bookmobile there is potential for future adult readers using and bringing their own children to a public library; the memory, the smell, the experience of libraries will be impressed on the brain of the child.

Each child who comes on board has a reading opportunity that would not be present if the mobile unit were not parked for easy access to books. This is time otherwise spent on video games and television entertainment. But a bookmobile visit can create a special kind of excitement in a child. Empowering a child with a library card and an opportunity to select books for personal reading is a great step forward toward a future strong reader. Reading can be active and involving, but it is a skill lost if not nurtured. It is a skill that needs exercise to get stronger and efficient.

SPECIALTY BOOKMOBILES FOR SCHOOL-AGE CHILDREN

Some libraries have specialty bookmobiles for children. Children's bookmobiles visit schools during the school year. Additionally, some systems visit underserved areas with large numbers of children to promote reading with afterschool visits. This type of bookmobile service fills the summer time by promoting summer reading programs and working to help reinforce reading skills when schools are not in session. The collection for this sort of bookmobile is different from that of a community bookmobile. It will consist of a juvenile collection divided into age-appropriate categories and a small amount of children's reference material. Audiovisual materials may be available. It is less common to see public access computers. Some bookmobiles for children also have a programming component and schedule regular storytimes.

This chapter explains how to provide bookmobile services to school-age children. For more information about services to preschoolers, see Chapter 7.

VEHICLE DESIGN

Fixed Features

Bookmobile vendors and consultants are excellent resources for designing a mobile unit for children, but a few things should be noted here. A good design plan will maximize all available space and use every square inch. Children's books tend to be thin and oversized, so adjustable shelving offers you the ability to make changes to accommodate different sized materials. Make sure storage and hanging shelves are included in your plan. Closets and cabinets can be tucked in creative spaces.

Lighting is important. Think about how light will reflect off walls and ceilings. Skylights might help.

Children come in all shapes and sizes, so plan on providing some sort of step stools so that taller shelves can be accessed. If programming is part of your plan, think about seating for the children. Risers or padded wheel well covers make nice seating. Remember that rainy and snowy days can make a floor too wet to sit on during a storytime.

Bookmobile shelving is very important. Almost all new shelving is adjustable, whether it is lightweight aluminum or stained wood. In a bookmobile dedicated to children's services, labels are important and most new shelving will accommodate subject labels. A Dewey Decimal poster and accompanying bookmark can be helpful, but labeling is the real key and it is quicker for a child to understand. The end goal would be the ability of a child to locate his own material. Words work well for older children, but pictures work well for everyone. Colorful clip art that can be attached to a shelf is helpful. A picture of a truck or plane in the transportation book area, a cat and dog near pet books, dinosaurs in the prehistoric animal area, all draw eyes to the right spot. Free clip art is available all over the internet and can be printed, laminated, and attached to a shelf. Visual clues are very helpful to young readers, and it makes a space inviting, welcoming, and helps customers find materials.

On a bookmobile, books travel better if the materials on the shelves are somewhat tightly packed, but materials cannot be so tight that the child has difficulty pulling a book out to examine. If the books are too tight, the tops of spines on many books will be damaged by small fingers trying to pull books off the shelf. Leave some space for easy handling.

Décor

Attractive interiors are always welcoming. You don't have to spend a lot of money for décor. Glossy book covers and pictures from older calendars can be used to decorate the bookmobile unit. Book covers create an attractive, literature-inspired, and cheap decorating scheme, but be warned. Children will hone in on the cover and want that book. So, if you decorate with book covers, be sure you've got easy access to the books themselves.

There are many colorful borders and posters available through numerous catalogs and local parent-teacher stores. One can use colored paper and die-cut letters to decorate. Little school house shapes with the school name on it are popular. There is not much space to decorate because most space is used for shelving and desk areas. Doors, ceiling, and windows are usually available for decorations. Sometimes it takes a little creative thinking. A large window might make a perfect aquarium with suspended fish and clear blue sheeting used as the water. A ceiling can be a solar system. In some bookmobiles, yearly themes can be used like origami, flying frogs, and book characters.

COLLECTION DEVELOPMENT

Books

School units and preschool units have different collection needs. Bookmobiles don't try to compete with the large assortment of materials available at a branch library. Space is very limited. If a unit goes to a school, a variety of circulating nonfiction material for reports and research school projects is needed. Definitely consider states, countries, and presidents, and shelve them alphabetically to allow a child to find material easier. It makes no sense to separate Greece from Greenland when a child is looking for a country that starts with the letter "G."

Children favor realistic illustrations rather than idealized illustrations—a photograph of an animal over a drawn picture of one. Even though we can only imagine what a dinosaur or alien from outer space might look like, the more realistic the illustration the more popular the book will be. DK (Dorling Kindersley) or Kindersley-like dictionary formats with big, bold colorful illustrations are extremely popular. A 100-page book on the Civil War with good research notes will sit on the shelf, but vibrant colorful books on the same subject find their way into children's hands. There will always be books that are so popular that the bookmobile will never have enough in their collections. Included in this category are wild animals, pets (especially cats and dogs), any joke or riddle book, any sports star or sports team, dinosaurs, aliens and UFOs, drawing books, and scary books.

Paperbacks are extremely popular, especially the ones promoted by the school book vendors or a book version of a television series or a movie. The best way to decide what is hot is to look at the sales flyers brought home by elementary school children. Visit book stores to keep track of new series. Check vendor catalogs and Web sites. Here again, children are greatly influenced by interesting and stimulating cover illustrations. R. L. Stine-like covers with ghoulish graphics are very popular. Children love series and the consistency of reading about the same people over and over. A great example is Anne M. Martin's Babysitter Club books, which are finding a new audience with the graphic version. *Nancy Drew* is still popular and has many offshoots, including graphic novels, even after all these years.

One issue that will always be a part of children's service is the problems related to lost and damaged materials. Paperbacks are disposable and easily and inexpensively replaced. They don't weigh a backpack down. Since parents usually are not on the bookmobile when a child selects the book, parents are less angry if they have a replacement charge for a lost or damaged paperback than a hardback book.

When purchasing books for a children's bookmobile, nonfiction is more popular than fiction. Children are curious about things, and a colorful book is a perfect introduction to a new subject. Probably a good ratio would be about 60–65 percent nonfiction and 35–40 percent fiction. Include a large percentage of paperbacks in the fiction area. Within these percentages, make sure the collection is divided among the different reading levels. This may mean that the same information is covered several times in several age groups. If the bookmobile will visit preschools, then additionally the unit would need a supply of board books, concept books, very easy stories, and nonfiction.

If you visit many schools and places where kids congregate, consider purchasing multiple copies of the most popular materials. While this might seem excessive in branch terms, it is not for a children's bookmobile. Most children's material is transitory, but heavily promoted. Hannah Montana is what every girl wants today. A few years ago, you couldn't buy enough Olsen Twin books. Buy multiple paperback copies and spread them out at various sites during the course of the schedule. Then, there are beloved classics. Beverly Cleary and E. B. White will always have a place on a children's bookmobile, but most materials are popular for only a short time. Multiple copies of paperback materials will get more of this popular material in the hands of children faster. It keeps the collection fresh, and it is a great marketing tool to get kids in the bookmobile.

Other Materials

Depending on the library collection, there are other materials that can be made available on a children's bookmobile. Magazines for children are popular. It doesn't take long for them to get very ragged, but children love them.

Many children enjoy audio books. These are good for reluctant readers and children with learning or visual disabilities. Some bookmobile libraries have a long tradition of carrying this sort of material, whether in the form of storytime sets, which include a book as well as an audio book, or stand-alone audio books. The latest innovation in this area is the purchase of Playaway audio books. These MP3-type audio players are becoming more popular because they are simple to use, don't require the listener to change a tape or CD, and have an expanding catalog of popular children's titles available for purchase.

The children's bookmobile might supply a collection of children's videos. The DVD is the most popular video format. If purchased for a children's bookmobile collection, a DVD title should tie into the book collection. Fiction and nonfiction are needed. Movie and television versions of a popular book and series are popular. Science, animals, pet care, and sports are good choices for nonfiction. How the bookmobile circulates this sort of material is a matter of library tradition and policy. Many libraries restrict the circulation of these materials to adults or teachers. Some bookmobiles will have a teacher's resource area for teachers to make selections. Other mobile units put this sort of material out of the reach of children so that it is only available to adults. If the material is available to children, it may be restricted by age-appropriateness or number allowed per child.

You could supply "Big Book" read-a-long books that teachers can use in their classrooms, as well as games, puzzles, and toys. Materials such as kits, games, and puzzles can be a problem because pieces can be misplaced. Some libraries number and mark on each piece and this information is noted in the catalog record. Most libraries don't want to invest a lot of time or money into this sort of collection. Some libraries provide puppets and stuffed animals. Keeping this sort of collection clean is a concern. Some things can be washed and some cannot. There are antibacterial dry sprays available and can be sprayed on materials to disinfect, but just as in a book collection, there is a time when a piece of realia needs to be discarded. Some libraries love providing this sort of service to parents and teachers, while others should not start this sort of service unless all aspects of circulation have been examined.

ORGANIZING THE COLLECTION

Organizing the collection is critical to controlling behavior and promoting a calm environment on a children's bookmobile. In a perfect world, children would come out quietly to make their selections. However, children are rarely perfect. They do not come on board in a quiet and orderly way. Coming on a mobile unit is just too exciting and filled with too much anticipation. It might be the highlight of the month. A well-organized bookmobile can have a calming influence.

It is necessary to spread the collection out in order to spread the kids out. Organizing reading materials up and down may work at a branch, but doesn't make sense when spreading materials out can disperse the children throughout the bookmobile. You don't want 15 children in the same place at the same time because that makes behavior more difficult to control.

When evaluating the placement of children's material, squat down as low as possible and look up and imagine how the display looks through a child's eyes. Think in terms of placing the easy books on the bottom. This could include board books, concept books, easy nonfiction, picture books, lower grade paperbacks and readers. Spread them out all over the bottom shelves to make it easier for younger children to locate books.

Consider having specialty shelves for paperbacks. Paperbacks are extremely popular. Three or four paperback shelves strategically placed throughout a mobile unit are not a bad idea. Series can be shelved together or apart, depending on the strategic purpose. For example, you could salt a few R. L. Stines and other scary titles or popular titles to spread the kids out, but put large long-time series together like *Nancy Drew* or *Saddle Club*, which helps those readers who are looking for #45 and #64 to complete their reading challenge.

Bookmobiles will always need a variety of materials, but you don't always need everything everyday. Materials like biographies, states, countries, presidents, and award winners can be tucked away out of the main traffic areas. On the fringes or on higher shelves is a good place for award winners. Materials such as graphic novels, which are age-appropriate for older readers, can be placed on high shelves out of reach of younger children.

On the other hand, hot material needs to be clearly visible at eye level. If the shelves are not too full, try some bookstore marketing. As the shelves loosen throughout the day, face an occasional cover out to grab attention. Have specialty shelves for a monthly feature, like "Valentines Day" or "Black History Month." Have books in baskets or small totes. If your bookmobile carries audiovisual material, storytime kits, and realia, think about who is allowed to check out these materials. If it is for teachers and adults, then put the material high or close to the circulation desk. If children can check out the materials, then locate them closer to the user's eye level. You can avoid a lot of behavior problems by spreading the collection and the children out. While it is not the way you would do it in a brick-and-mortar library, it makes sense in the close quarters of a bookmobile.

The way materials are shelved and organized is important not only because it looks good, and disperses children, but it also adds to the efficiency of the classroom visit. Most classroom students will only have 15 or 20 minutes to visit the bookmobile, and making things easy to find will get the children in and out quickly and keep the bookmobile staff on schedule and the day flowing. That makes everyone happy.

SETTING UP SERVICE SITES

The Importance of Communication

It cannot be overstated that success hinges on the library's ability to sell the service to the principal, the teachers, and the school secretary. On top of the hierarchy is the principal. If he or she is excited about the service, then the teachers will be encouraged. If the principal is uninterested, most of the teachers will be, too.

Trying to call a principal is frequently difficult. They do not always respond to voice mail or messages. An e-mail address is a valuable tool for direct communications.

The reality is that teachers will gripe about the inconvenience of their time slot or the time that a bookmobile visit takes away from their teaching. Some will complain about the responsibility for the books and severely limit their students' selections. The bookmobile staff can overcome most problems by becoming ambassadors of the library. It is all about service and extending that service to the schools and especially the teachers. Visits before the school year starts are helpful to detail the services you can provide. Offering to bring extra material for their special curriculum units can inspire loyalty.

Only good things can come from a good relationship with school secretaries. They are the ones who have the organizational skills to facilitate the schedules. It is essential to have these people on your side for those times when you have a problem they can help resolve. Make sure you go into the office each visit to say hi and get information about field trips and changes in the schedule.

Schools need to be reminded about visits. A phone call or a mailed reminder before each visit works well. Schools are busy places, and a bookmobile visit can get lost in the shuffle. A reminder is always a good idea.

Parking

Before the school can be scheduled, it is important to ensure that there is a safe place to park the bookmobile. This will require a site visit to discuss with the school administrators the mobile unit's parking and power requirements. Some mobile units are powered by generators, but others will use a shore line, a 220-volt power cord that allows the bookmobile to plug into a building's electrical system. It is also important that the children have a safe path between the school and bookmobile. After it has been determined that the bookmobile has a good parking spot, then it is time to schedule the visit.

Setting the Schedule

With the exception of one-of-a-kind events, such as parades, a bookmobile designed for children needs a consistent and regular venue. Weekly, biweekly, or monthly are the most common schedules.

Finding a time that meshes the mobile unit's availability and the school's schedule is usually a matter of compromise. A visit scheduled at the wrong time is doomed from the beginning. It sometimes takes some work to negotiate this, and hopefully the school has some flexibility to rearrange some parts of its schedule.

If a bookmobile service is set up to visit many schools, then more detailed information is needed to coordinate all the schedules. Traditionally, schools begin the year in August or September, but the bookmobile schedule needs to be complete by midsummer in order to notify each school of their visit dates and times. A good information gathering time is right before school recesses for summer break.

The scheduler needs much more information than just when school starts and ends for the day. They need to know bus schedules, the number of classrooms, and grade levels of the classrooms. A school calendar is a valuable tool to schedule around teacher in-service days, parent-teacher meetings, and school holidays. An example of an information sheet sent to schools each spring is included in this chapter.

Some mobile units visit schools for a short time and only students who need to check out or return material are allowed to come out to do library business. The visit may be an hour or longer. A more traditional approach is used by most schools which schedules students by classroom throughout the visit. Depending on the school population, this might be a half day, a whole day, or two days.

If this is a school that has had bookmobile visits in previous years then not much ground work is needed. However, if it is a new school, the principal and teachers will need the scheduler's help. The scheduler will know how much time can be allocated for the visit. It is highly encouraged that the school has a schedule for class visits to the bookmobile. Most classes are scheduled for 15 to 20 minute increments. Sometimes school personnel forget that library staff need to have a time for lunch included if the bookmobile unit stays for the whole day.

For a new school, the only way to determine the duration of a visit is by student population. Generally, school populations under 200 can be seen in a half day, so if the school population is 323, then a full day should be scheduled. For each 200 students add an additional half day.

Circulation is the best way to determine the length of time for established service sites. If circulation activity is between 250 and 400 per visit, then a half day is needed. Library circulation that is between 400 and 800 per visit require a full day. For each additional 400 circulations, add a half day. If the school circulation needs an additional half day, it is better to schedule it after the full day. Half day visits before a full day tend to be wasted time because teachers are inclined to ignore their scheduled time, knowing they can come the following day.

Evaluation

One of the best assessment tools for school stops is asking staff assigned to the stop to evaluate it at the end of the year. The assessment should include any special circumstances such as students with disabilities or schools with parking, power, or connectivity issues. Looking at the assessment along with school circulation and school population gives you the most realistic look at the school. If numbers are up, then time is added. If numbers are down, it gives you a chance to talk to the school about the situation. Keep in mind that some schools are more difficult than others and may require more time even though the circulation does not warrant it. This is especially true if the school has special- or high-needs students or many students with overdue materials.

MARKETING

If your library has a Web page and school stop information is featured on it, make sure that school teachers, secretaries, and principals know where it is. It might save time and a phone call when they know where to find routine information. Consider sending a newsletter at the beginning of each year that includes pictures of the staff, basic information and expectations. When it is distributed, make sure each classroom teacher gets a copy. Use card stock and make posters to be placed in the school office and teachers' lounge for important bulleted reminders like:

- Make sure each child has a card in hand
- Come at the time your class is scheduled
- Teachers need to give the bookmobile staff two weeks notice for special material requests

Every bookmobile operation will have other printed reminders as well.

At the St. Louis County Library a visit reminder is printed on a standard piece of paper with a picture of a bookmobile and the tag line "The Bookmobile is coming". The school name and next visit date are inserted and the reminder is mailed a week before the visit. All marketing material and reminders are excellent places to include information such as the bookmobile office phone number and Web site address in bold writing.

LIBRARY SERVICES

Services to Teachers

Bookmobile visits can be a valuable resource to teachers. Besides supplementing the school library, a school unit can bring many additional materials for classroom use. While it is true that the bookmobile has a small collection, when the branch library resources are included it becomes a very rich collection. Market this service by distributing request forms to the teachers. It will encourage them to use the resources of the library. It will also encourage them to bring their children to the bookmobile.

Teachers are library users and find the bookmobile very convenient, so it should not be surprising that they might enjoy having a small popular adult collection on board. Rarely will a school bookmobile have the resources to provide a current selection of best sellers, but the best sellers of six months ago are obtainable as interest wanes at the branches or main library. Putting this type of material on a children's unit can act as a teacher magnet, giving the librarian or clerk an opportunity get to know the teacher.

Services to Children

While it is true that bookmobiles help the schools and the teachers, it is really the children who are the main beneficiaries of bookmobile services. Getting their first library card can empower them and lead to a lifelong love of reading. Selecting his or her own reading material will be one of a young child's first independent decisions without a parent. It is important that bookmobile librarians and staff find positive ways to channel this enthusiasm and make it a pleasant experience.

Children need to be guided, because without guidance there is chaos. As mentioned previously, a well-designed, well-labeled bookmobile can help with the guidance, but there are other helpful actions as well. Many teachers will help the children, but some will not because they will consider it your turf. Some teachers will not accompany the children, leaving it to the librarians to manage the class. Stand at the door, welcome them on board, and remind them of your high expectations. If there are two staff members on board, then spread out for more coverage. There will be lots of questions coming from many directions at once. Besides handling the questions, the staff will also be checking material in and out, registering new students, and dealing with overdue materials. It is important that the bookmobile is designed so that everything is conveniently reached and secured. Identifying potential problems is mandatory before the first visit because everything is more confusing and chaotic as children enter the mix.

Managing Children's Behavior

As positive as we try to make the experience for everyone on board, sometimes there are problems that require additional attention. Just as teachers have problem students in their classroom, those same students will cause similar problems on a bookmobile. A multistep approach similar to a teacher's approach is a good start. It is always a good

Checklist for a Well-Organized School Visit

The combination of lots of children and short time spans can be troublesome, but bookmobiles that are designed for this sort of service take on the challenge every day. There are several procedures that will help make the visit go easier.

- Preregister children for library cards. Take registration forms over to the school early. After they are filled out, process them so you will be able to deliver the cards on or before the first visit.

- Provide the school or agency information on registration rules and library policy.

- Ask the school to provide an alphabetical list of students' names and addresses so that library cards can be renewed, addresses updated, and new children can be registered quickly. It provides independent verification of addresses.

- Using the library database, run a similar alphabetical list of all the kids at a particular school. (This does require that there be some sort of searchable school or school number field in the library database.) These two lists can be compared for registration and renewal purposes. Updates of customer information can be keyed into the library database at a later time.

- Make duplicate library cards and keep them on board. Give one to the child to take home and keep a duplicate to use on the mobile unit. There are many varieties of duplicate cards available from library card vendors.

- Organize the cards by classroom and keep them in your school file.

- Make sure that everyone has a card before they come on board. Teachers can help with this. With 15–20 minutes per class, you can't waste time looking up everyone's number.

- Once or twice a year, run a list of children who have exceeded the fines threshold. Then, reminders can be made and delivered to the child.

- Create next visit bookmark reminders, especially if you cannot set due dates to accommodate school holidays or if the receipt printer has lag time issues.

- Organize books to resupply the shelves quickly. Put like things together. If the bookmobile has storage areas, make sure the material in storage is well marked for quick access. If your top shelf is a storage area, make sure corresponding material is over the area where it is shelved.

idea to keep a close eye on all the children, looking for potential problems. When a potential problem is observed, a gentle reminder is in order. When a child is trying to tug material from another child, make sure to talk to him or her, saying, "Please make your own selections and keep your hands to yourself." If the child continues bothering other children, separating him from the others might be a good idea. Most bookmobiles have areas where a child can sit quietly for a minute or two as the others check out and leave. With a smaller group and less stimulation, the child might be able to select books. But there are times when positive reminders do not work. It is appropriate to ask the child to leave, but please inform the teacher of the problem. Sometimes, a disruptive child will be fine with less stimulation (i.e., fewer other children) or when accompanied by a teacher or teacher's aide.

Then, there are times when a whole class comes on board overstimulated. This is a situation when speaking to the classroom teacher or school principal is suggested. This situation can be turned into a positive experience for all when everyone is working together toward this goal, but it will not happen without communication between the bookmobile personnel and the school personnel.

Nothing will break your heart faster than a first grader sobbing inconsolably because he or she doesn't have a card, hasn't returned a book, cannot pay a fine, and cannot check out. These young children don't understand library rules. In these cases, have a form that explains the situation ready to fill out so the parent or teacher will know what it going on. Some children's bookmobiles keep freebie books that were donated or deleted from the collection to give as a way to appease the child.

Deposit Collections

In some library systems, deposit collections are used to serve children. In this case, the students probably do not select the material. The material is selected for them at the suggestion of the teacher and used for classroom projects. In this type of system, the books are selected and checked out to the classroom using an institution card or a teacher's personal card. This sort of operation is staff-intensive because the librarian or library clerk will have to select material according to a theme, check out and produce an invoice sheet and reverse the process when the materials are returned. However, it may be the only option when a library does not have a bookmobile large enough to accommodate visiting children.

Programming

Some children's bookmobiles are focused on circulation, while others have a dual purpose and can use a bookmobile as a programming vehicle. Programs can be as simple as a quick sit down storytime, or if time permits, you can offer a full-blown storytime with songs and a craft. Sometimes bookmobiles are heavily involved in school circulation during the school year, but have time to transform their mission during the summer months.

For many librarians, programming is the cream, the best thing about bookmobile service. They design sets, flannel boards, puppets, and masks to tell a story and entice those reluctant readers into the bookmobile. These employees are creative people. They would be a success anywhere, but they enjoy taking their act on the road and are stimulated by the spontaneity that is always a part of bookmobile service.

Fines

It is strongly suggested that a children's bookmobile be a fine free zone. One could argue that damaged or lost library materials should be billed and most libraries do have this as part of their procedures. When a book has been lost, damaged, or billed, it may be necessary to deny a child bookmobile privileges. Fining children for late returns, however, is a different matter. It is counterproductive and has no positive results. Most children are discouraged from bringing money to school and most bookmobiles do not carry much cash. It is important to remember that bookmobile services to children are about encouraging library use, promoting reading, and expanding a child's universe.

STAFFING

Working with children in small confined spaces is a challenge. The first of many criteria for a manager to consider is finding the right person for the job. Staff members who work on a school unit must like working with children. This person needs to blend patience with the ability to control a crowd for the safety of the child. They cannot be flustered by lines of noisy children, computer failures in the middle of transaction, and youngsters who sob when you tell them you cannot check out to them. Staff need to be inventive, efficient, and able to think on their feet to devise instant solutions to complex problems. This job requires thinking outside the box.

Another important consideration is a sufficient number of staff to provide a safe environment for the children. A bookmobile is a small place, and when it is crowded with children, it can become an uncontrolled place. Two people can control the space better than one. Children sometimes get sick, have accidents, or get angry on a school unit. There have also been instances when a child or children have accused a library staffer of wrongdoing. It is better for everyone if there are two adults on board, witnessing the situation, and handling the problem with calmness. If the library can not provide two staff members on the bookmobile, then a teacher, a teacher's aide, or a parent volunteer should be used to insure a safe visit.

CONCLUSION

Bookmobile service to children can be challenging and unpredictable. It requires careful planning and preparation to be successful, but most obstacles can be overcome. Selecting an appropriate collection and displaying it in a child-friendly way are key. A carefully planned and loaded bookmobile can disperse children and make the whole experience more pleasant and safe for everyone. Working with school personnel will lead to successful visits. It is a beneficial service that will enrich children, benefit the library with high circulation numbers, and create a generation of new readers.

ADDITIONAL RESOURCES

Please return form to:
Library Name
Library Address
Fax Number

Return Form by:

Bookmobile Information for
School Year 2009–2010

School Name: Principal's Name: _____
School Address: Contact Person: _____
City, State, Zip: Librarian's Name: _____
School District: Phone Number: _____
                                       E-mail: _____

Do you wish to have Bookmobile Service? (*circle one*)   Yes   No
(School Bookmobile Service consists of 8 check out visits and **one final pickup only** visit)

What radio/television stations do you notify to cancel due to weather? _____

First Day of School (*month/day*) _____ Last Day of School (*month/day*) _____

Winter Break Dates: (*first date off*) _____ School resumes: _____

Spring Break Dates (*first date off*) _____ School resumes: _____

Dates you will not be in session or have early dismissal: _____

     School Testing Dates: from _____ to _____

     School Day: Hours _____ A.M. to _____ P.M.

     What time do buses/cars leave in the morning? _____ A.M. Return? _____ P.M.

     Please circle day/s of week that are bad for you   Mon   Tues   Wed   Thurs   Fri

     Why? _____

Estimated enrollment _____ Number of classrooms that will use the bookmobile ____

Do you have a school library? (*circle one*)   Yes   No

Please Note:

In some situations schools may be required to provide adult supervision on board the bookmobile.

The library needs the school's cooperation to verify student addresses and to deliver notices to students.

We try to schedule all schools that request service, however more schools ask for service than we can accommodate.

The library will monitor circulation statistics and rates of return. Service may be modified or suspended at the discretion of the library.

Figure 8.1: Bookmobile information for school year 2009–2010

From *On the Road with Outreach: Mobile Library Services* by Jeannie Dilger-Hill and Erica MacCreaigh, Editors. Santa Barbara, CA: Libraries Unlimited. Copyright © 2010.

Bookmobile: Sample Classroom Sign-Up Sheet

The library allows a 45-minute lunch period for staff.
Please schedule a lunch period for us. Thank you!

TIME	TEACHER	GRADE
9:00–9:15		
9:15–9:30		
9:30–9:45		
9:45–10:00		
10:00–10:15		
10:15–10:30		
10:30–10:45		
10:45–11:00		
11:00–11:15		
11:15–11:30		
11:30–11:45		
11:45–12:00		
12:00–12:15		
12:15–12:30		
12:30–12:45		
12:45–1:00		
1:00–1:15		
1:15–1:30		
1:30–1:45		
1:45–2:00		
2:00–2:15		
2:15–2:30		

Figure 8.2: Bookmobile: sample classroom sign-up sheet

From *On the Road with Outreach: Mobile Library Services* by Jeannie Dilger-Hill and Erica MacCreaigh, Editors. Santa Barbara, CA: Libraries Unlimited. Copyright © 2010.

PUBLISHERS OF ELEMENTARY-LEVEL BOOKS

Dorling Kindersley. http://www.dk.com/.

HarperCollins. R. L. Stine Books. http://www.harpercollins.com/authors/14471/RL_Stine/index.aspx.

Penguin Group. Nancy Drew Series. http://us.penguingroup.com/nf/Search/QuickSearchProc/1,,Author_1000039803,00.html.

Random House. Saddle Club Series. http://www.randomhouse.com/author/results.pperl?authorid=3618.

9

Books-by-Mail

By Kathleen Mayo

Books-by-mail is a cost-effective approach to providing library service for persons who have difficulty getting to a library for any number of reasons. It is a common alternative to in-person delivery to homebound patrons, especially where library staffing is limited or the patrons are geographically very distant from the nearest library. Similar to homebound delivery, library staff selects, checks out, and bundles materials for patrons. Unlike homebound delivery, communication between staff and patrons is generally limited to phone, e-mail, and good old fashioned letters and notes.

Library customers place requests by mail, phone, fax, and e-mail, and libraries mail out the materials in reusable bags. Today, typical books-by-mail customers are persons who lack transportation and who are recuperating from an illness or have a long-term physical or medical disability. There also are many books-by-mail programs that target rural residents and communities with no full-service library.

Books-by-mail gained national attention in the 1970s and 1980s when the America Company started a commercial venture to sell libraries printed customer catalogs and paperback books for their mainly rural residents. Many communities liked the service model and libraries soon started their own variations. While most programs are operated by public libraries, some are projects of regional library cooperatives or state library agencies.

Books-by-mail is the most common name for these programs. Others are called Mail-a-Book, Mailbox Books, or have distinctive names such as Connections (Miami-Dade Public Library System), Special Delivery (Public Library of Youngstown and Mahoning County), B-Mail (Polk County Library Cooperative), and L-STAR (District of Columbia Public Library).

In starting a new books-by-mail program, there are several issues to consider: criteria for eligibility, program location, staffing, mailing parameters, loan procedures, and scope of collection. These factors will determine the size and nature of the service.

A TYPICAL DAY IN BOOKS-BY-MAIL

A typical day in a books-by-mail program has many variations, but it generally involves the following activities:

- *Receiving customer requests.* These come in the form of phone calls, e-mails, and mailed lists sent with returned bags or separately. Sometimes customers contact the library just to say that they are ready for more materials. During the day, staff will take time to place holds on those items that are not on the shelf.

- *Working directly with customers.* Answering the phone and responding to phone calls and e-mail messages from customers who want to converse with staff. Often this involves speaking with potential customers who are calling to find out about the program and to get an application.

- *Checking in materials.* Mailing bags are delivered by the letter carrier or come through the library delivery system from another library building. Most programs ask branches not to open bags, but to forward them to books-by-mail for check-in. Some of the items will need to be shelved and others will be holds that books-by-mail customers have requested.

- *Preparing orders to be shipped out.* This involves pulling items from the collection and the holds shelf, checking them out, and attaching the packing list/receipt. Staff place these items in a bag and add any additional items such as order forms, plastic security ties, or bookmarks. Staff add a mail tag with the customer's name and address on one side and the books-by-mail return address on the other. When bags require postage, staff weigh the bags and affix the appropriate postage to the mail tag. Bags are now ready for pick up or for delivery to a library mail center or Post Office.

- *Setting up new customers for service.* This involves taking information from the application and phone calls to set up new library accounts or make changes to existing ones.

- *Housekeeping.* Extra time is used to shelve materials, process new items, mail out applications and flyers, update customer records, work on catalog or newsletter, order materials, and plan special programs or promotional activities.

IDENTIFYING YOUR CUSTOMERS

The decision about who you will serve through a books-by-mail program should arise from your library's mission as well as needs assessments. Ask yourself, who has difficulty using your library service? What requests for service do you get from customers, family members, and staff? A close look at your demographics and a community scan of service patterns should help to clarify this target group of potential customers. While many communities use books-by-mail to reach persons with medical and physical disabilities, others have focused on serving older adults, persons with transportation problems, rural residents, or all of the above.

Libraries should clearly define who is eligible for service and include that statement in all of their service descriptions and promotions. It's probably better to start small, and broaden your target audience as your program develops. For example, some programs started as services for older adults who had difficulty using a library due to medical and physical disabilities. These libraries later expanded their services to include persons of any age with those limitations, individuals with a temporary disability, and caregivers. Some libraries such as Atlantic County Library System make their service available to all library customers.

WORKSPACE CONSIDERATIONS

Sometimes the best location for a books-by-mail program boils down to where you have available space, but ideally you should consider some other factors, too. If you have more than one library facility, you'll want to choose a site with good access to a Post Office or delivery service that can handle your volume of deliveries. Inside the building, book-by-mail operates well near the mail and courier delivery area. In most cases, there is no need for it to be located in a public service area. And it's advisable to locate a books-by-mail program in a main or regional library with access to a large collection.

Books-by-mail operations need work areas for staff with room for their phones, computers, printers, and files; a sorting/processing area for preparing orders for shipment; a mail area for holding the postage machine and the bins or bags for the Post Office; space to accommodate book carts; and shelving for a core collection and holds. The size of all this will depend on the program, the number of customers served, and the type of collection it uses.

MAILING MATERIALS

Postage

Some libraries pay both outgoing and return postage while others just pay outgoing postage. In the latter case the customer can then pay return postage (putting on the same amount as it cost to send out) or have someone drop off the bag of materials in a book drop. It's difficult to cut back on service once you have offered it, so it may be wise to start by paying only outgoing postage. Most programs use either Media Mail or Library Mail rates as well as Free Matter for the Blind and Physically Handicapped. Library Mail is slightly cheaper than Media Mail and seems to be the best option for a general postal rate. A few libraries use companies such as UPS to handle their deliveries.

Free Matter postage is available for individuals who need to use large print, audio, or Braille formats because of a visual or physical disability that prevents them from reading standard print. Medical certification is required to prove eligibility. Libraries can provide certification forms for this purpose and keep them on file for possible review by the Post Office.

For more information on the Free Matter for Blind and Visually Handicapped Persons rate, check out the U.S. Postal Service Web site at www.usps.com. To find the useful brochure, "Mailing Free Matter for Blind and Visually Handicapped Persons; Publication 347," follow this path: About USPS & News, Forms & Publications; Postal Periodicals & Publications; and Publications.

It's important to speak with your Post Office manager before starting a program. That person will have suggestions for procedures and efficiencies and will answer any questions you have regarding Free Matter postage. The manager also needs a heads up about this new service as it will increase Post Office business and may impact delivery schedules and arrangements with contracted carriers who use their own vehicles.

Although the U.S. Postal Service has standardized procedures, each community experiences local interpretations of postal regulations. For example, some letter carriers are allowed to personally deliver bags to their customers' doors, while others must leave them in the mail box. Mail delivery often becomes a subject of conversation with customers who think that the library has some control over this federal agency.

Mailing Equipment and Supplies

Letter carriers will provide bins or large containers for your use in addition to picking up your outgoing bags and dropping off returned bags. Many libraries have an electronic scale and their own postage machine for affixing postage, while others send them to a centralized mail center to handle this process. Libraries generally own their scales and rent the postage machines on a monthly basis. Libraries have the most success with zippered nylon bags that are imprinted with the return address and the mail rate. They have a clear plastic window for inserting the mail card. The cards have the patron's address on one side and can be turned over to show the library address for returns. These bags can last for over a dozen years, are water resistant, and can even be washed. Canvas bags are heavier, but are difficult to clean and are not water resistant. A few libraries use standard padded envelopes. The A. Rifkin Company is the most commonly used bag manufacturer, but several library vendors also sell bags for this purpose.

You should get bags in two or three sizes to accommodate different size materials. Also consider putting your Library Mail deliveries in one color bag and use another color bag for the Free Matter deliveries. Check with your local post office for advice on which colors to use. You want ones that are unique for your area.

Here are some other considerations. Some customers have difficulty lifting heavy bags so they ask staff to put only one or two items in a bag. Others have mail boxes that will not accommodate larger bags. Sending DVDs and audio books on CD in their own cases works fine for most libraries and they do not require additional padding.

STAFFING

There are many staffing models for books-by-mail programs. Some libraries have positions dedicated for books-by-mail only, but most have support from staff who share their time with other services—usually senior services, outreach programs, bookmobiles, or general library circulation. Logical operations for cross-training with books-by-mail are Talking Book sub-regional libraries, mail services that assist some of the same customers. A good example is the program operated by Pinellas Public Library

The Best Things in Life Are Free

In addition to paid staff, many programs use volunteers to help with functions such as pulling requests from the shelves, shelving returned items, preparing bags and adding postage, handling special mailings, and filing mail cards. In fact, volunteers from the Friends of the Cedar Rapids Public Library operate their books-by-mail program entirely!

Cooperative. These different staffing models reflect the size of the program, staffing patterns for the individual library, and availability of positions. Most programs prefer to have positions that are dedicated to books-by-mail with additional help available from other areas.

Because most books-by-mail programs involve extensive reader's advisory responsibility, they work best with librarians and other skilled library staff to handle selection functions. In programs that receive many phone calls from customers placing requests, it's important to find staff with great communication skills and an understanding of their customers' needs and situations.

COLLECTIONS

Nationally, books-by-mail collections vary as much as the programs themselves. Many libraries have dedicated core collections that serve only books-by-mail patrons. If they do, these collections usually concentrate on specific formats (paperbacks or large print) or bestsellers. Some use leased materials to keep their collections current. Core collections are often part of a larger outreach or branch collection that supports home deliveries, deposit collections, or bookmobile programs. Generally core collections don't show up in the public catalog so that they won't be used to fill holds for other patrons.

Some books-by-mail programs fill requests from the entire collection of the library or system. Books-by-mail staff place holds and/or pull titles from the library. This is not always effective for providing timely access to bestsellers and popular materials. However, most programs use both: a core collection that they augment with materials from the general collection. This gives customers access to the broadest array of materials.

While some books-by-mail programs limit their offerings to books or to the materials in their core collections, it is also common for programs to provide any materials from the library collection that will fit in a delivery bag. A number of libraries also offer interlibrary loan services for materials that are not available through the library system.

AUTOMATION: SPECIAL FEATURES

Most major automation vendors have integrated library systems (ILS) that can support the special record-keeping needs of books-by-mail and home delivery services. When considering ILS features, the following are particularly useful:

- The ILS should allow books-by-mail to maintain reader histories and let customers enter numerical ratings for the titles that they

Something for Everyone

Many books-by-mail patrons have very predictable and narrow reading interests, while others are open to new subjects and authors. Lee County's quarterly newsletter, *The Mail Bag*, includes comments and recommendations from customers, annotated lists of new materials in large print or on CD, and sometimes features of the customers themselves. One gentleman faithfully watches C-SPAN's Book TV and calls in his requests while the show is on! Others are pursuing college lectures from the Great Courses series, want all the new knitting and crochet books, or focus on very specialized niches of the Christian fiction market.

have read. These two features are important tools for staff that provide reader's advisory help.

- It's useful to have an alert for staff when the customer has borrowed the item before. Alerts should show up when staff place a hold or check out an item.

- Automation systems can generally produce a customized packing list to include in a shipment. It might include the customer's name and address, a list of the items checked out, a place for customers to rate the items they are returning, space to request additional materials, and additional information about the account. Customers return the list with their bag of books.

- Other useful features include notification when a customer hasn't received service for a designated period, the option for customers to select books-by-mail for their holds, and the ability to print mailing labels for each order.

PROCEDURES

Books-by-mail programs generally follow the policies and procedures of their libraries, but they have differences due to the nature of a mail service and the needs of the individuals who are served. Most programs have longer loan periods and/or they do not charge late fines. Some allow customers to exceed quantity limitations for items such as DVDs or the number of holds that can be placed. Others have limitations on such things as the number of requests placed per phone call or the number of items that will be mailed. Programs also have varying standards for service delivery. For example, a books-by-mail program may have a 24-hour turn around on filling requests or a two-day limit for processing new materials. The one consistent fact is that each program is different, and their policies run the gamut from open and user-centered to rigid and restrictive.

The forms used by various books-by-mail programs are similar. Programs serving older adults and persons with disabilities need to use large print forms. Many programs include their applications on their Web sites for either printing out or for on-line submission. The following is a list of forms you should consider using in your books-by-mail program:

- *Books-by-Mail application form.* This typically includes basic identifying information (name/address/phone/e-mail); a secondary contact name; acknowledgement that the person meets any eligibility requirement; special formats/languages; a checklist of genres, reading interests, favorite titles or authors; and a signature line. The checklist serves as a reader profile to help staff provide reader's advisory assistance. See "Sample Forms" at the end of this chapter for a sample application form.

- *Application for Free Matter postage.* This can be a simple, one page document. Keep it in a file for the unlikely event that the Post Office may request to see them. The Postal Service does not have a standard application for Free Matter. See "Sample Forms" at the end of this chapter for an application developed by the Lee County Free Library based on Postal Service requirements.

- *New customer letter.* This is used to welcome individuals to the program, explains the service, and includes tips for getting the best service. It's usually mailed out with the first order. Attaching a large print card with the books-by-mail phone number and address gives customers a helpful tool to keep near their phone.

- *Order forms.* These are often postcard-size with the books-by-mail program's address on the back for people who want to send them in separately. You could also use a business reply mail card. Order forms are usually included in each shipment of materials.

SELECTION TOOLS

While some customers have easy access to book reviews and bestseller lists, others need some help from the library. Books-by-mail programs often produce extensive catalogs of titles with short annotations. Catalogs, like the extensive ones produced by Arrowhead Library System and the Central Kansas Library System, are especially valuable for programs that limit circulation to the items in their core collections. Some programs produce regular newsletters with information about library and community activities and annotated lists of new materials. Books-by-mail programs also produce specialized genre lists and bookmarks of the "If You Like" variety, as well as lists from sources such as Novelist. A few programs distribute copies of Book Page, the review tool available in many public libraries.

PROMOTING THE SERVICE

At a minimum, most programs need a books-by-mail flyer that clearly defines program eligibility and describes how the program works. Flyers should be available for the public at every library outlet as well as through community services that address eligible groups and individuals. Here are some additional promotional practices:

- Keep staff informed of books-by-mail through new employee orientation and reminders in staff newsletters and other forums. Most referrals come from library staff, so they need to be comfortable describing books-by-mail to potential customers.

- Feature books-by-mail in general library promotional materials and specialized flyers and brochures aimed at the target group.

- Include information about books-by-mail on the library Web site in an easy to find location, along with the application form, current catalogs and newsletters, and contact information. This is a good place for connecting customers to other library resources available from home, too, like downloadable audiobooks, telephone reference, and online book clubs.

- Solicit coverage for books-by-mail with all types of media, including specialized and free publications like shopping guides, electronic co-op newsletters, and local weeklies. Books-by-mail service makes for a good human interest story while featuring examples of superior customer service. No one can

> ### Keep an Ear Out
>
> The Lee County Library System asks its staff to listen for two types of clues. The first is from customers who say they're having surgery or some other procedure and won't be able to get to the library for a while. The second is from customers who say they are selecting materials for their family member or neighbor who can't make it to the library. Both of these statements should prompt staff members to pull out books-by-mail flyers and tell them about the service.
>
> ### Hospice Services
>
> With the local hospice including books-by-mail flyers in each of its packets for new patients, Lee County's books-by-mail serves many people at the end of their lives who want to re-discover favorite titles and movies or find the ones they never got to read. Over the years books-by-mail has received many gifts and a few bequests from customers and their families who appreciate the personalized service that they received.

promote books-by-mail quite like the customers who depend on it for their reading lifeline.

- Tell the books-by-mail story through presentations to community groups and faith-based organizations. Although the audience members may not be eligible themselves, they often have family members and neighbors who are. Having tables at senior health fairs and other events for older adults is another way to reach this targeted market.

- Spread the word through community partners such as home health agencies and congregate meal sites that are already invested in the program. Provide flyers for their staff and clients, prepare articles for their newsletters, and have links to books-by-mail from their Web site. Many programs ask Meals-on-Wheels drivers to deliver flyers and applications to their meal recipients.

BUDGET

Most programs have difficulty identifying exact operating costs since they are usually part of a larger department's budget. Many of them start as grant projects and use that funding to pay for the start up costs of purchasing bags, initial collections, and equipment. Generally, these are the categories to include in new and existing program budgets:

- *Postage.* The amount spent on postage depends on the program focus and the library's policy on covering postage one way or both ways. Some programs send out at least half of their bags at no cost using the Free Matter postal provision. Postage for newsletters and catalogs can vary based on the postal rate used.

- *Postage machine.* Digital postage machines are usually rented with a monthly contract that includes servicing. The electronic scales that connect to those machines are purchased. Check the yellow pages under "Mailing Machines and Equipment" to locate local vendors.

- *Mail bags.* Preprinted nylon zippered bags are a significant up-front investment. Their costs vary depending on their size and the number purchased.

- *Core collection.* The costs to create and maintain a current core collection vary widely based on the size of the collection and the formats that are circulated.

- *Supplies.* The cost for general office and library supplies used by books-by-mail is comparable to other library services. There are some additional costs for postage machine supplies such as postage labels and ink cartridges.

- *Printing.* This includes the cost to print forms, catalogs, lists, and newsletters.

- *Salaries and benefits.* This is usually the largest item in any books-by-mail budget. Since many programs use at least some shared staff time, this is generally calculated in full time equivalents (FTE).

- *Staff training.* Continuing education costs are comparable to those for similar library positions.

OTHER SERVICE MODELS

This chapter describes traditional outreach programs operated by public libraries and library systems. However, other models exist.

- *Mailing on-hold items to all patrons.* For over 30 years, the Orange County Library System has used a local courier service and the U.S. Postal Service to deliver its holds directly to customers. Missoula Public Library and a group of public libraries in Montana are testing out a similar program to reach its mainly rural residents.

- *Mailing on-hold items for a fee.* Other libraries have experimented with mailing requested items to any customers who pay a per item fee. Multnomah County Library, Miami-Dade Public Library System, and Contra Costa County Library all charge for this convenience.

- *Mailing all items to rural residents.* The Maine State Library has a well-established program to mail materials to any residents of Maine communities where there is no full service library and to people who are homebound for medical reasons. Their Web-based program has an on-line catalog and conducts most transactions on-line.

- *Large print books-by-mail.* A number of Talking Books libraries have loaner collections of large print books in addition to their audio materials. The Talking Books Library at Worcester Public Library operates their program for Massachusetts residents who are registered for talking book service. Their catalog is available in both print and online formats.

CONCLUSION

A few closing words of advice are worth mentioning. Keep your program as simple as possible to minimize paperwork and staff time. You should be able to keep all the customer and transaction information you'll ever need on the on-line records. Simplify your program by eliminating fines for overdue materials and extending loan periods.

Allow customers to use both libraries and books-by-mail. Folks with medical and physical disabilities have good periods when they feel up to visiting the library and selecting their own materials. That's a good thing even if it complicates your life a little.

Larger type is a wonderful thing for customers and staff. Use it for your forms and publications.

Search the Internet to find some examples of books-by-mail flyers, applications, and Web sites. Steal the best features for your own program.

You'll probably have a few customers who don't really qualify for your program. Think twice before adding extra restrictions just to catch the cheaters. Every service has a few people who spend their lives trying to get something for free.

While this chapter describes a program with many steps and procedures, books-by-mail is still a very personal service that brings independence and enjoyment to the many people who use it. Books-by-mail staff often discover that they are a vital part of their customers' lives; some days, they are the only link that an individual might have with the outside world. This is heady stuff and one of the reasons that books-by-mail staff know they are making a difference in people's lives.

Sample Books-by-Mail Application for Service

For purposes of printing, the following documents demonstrate content only.

When creating your own letters, applications, and other forms specifically targeting seniors, keep in mind that many of your patrons may have some form of visual disability. Text in at least a 14-point font printed on a high contrasting color of matte (non-glare) paper works best.

The following documents feature the Arial font in 16-point and 14-point sizes.

LEE COUNTY LIBRARY SYSTEM
BOOKS-BY-MAIL SERVICE
(239-390-3232) (800-660-6420, Ext. 4) (TTY 239-498-6425)

APPLICATION FOR SERVICE – ADULT

NAME: _____

ADDRESS: _____ APT #: _____

CITY: _____ STATE: _____ ZIP: _____

PHONE: _____ DATE: _____

I am a resident of Lee County who is unable to use the Lee County Library System because (check one):

_____ I have a physical disability or chronic illness.

_____ I am convalescing from surgery or illness.

_____ I experience a loss of mobility associated with the aging process.

_____ I am a caregiver for a person with one of the above limitations.

I give permission to the Lee County Library System to keep a record of the library materials sent to me in order to avoid duplication. This information is confidential.

Signature: _____

PLEASE CHECK ALL THAT APPLY:

_____ I prefer large print books.

_____ I prefer paperback books.

_____ I have trouble holding large or heavy books.

Figure 9.1: Sample books-by-mail application for service

From *On the Road with Outreach: Mobile Library Services* by Jeannie Dilger-Hill and Erica MacCreaigh, Editors. Santa Barbara, CA: Libraries Unlimited. Copyright © 2010.

_____ I would like to receive:

     _____ CDBs (Books on CD)

     _____ DVDs

_____ I am also a registered Talking Books reader.

Please check your favorite categories. Choose at least *three* areas so we may send a variety of good books.

FICTION / STORIES

_____ Mystery
_____ Generational Sagas
_____ Historical Fiction
_____ Romance
_____ Classics
_____ Westerns
_____ Humor
_____ Adventure
_____ Occult and Horror
_____ Crime, Police
_____ Espionage & Spy
_____ Science Fiction
_____ Animal Stories
_____ Family Stories
_____ Short Stories
_____ Florida experience
_____ African-American experience
_____ Hispanic-American experience
_____ Southern experience
_____ Jewish experience
_____ Christian experience
_____ Bestsellers
_____ Other: _____

NONFICTION / INFORMATION

_____ Philosophy
_____ Religion and Inspiration
_____ Computers
_____ Psychology
_____ Politics
_____ True Crime
_____ Languages
_____ Nature and Animals
_____ Science and Technology
_____ Cooking
_____ Gardening
_____ Health & Medicine
_____ Fitness & Exercise
_____ Art, Crafts & Hobbies:
_____ Music: _____
_____ Poetry and Plays
_____ Travel and Geography
_____ Military
_____ History
_____ Biography:

    Hollywood_____

    Political _____

    Historical _____

_____ Florida
_____ Other: _____

Additional comments and favorite authors:

_____

_____

_____

Mail completed application to:

Books-by-Mail

Lee County Library System

21100 Three Oaks Parkway

Estero, FL 33928

Figure 9.1: (continued)

Sample Free Matter Application

LEE COUNTY LIBRARY SYSTEM

BOOK-BY-MAIL SERVICE

(239-390-3232) (800-660-6420, Ext. 4) (TTY 239-498-6425)

APPLICATION FOR FREE MATTER POSTAL PROVISIONS

Some people need to use large print books, audio material, or descriptive videos because of a visual or physical disability that prevents them from using standard print. They are eligible to receive these materials postage-free through the postal provisions called "Free Matter for Blind or Disabled Persons."

To receive this benefit, the U.S. Postal Service requires individuals to certify their eligibility. Please return this completed form to the Books-By-Mail Service by refolding it, with the library address showing on the outside.

CERTIFICATION OF DISABILITY

I certify that:

NAME: _____

ADDRESS: _____ APT #: _____

CITY:_____ STATE: ____ ZIP:_____

PHONE: _____ DATE: _____

is unable to use or read conventionally-printed material due to a physical or visual disability. I am a(n):

_____Licensed Medical Doctor

_____Ophthalmologist or Optometrist

_____Registered Nurse

_____Professional staff member of a hospital or other health/social service agency

Certified by: (signature) _____

Printed or typed name: _____

Address: _____

_____

_____

Date: _____

Figure 9.2: Sample free matter application

From *On the Road with Outreach: Mobile Library Services* by Jeannie Dilger-Hill and Erica MacCreaigh, Editors. Santa Barbara, CA: Libraries Unlimited. Copyright © 2010.

ADDITIONAL RESOURCES

The following is a list of the books-by-mail programs mentioned in this chapter, "Books-by-Mail."

Arrowhead (MN) Library System
Mail-a-Book
218-741-3840 or mailbook@arrowhead.lib.mn.us
www.arrowhead.lib.mn.us

Atlantic County (NJ) Library System
Books-by-Mail
609-625-2776 x 6324
www.atlanticlibrary.org

Cedar Rapids (IA) Public Library
Books by Mail
319-398-5123
www.crlibrary.org

Central Kansas Library System
Books-by-Mail
620-792-4865
www.ckls.org

Contra Costa County (CA) Library
Books by Mail
800-984-4636
http://ccclib.org

District of Columbia Public Library
L-STAR
202-727-2144
www.dclibrary.org

Lee County (FL) Library System
Books-by-Mail
239-390-3232 or booksbymail@leegov.com
www.lee-county.com/library

Maine State Library
Books by Mail
207-287-5650
www.maine.gov/msl/outreach/booksbymail/index.htm

Miami-Dade (FL) Public Library System
Connections and Borrow-by-Mail programs
305-474-7251
www.mdpls.org

Missoula (MT) Public Library
406-721-2665
www.missoulapubliclibrary.org

Multnomah County (OR) Library
Books by Mail
503-988-5404 or lib.adult.outreach@multcolib.org
www.multcolib.org

Orange County (FL) Library System
MAYL—Materials Access from Your Library
407-835-7323 or mayl@ocls.info
www.ocls.info

Palm Beach County (FL) Library
Books-by-Mail
561-649-5500
www.pbclibrary.org

Pinellas (FL) Public Library Cooperative
Books by Mail
727-441-9958
www.pplc.us

Public Library of Youngstown and Mahoning County (OH)
Special Delivery/Library by Mail
303-792-3869 or SpecialDelivery@libraryvisit.org
www.libraryvisit.org/specialdelivery.htm

Worcester (MA) Public Library/Talking Books Library
Large Type Books by Mail
508-799-1730 or talkbook@cwmars.org
www.worcpublib.org

10

Homebound Delivery Service

By Joyce Voss

Public library outreach services exist because some residents cannot make use of library resources in traditional ways. One aspect of outreach is service to the homebound, those unable to get to the library due to illness (temporary or long term), age, or disability. Candidates for homebound delivery may live in individual homes, group housing, retirement apartments, or other kinds of living facilities. Not only are they residents of the library's population area but, because of their present limitations, they are especially in need of library collection access.

As one of the oldest forms of outreach services, homebound service is found in a great majority of public libraries. Selecting materials and then delivering them to the homebound person is the basis of the service, but how this is accomplished varies. This chapter discusses several factors to consider when setting up this homebound service, including determining the need for the service; securing funding; fundamentals of providing homebound service, such as determining who qualifies and registering patrons, selecting and delivering materials, and keeping patron reading records; staffing, particularly the use of volunteers; and marketing the service.

DETERMINING THE COMMUNITY'S NEED FOR HOMEBOUND SERVICES

The need for homebound services to your community can be expressed in many ways. Patrons themselves may inquire about homebound services at your library. Often, children and neighbors of homebound people make the inquiry. And sometimes, senior residences in your area will approach you.

You can also do the asking. Information gleaned from a library survey can help in decision-making. So, too, can approaching agencies that serve seniors and disabled members of the community for information about their customers.

You can always look at demographic data. What does your census tell you about the ages of your citizens? Where do seniors—the most traditional recipients of homebound services—live? Are there senior residences or other assisted living facilities in your area?

Instituting homebound services gives you an opportunity to evaluate outreach services operations in other libraries. If there are libraries in your area running homebound

Margaret, an Armchair Traveler

Margaret, a middle-aged woman, lives in group housing, due to some physical challenges. She loves new ideas, and is a fan of biographies and nonfiction that take her to places she may never go. To get to the library is extremely difficult, and even if she could, the process of getting materials from shelves, checking out, and so on, is more than formidable. Homebound Service suits her to a tee. Margaret has an extensive conversation with her homebound selector once a month. She wants to be sure she gets the most recent exciting adventure. The selector in turn seeks feedback about the items recently sent. This productive give and take has a wonderful resolution. It allows Margaret to be a world traveler without leaving her armchair.

services, visit with a few of them to see different ways of providing the service.

FUNDAMENTALS OF HOMEBOUND SERVICES

Fundamentals of homebound service include determining who qualifies for service; registering patrons; assigning staff or volunteers to select materials; establishing a delivery schedule and method(s) of delivery; and keeping accurate records of the materials a patron has received and usage statistics.

Determining Who Qualifies

First, the library's qualifying criteria for homebound service should be established. Does the applicant need to reside in the library district? What is the nature of his inability to visit the library itself? Request an explanation of the person's need for homebound delivery. If your service grows very large, you might even require a doctor's note verifying an individual's homebound status.

Registering Patrons

In some cases, to institute service, a patron is simply pointed to a library phone number to call. When the call comes, a staff member fills out an application form for the patron. More often, the application form appears on the Web for patrons to fill out. After the patron fills it in and sends it back to the library, staff can call for any clarifications needed. Many examples of these applications can be found by checking public library homepages and through an Internet search of "library homebound delivery application." You may also refer to the sample at the end of this chapter.

Ideally the form should request the patron's identifying information: name, address, and phone number. It is then wise to ask for a secondary contact in case the patron cannot be reached. If there is concern by staff about other situations, for example, loose pets or cleanliness of the home, this could be added into an "Additional Information" section. For the sake of public relations, the questions should not be printed on the form. But staff, after reviewing the application and during their first conversation with the patron, can ask them.

Should homebound borrowing privileges differ from those of regular patrons? Homebound patrons are often given special status library cards which are coded to not charge fines and to direct any overdue notices to the outreach staff as opposed to having the overdue mailed to the homebound patron. The question of lost items, to charge or not to charge, also needs to be determined when instituting the service. Many libraries view occasional lost or damaged items as part of doing business with the homebound population.

Materials generally stay in the home, which mostly eliminates the loss and damage that results in fines. For 95 percent of homebound patrons, losing items is not an issue, especially if pickup is regular and a two-bag system is used (i.e., exchange a bag of new items for a bag of items the patron is finished with). Damaged items should only become an issue if damage is an often-repeated offense. When there have been several occurrences of problems, then you should inform the patron that the service will be stopped if the problems do not improve.

Selecting and Delivering Materials

Selection Strategies

To be able to satisfy a patron's requests, you need to determine what kinds of material he or she wants. What are the preferred formats, for example, large type, DVDs, or audio books? What are the patron's reading or viewing tastes? Some forms simply ask the patron to list fiction preferences, nonfiction preferences, favorite authors, favorite musicians; others provide a list of them for the patron to check off. Under each genre, more delineation might be wanted. With mysteries, for example, does the homebound reader/listener want to avoid books and movies with strong language, violence, and sex? Does he or she prefer CSI-style, psychological, or historical mysteries?

A checklist is a good starting point, but continued selection for the patron will need more refining. The point is that you can create patron profiles as general or detailed as you want to, keeping in mind that after working with a patron for several months, you will fine-tune your understanding of the types of material the patron desires by seeking feedback on how the patron's needs are being met. In addition to conversing with patrons about how they like the materials they receive, you can also solicit feedback with a simple feedback response sheet placed in the homebound delivery bag. A sample is featured at the end of this chapter.

Selection and Delivery

Some libraries begin with a few homebound patrons and may have a casual approach to who fills the request and who delivers, but if the number of individuals seeking service gets to be above 10, more structure is probably needed. There are several selection-delivery options to choose from

STAFF SELECT—STAFF DELIVER

Here the selector will have more training in advisory and if that selector also delivers, the direct contact should lead to refining the matches of book to customer at a faster rate. The cost is greater because of more staff time and may impact ability to execute other outreach efforts.

STAFF SELECT—VOLUNTEERS DELIVER

Trained to select, the selector asks the right questions in feedback discussion. Staff time saved in having a volunteer deliver could be directed to other outreach services.

It also provides a volunteer opportunity for someone and may mean more time spent with the homebound patron.

Volunteers Select—Staff Deliver

This can be successful if volunteers are people with wide reading taste and are motivated to increase their knowledge of genres. Staff delivery means more direct contact with the patron, enabling that staff to work more closely with the volunteer selector to find the right materials for that individual.

Volunteers Select—Volunteers Deliver

With the right skills, a volunteer could select. Working in unison with feedback from the volunteer who delivers, the volunteer selector is able to find materials that meet the taste of the homebound patrons. Staff have less control, but save more time.

Patrons Select for Themselves—Staff or Volunteers Deliver

A scenario in which patrons select materials for themselves (usually online) would work for that reader who always knows what he wishes to read, view, or listen to. Even with this independence, the patron should be called periodically to see how things are going and also to be reminded that the library is there to be of help if it is desired. A volunteer to deliver would be ideal in this situation.

Staff or Volunteers Select—Non-Library Staff Deliver

In this scenario, it's typical for a family

One Library's Selection and Delivery Model

Arlington Heights (IL) Memorial Library has a two-part homebound service called the Library Visitor Program. Part one involves delivery to homebound residents in several health care sites, totaling 50 patrons. Two senior services staff do all selecting for the health care sites. Staff delivers to institutions with more than 10 patrons, and a volunteer delivers to institutions with less than 10 patrons. Delivering to facilities with more than 10 patrons, staff use a delivery van, bags, and rolling carts. Delivery volunteers use their own cars, must carry their own insurance, and are not reimbursed for mileage.

Part two is delivery to individual homes and has, at any given time, between 20 and 30 patrons. Deliveries are scheduled throughout the month and each patron receives delivery once a month. Each week six to seven homebound clients are served with a total of 70 or so items delivered by a volunteer.

Six selectors work with patrons' requests. Four of them are main library Advisory Service staff. The other two are Outreach staff, including the Outreach administrator. After completing the selections, staff place materials in a central location. This is a group of designated shelves in the outreach area, near the loading dock. On Friday, a volunteer comes in to check out and bag the library items. A copy of *Book Page, America's Book Review* is included in each bag, plus the feedback sheet, bookmarks and other library promotional material. Directions to the patron's home and any special instructions (i.e., presence of a dog) are provided with each bag. On Monday morning, all is ready for the delivery volunteer. Patrons know approximately what time the driver will arrive because this will have been established in a phone call during the previous week between the patron and the library staff. The delivery volunteer drops off the new bag and picks up the previous visit's bag containing items to be returned. When the delivery volunteer comes back with the patrons' returns, they are checked in.

member or group home director to pick up and return materials. This is a great option especially if the library cannot or is very limited to how often deliveries can be made.

STAFF OR VOLUNTEERS SELECT—NON-LIBRARY AGENCIES DELIVER

In this scenario, volunteers from non-library agencies, like Meals-on-Wheels, might pick up patrons' library materials at the library. But it's more likely that the library will have to transport the homebound delivery bags to a central location. Using the Meals-on-Wheels example, this central location might be a nutrition center.

STAFF OR VOLUNTEERS SELECT—MATERIALS ARE DELIVERED BY MAIL

This is especially effective if your service area is geographically very large. For more information about books-by-mail programs, see Chapter 9.

Delivery Methods

You also need to consider where your delivery points will be. If you're delivering to senior centers or group homes, you need to determine if staff and volunteers will deliver directly to patrons or exchange materials through the facility staff. You also have to decide if you'll provide services only to critical mass points, like assisted living facilities with more than 10 homebound patrons. This is usually a good option if you're very short-staffed and the demand for homebound services is very high. With adequate staffing, however, you can provide door-to-door delivery to each room at the institutional sites.

You have some choices about how to transport materials. One option is to assign a library vehicle, usually a car or van, for a staff member or volunteer to use for deliveries. This method works best if the delivery schedule is consistent. For more flexibility, staff and volunteers can use their own vehicles to deliver materials. If you rely on this method, you need to make sure the library either carries appropriate insurance or obtains written liability waivers from staff and volunteers. See the end of this chapter for a sample liability waiver.

Managing Staffing to Meet Patron Demand

There are some other ways of managing staff-to-demand. Setting limits on the number or weight of materials per delivery is one. Limiting the number of deliveries per month is another, although remember that if you are visiting homebound patrons outside the regular materials checkout window, you'll need to take steps to ensure that homebound patrons don't receive overdue notices in error.

Another effective solution to short-staffing/high-demand is delivering deposit collections. This is a particularly effective service model for assisted and independent living sites. A deposit collection is often 100 or more items placed at an institution for a specific period of time—one month or two. Then, a new collection is brought in and the first might be moved to a second institution or returned to the library. Staff at the institution receiving the deposit collection decides how to circulate the materials. It

of mileage and stating what personal car insurance is held. You will also need a driver's license number and expiration date, make/model/year of their automobile, and their license plate number.

If delivering homebound materials, volunteers should be informed about the weight of the bags and how they can be transferred to a vehicle. Delivery is done in all seasons. There should be a conversation about the comfort level of driving in rain and snow and the extent of the delivery area.

Many public libraries now run background checks on volunteers who deal with certain segments of the clientele, such as children and homebound patrons. A decision about background checks should be made and reasons for the decision clearly stated. Background checks need to be an administrative decision by the library and considered for other areas of the library, not just outreach. A written policy statement is also a good idea. A sample background check policy appears at the end of this chapter.

In the library world, there has been discussion of doing similar background checks on homebound patrons, but as of this writing, this author knows of no library that has actually done this.

Motivation and Retention

A library director once related that although there was a need for homebound delivery service in his county system, the library was unable to find enough volunteers to keep the service going. How can such a situation be remedied? One way is to hang on to the volunteers you already have. But motivating and retaining volunteers is no small task.

The volunteer supervisor's role is to be welcoming, to be available to the volunteer when she or he is working, and show appreciation for what the volunteer does. Talk to the volunteer about why the service is important and how it flows from the library's mission. Walk through the job to be done, supplying clear guidelines for both the tasks to be accomplished and how to conduct oneself in performing the service. Discussion about materials selected and looking over what has been pulled for the first few visits are important training components for a volunteer selector. When the delivery volunteer returns, ask about the deliveries made that day and the people visited. Be interested. If it is a rote request, real answers will not be forthcoming. What if the volunteer cannot come on a day assigned? Does s/he should know how to notify the library? Staff in turn should have a back up plan for serving the homebound affected.

Honoring volunteers during April, Volunteer Recognition Month, is a more spectacular way to say thank you. A note and small gift is good. Some libraries provide a luncheon to which all volunteers are invited and awards given out. The expense of this is often a project that the Friends of the Library might sponsor. Also remembering birthdays or extending special greetings at holiday time are thoughtful gestures to your volunteers.

Another way of making the work rewarding is pairing volunteers with particular patrons for whom they select and/or deliver materials. This often leads to strong connections between volunteer and patron, especially if volunteers are able to visit their patrons for a more extended time beyond that required just for delivery.

Safety Precautions

When library services take place outside the library, certain security precautions should be addressed. Delivery staff and volunteers, since they enter people's homes, have special responsibilities and risk factors which need to be set forth in written guidelines or expectations. These include, but are not limited to, the following.

> **A Little Effort Means a Lot**
>
> One library volunteer in Niles, IL, shared this story about a homebound connection. "Martha is one of our regulars at a complex called The Huntington. We heard she had been in the hospital and was recuperating at Ballard Nursing Home, which is also in Niles. We made a goodie bag of magazines and paperbacks from the Friends of the Library sale room and paid a surprise visit. I'll never forget the joy on her face when she saw her two Outreach buddies. Her only son is in Korea. With no family here, we have become almost like relatives to her. Martha is back home and mentions our nursing home visit every time she sees us."

Privacy

Keep all information about the patron confidential. This includes information about the items they borrow, their living arrangements and medical conditions, and so forth.

Absences

Notify your Volunteer Supervisor as soon as possible if you need to be absent for any reason.

Communication

Listening to the patron is crucial. Be sympathetic, objective, and respect confidences. Keep your conversation upbeat. It isn't appropriate to discuss your own problems. Relate patron requests back to your Library Supervisor in a timely manner as to selection preferences or other special requests. All contacts initiated by the patron between visits should be directed to your Volunteer Supervisor. The volunteer should be responsible to the homebound individual only when doing the library work and at the time of regular homebound contact.

Awareness

Be mindful of your own safety in all circumstances. If you observe a situation that concerns you, report it to your Volunteer supervisor. If something appears life threatening call 911 immediately.

Appropriate Boundaries

Do not give your personal telephone number or home address to the patron; run errands or complete household chores like walking the dog; provide transportation; or accept gifts or tips.

Too Close for Comfort

One staff person who delivered monthly to a disabled woman freely shared her phone number. At first, the patron called occasionally, but all too soon she was calling daily. This interfered with the staff member's work and it took the intervention of a supervisor to resolve this difficult situation. What seemed like a harmless friendly gesture turned into a bothersome situation. The supervisor explained that if homebound service was to continue the calls needed to stop, and the two could continue discussing their mutual interests during their monthly homebound visits. It took a few months for hurts to heal, but the two got back to friendly visiting.

FUNDING

When starting up a homebound service, you need to carefully plan how much it's going to cost you. Factors that influence the cost of running a homebound service include:

- Size of the service population
- Number of clients
- Research and planning time
- Number of staff hours needed
- Cost of supplies
- Mileage reimbursement, if any
- Liability insurance

With a few homebound patrons, the library's existing budget probably can absorb the costs involved in executing selection and delivery. However, once the numbers rise, staff hours, use of volunteers, and organization of information and delivery may need additional dollars. A straightforward way is to allocate money from the existing library budget, a feasible answer if the need is very obvious and a small service has already begun.

You should also do some internal research. Consider if your homebound service can piggyback an existing outreach service at your library, like the bookmobile. You might find that it is time to discontinue some other service. Dollars realized from this could be applied to homebound delivery.

Working cooperatively with another agency, such as Senior Van Center or Meals-on-Wheels, to fill the delivery function might be the answer to limited funding. Many libraries solve the problem of staffing by employing small armies of volunteers just for homebound delivery.

Initial seed money might also be sought through the library's Friends Group, the library's Foundation, if it has one, plus federal, state, and private grants. The library's reference department can supply a listing of other possible associations willing to support the homebound service. Interestingly, some Friends groups undertake the delivery of homebound materials as one of their projects.

MARKETING

There are small ways and big ways for a library to promote homebound services. One of the big ways is the library's Web site. The site put up by the Topeka and Shawnee County (KS) Public Library is a good example, featuring a well-written narrative and photographs of different phases of its Red Carpet Deliveries. It certainly merits a look if your library is just beginning to develop a Web presence for homebound. Some Web sites also include an FAQ-type page to detail what is involved in homebound service. Poudre River (CO) Public Library District has this feature at its link, "Helping Hands." (Poudre River Public Library District, n.d.)

Still other libraries, like the Washington County (OR) Cooperative Library Service, feature patron tributes to homebound service on their Web sites. A video link on Kenton County (KY) Public Library's Community Outreach page shows the homebound delivery service in action, delivering materials and services to congregate facilities and to individuals of the county. Staff reveals satisfaction in providing the service, and smiling residents selecting items demonstrate why a picture is worth a thousand words.

Many libraries provide a link on their Web sites to the homebound application form. However, far too many bury that information deep within the site, making it very difficult to find. If you have homebound service included on your library Web site, be sure to check and see how easily (or not) homebound delivery information can be found by the patron in need.

Some smaller ways of marketing include sending an annual letter to each of the churches in your community with a ready-made blurb about homebound service that can be copied into the church bulletin. Perhaps medical offices would allow a small poster featuring details of homebound delivery. Ask Meals-on-Wheels drivers to drop off brochures when delivering meals. Is there a library column in the local paper you can use to promote the service?

Anytime a speaker from the library gives a talk, ask them to take some promotional material about homebound. Maybe during final remarks a personal story could be added to illuminate what a difference delivery of materials makes to the isolated individual. Perhaps this would not be suitable at a storytime, but presentations to service clubs or during a library tour are appropriate occasions.

Make sure promotional material is eye-catching. Logos and layouts used five years ago will probably look a bit staid today. Does your library do promotional giveaways? How about a homebound magnet! Door hangers advertising the service can be placed on room doors in nursing homes and other spots outside the library to help generate business. Honnold and Mesaros present more good ideas on creating printed publicity in their book *Serving Seniors.*

CONCLUSION

As with any library service, staff need to continually evaluate, make adjustments and provide statistics to support the necessity of the program. Of course, homebound circulation can never compete with regular circulation, but circulation is not the end of the story. It is good public relations to serve the homebound, for it illustrates that library services are for all of the community's citizens. The majority of customers are seniors, but representatives of all age levels are served.

Whether it is called Red Carpet Service, Library at your Door, Library Visitor Program, Library Express, or simply Homebound Delivery, the purpose is the same. The library is a transformational force and it transforms in myriad ways. For the homebound customer, it means caring, sharing, intellectual stimulation, lifelong learning, entertainment, and much more.

REFERENCES

"Book Page, America's Book Review." *Promotion, Inc.* Available at: http://www.bookpage.com/.

"Helping Hands." Poudre River (CO) Public Library District. Available at:: http://www.poudre libraries.org/information/outreach.html.

RoseMary Honnold and Saralyn A. Mesaros. *Serving Seniors: A How-to-Do-It Manual for Librarians* (New York: Neal-Schuman Publishers, 2004).

"Library Visitor Program." Arlington Heights (IL) Memorial Library. Available at: http://www. ahml.info/services/special_needs.asp.

SAMPLE FORMS

For purposes of printing, the following documents demonstrate content only. See Chapter 9 for discussion about making print materials more accessible to patrons with visual impairments.

Sample Homebound Services Welcome Letter

Materials delivery to persons who are temporarily or permanently homebound is a service provided by the Everywhere Public Library. This program is available to all residents who cannot get to the library because of illness, age, infirmity, or disability.

To participate in this program, you must have an Everywhere Library Card, live within the library's service area, and complete the attached application and interest checklist. If you do not have a library card, you will be able to register for one.

Once your application is completed, a library staff member will contact you to discuss your needs and interests and, if necessary, register you for a library card. After you are accepted into the program, a Library employee or volunteer will deliver materials to your door. Every three weeks, we will pick up materials and deliver new ones.

Overdue fines are not charged, but you are responsible for lost or damaged materials.

For more information about the homebound delivery program, contact the outreach coordinator at 555-READ.

Everywhere Public Library
1234 Street St
Anywhere, US 56789

Sample Homebound Services Application

Date _____

Name _____

Everywhere Library card number _____

Name of Retirement Home (if applicable) _____

Street Address _____ Apt. no. _____

Phone number _____

Best time to call _____

E-mail address (optional) _____

Reason for requesting service _____

_____

Your signature _____

For staff use only

Date received _____   Date contacted _____

Date of first delivery _____

Figure 10.1: Sample homebound services application

From *On the Road with Outreach: Mobile Library Services* by Jeannie Dilger-Hill and Erica MacCreaigh, Editors. Santa Barbara, CA: Libraries Unlimited. Copyright © 2010.

Sample Homebound Patron Interest Checklist

Name _____

I am interested in reading (check all that apply):

Fiction

- ❏ General
- ❏ Classics
- ❏ Mysteries
- ❏ Short stories
- ❏ Science fiction
- ❏ Historical fiction
- ❏ Fantasy
- ❏ Crime
- ❏ Romance
- ❏ Westerns
- ❏ Bestsellers
- ❏ Other (please list) _____

Nonfiction

- ❏ Autobiographies
- ❏ Poetry
- ❏ Hobbies
- ❏ Biographies
- ❏ Arts & Crafts
- ❏ Humor
- ❏ History
- ❏ Cooking
- ❏ Sports
- ❏ Religion
- ❏ Gardening
- ❏ Science
- ❏ Health
- ❏ Other (please list) _____

Figure 10.2: Sample homebound patron interest checklist

From *On the Road with Outreach: Mobile Library Services* by Jeannie Dilger-Hill and Erica MacCreaigh, Editors. Santa Barbara, CA: Libraries Unlimited. Copyright © 2010.

Please specify hobbies, crafts, etc. _____

_____

How many books would you like every 3 weeks? _____

Do you need large print? _____

Would you like books on audiotape or CD? _____

Are you interested in receiving magazines? _____

What magazine subjects or titles would you like? _____

_____

Are you interested in receiving movies? _____

Would you prefer DVD or VHS format? _____

_____

What types of movies would you like? _____

_____

How many movies would you like every 3 weeks? _____

(Note to reader: A Patron Interest Checklist is also commonly referred to as a Homebound Services Questionnaire or Patron Profile.)

Figure 10.2: (continued)

Sample Volunteer Liability Waiver

"As a volunteer whose accepted volunteer role requires me to drive my own vehicle, I have been informed and fully understand that my personal insurance would apply in the event an accident or injury should occur while performing that volunteer role. I, therefore, agree to indemnify and hold harmless the Everywhere Library and the City of Everywhere and their officers, agents, and employees from any and all liability resulting from performance of my volunteer role.

Further, by signing this agreement, I agree to maintain in force insurance coverage as required by the State of Anywhere and in sufficient amounts as I've determined for my own protection for the duration of my volunteer service."

Signature of Volunteer _____

Name of Volunteer (Print) _____

Date _____

Signature of <<Title of Library Designee>> _____

Name of <<Title of Library Designee>> _____

Date _____

Figure 10.3: Sample volunteer liability waiver

From *On the Road with Outreach: Mobile Library Services* by Jeannie Dilger-Hill and Erica MacCreaigh, Editors. Santa Barbara, CA: Libraries Unlimited. Copyright © 2010.

Sample Homebound Patron Feedback Form

Dear:

We hope you enjoy the books we selected for you! Help us to provide better service by putting a check next to the books you liked.

Title   Author

Figure 10.4: Sample homebound patron feedback form

From *On the Road with Outreach: Mobile Library Services* by Jeannie Dilger-Hill and Erica MacCreaigh, Editors. Santa Barbara, CA: Libraries Unlimited. Copyright © 2010.

ADDITIONAL RESOURCES

Sample Criminal Background Check Policy Statement

Because of a growing awareness of safety issues, the library is now incorporating criminal background screenings on staff and volunteers in selected positions who work directly with library assets, control library resources, or provide library services in patrons' residences. The purpose of these screenings is to identify individuals who may pose a risk in working with the library's assets or managing library resources, or who might endanger the safety of library patrons, staff, or volunteers.

To safeguard the welfare of all its patrons, staff, volunteers and resources, the library performs criminal background screenings for individuals 18 years of age or older who hold or seek positions in any of the following departments or services:

- Homebound Services
- Daycare Storytime Services
- Finance
- Security
- Any specific positions which may be designated as sensitive, such as Young Adult Services Librarian.

In addition to these categories, the driving records of staff who are authorized to operate a library-owned vehicle are checked on an annual basis as required by the library's insurance carrier.

If a criminal background screening reveals any information that, in the judgment of the library, renders an individual unsuitable for employment with the library, the individual's application or assignment will be dismissed or terminated. In reviewing criminal convictions, the library considers the nature and gravity of the offense, the recentness of the offense, and the nature of the library position sought or held. The library does not take into consideration sealed or expunged arrests and convictions.

The library contracts with a qualified outside firm to conduct criminal background screenings. All information obtained from screenings will be kept confidential to the extent required by law.

Homebound Delivery Programs Mentioned in Chapter 10

Arlington Heights (IL) Memorial Library
Library Visitor Program
http://www.ahml.info/services/special_needs.asp#

Clermont (OH) County Public Library
Library at your Door
http://www.clermontlibrary.org/servicelayd.shtml

Poudre River (CO) Public Library District
Helping Hands Library Homebound Delivery Service
http://www.poudrelibraries.org/information/helping-hands.html

Kenton County (KY) Public Library
Homebound Services
www.kenton.lib.ky.us/outreach/homebound

Topeka and Shawnee County (KS) Public Library
Red Carpet Services Delivery Service
www.tscpl.org/services

Washington County (OR) Cooperative Library Services
Homebound: Books-by-Mail
http://www.wccls.org/library_services/homebound

11

Lobby Stop Service to Nursing Homes and Retirement Facilities

By Bernie Garrison

Lobby stop service is a way of delivering browsing collections to patrons in the comfort of their own living facilities. Essentially, the service consists of a delivery vehicle and any number of carts of library materials. Carts are wheeled into a common area, like a lobby or community room, and circulation is set up on a table usually provided by the facility. Patrons can then browse materials at their leisure. The lobby stop service model can also be used to provide materials to daycares, recreation centers, and any other locations where patrons either cannot access a bookmobile (usually because of limited physical mobility) or where a full-sized bookmobile cannot park.

The goal of this chapter is to provide you and your organization with a schematic for determining if lobby stops are the best mode of service delivery for seniors in your community, and if so, how to orchestrate a plan for action. Using the Columbus (OH) Metropolitan Library as a model, we discuss how to assess existing services and alternatives; calculate a budget; make site selections; review vehicle options; manage staffing, scheduling, and collections; draft policies and procedures; conceive a marketing strategy, decide on peripheral services; evaluate the success of new services; and advocacy.

ASSESSING EXISTING SERVICES AND EXPLORING ALTERNATIVES

The first step is to develop pictures of how you envision a new or improved Outreach program. If you are expanding, shrinking, or considering other changes to your program, you need to know where you're at right now. As you assess existing services, you really only have three options: maintain the service as it is, cancel the service entirely, or amend the service to meet the new demands.

Developing a complete picture means looking at more than your circulation statistics and the demographics of your users. You need to look at population and residential

A New Service Opportunity

In 1990, Columbus Metropolitan Library opened a new branch in an area long serviced by the bookmobile. Outreach had a longstanding tradition of not providing bookmobile service within a two-mile radius of any branch, a practice meant to limit service duplication between the bookmobile and branch libraries. With the opening of the Southeast Library, Outreach lost almost a third of its stops.

At this turning point, the Outreach division took the opportunity to investigate underserved populations. We decided to maintain bookmobile service to suburban communities and eliminate rural locations in favor of urban neighborhoods and senior retirement facilities.

However, within a year of implementation most stops saw decreases in usage and circulation. An initial analysis revealed an increasing number of suburban users were abandoning bookmobile service for Columbus Metropolitan Library's newly renovated or enlarged branches. Urban borrowers, many of them children and young adults, had blocked cards curtailing their borrowing privileges. We also we realized seniors had difficulty boarding a bookmobile without a wheelchair lift and carrying items to and from the vehicle. Poor weather conditions further hindered their access. Things were looking bleak. For the first time in nearly 50 years, Outreach was in fear of losing its beloved bookmobile.

So, in 1992, we launched a full-fledged reassessment of existing bookmobile and outreach programs. We gleaned information from focus groups, brainstorming sessions, visits to other outreach programs, demographic analysis, and community needs assessments. Our research prepared us to discuss serving newly defined target groups, including the very young and the ever-growing senior population. Our analysis revealed an array of useful information, with the following points being key:

- The library's dedication to erecting new buildings, renovating others, and combining smaller branches into regional facilities was curbing the need for bookmobile service as we knew it.

- With approximately 15,000 new babies born annually in the county, new parents and their infants needed to be introduced to libraries and the importance of reading.

- Other organizations were replicating services we provided, such as storytelling sessions and new parent programs.

- Better informed customers expected increased quality customer service, convenience, accessibility, and access to popular materials.

- Trends supported an increasing need for innovative, easily accessible senior programming.

- Our 19-year-old bookmobile had about three more years of road service remaining.

We determined that, on too many levels, our bookmobile had outlived its usefulness.

construction trends in your service area as a whole. Comparing this information against the snapshot of your existing library service will provide the context you need to make decisions about where to go next. For more detailed information about planning for outreach services, see Chapter 1.

The list below provides a reference point for where the Columbus Metropolitan Library was prior to executing its new plan of action (see sidebar), including rationale for why particular services would be maintained, cancelled, or amended, and what new services were proposed to take their place:

- *Traditional Bookmobile Service* was amended. It was no longer the most viable method for connecting the Columbus metropolitan community with libraries and materials. A building program, blocked cards, the inability of seniors to easily access the vehicle, and decreasing circulation all played into ending this service in favor of a pilot program geared toward the needs of daycare children at risk for reading.

- *Homebound Service* was thriving and would be maintained. It would merge eligible books-by-mail and select bookmobile customers into its ranks.

- *The Talking Book Machine Program* was amended. This federally funded program provides, at no cost, cassette players and recorded books to people who are legally blind, visually impaired, and physically or reading disabled. Many man-hours went into the physical delivery and set-up of equipment; therefore, the division elected to change the program by mailing machines and referring out of district customers to the State Library.

- *Correctional Facilities* were maintained. Six facilities had donated materials delivered bimonthly. The service was deemed worthwhile and not a drain on resources.

- *Deposit Collections* were cancelled. These collections of books loaned to senior centers and residents were taking a big hit in terms of materials loss. Typically, there was little to no monitoring of the books or the customers using them. Some facilities neither had a convenient area for set-up nor had the area secured after business hours. For these reasons lobby stop was a solid choice to replace deposit collections.

- *Mobile Collections* similar to what lobby stop offered were cancelled. Boxes of books had been delivered by van to a senior site where they were hand-trucked in and set up on tables. Although we had few of these sites, this service would be cancelled and customers would be absorbed into the lobby stop service.

BUDGETING

Budgeting is crucial to your planning success. Without fastidious forethought you can easily find yourself and your organization in a precarious position. During the process you'll want to think about start-up costs, including purchasing a vehicle and its many components (e.g., shelving, lift, graphics, heater, insulation, wall panels, lights, carts, and circulation equipment). Carefully consider annual ongoing costs such as staffing, collection development, marketing, supplies, fuel, preventive maintenance costs, and any telecommunication costs associated with computer equipment and cell phones. Your administration will often be less concerned with start-up costs than ongoing costs.

If your library is unable to fund or fully fund a project of this size consider other funding opportunities. Can you combine existing services into one to expand on services while maximizing dollars? Does your library have a strategic plan to which your project can attach itself, in order to further the library's mission as well as your own? Do you have an existing vehicle that is being used for a dying service that can be retrofitted for a new program? These are just a few strategies you might employ as you weigh your options.

Should your library be underfunded you may still have options available to you. Start by investigating grant opportunities. Be aware there may be in-kind monies you

> **A Bookmobile Facelift**
>
> We experimented with retrofitting our traditional bookmobile when we realized its usefulness was no longer viable. As a three-year pilot project, the bookmobile was transformed into a children's bookmobile servicing children in preschools. This option allowed us to make use of an existing vehicle, bringing a much needed service to the community while maximizing dollars.

may need to contribute, in addition to the annual costs associated with staffing, preventive maintenance, and other ongoing expenses. Corporate sponsorship is another manner of securing funding for all or part of your project. Organizations may not be willing to fund an entire start-up program; however, you'd be surprised at how much they might be willing to contribute. Columbus Metropolitan Library's Outreach division received corporate dollars to fund a $10,000 graphics job on a bookmobile and over $30,000 to fund a new infant/parent reading program. Think creatively, keep connected to the library's strategic plan, and advocate for what you know your community needs. With lots of determination, you may find the capital needed to support your efforts.

SITE SELECTION

Identifying Potential Service Locations

As you begin your search for potential service sites at senior residences, there are a number of avenues to consider. Senior facilities can be found through local telephone directories, existing contacts at senior facilities, and through local publications aimed at seniors. You should also contact your county health and human services department for help in finding senior service and advocacy groups. It wouldn't hurt to do a little Google searching for these kinds of organizations in your area, either. Ohio has a Department of Aging that provides an exhaustive list of senior facilities, including information on each facility's client base, occupancy, and contact information. This is helpful in knowing if a particular facility's occupancy is low or high; if the residents are mobile or not; and if the facilities fall within your service boundaries. Check with your state or local department of health and human services to see if there is a similar resource available to you.

Determining Eligibility

As you identify eligible customers and facilities ask yourself a few questions. Who will compose your target audience? What are their mobility issues? What types of senior complexes are you targeting and why? Is there easy access to facilities and parking? You can make decisions about your audience and site's eligibility through the use of an intake form. (See the end of this chapter for a sample.) In essence, this tool is a two-fold survey. First, it evaluates facilities' desire and need for the service. Secondly, it provides information on the various properties' accessibility. Questions contained in the intake form can include:

- Are residents mobile enough to get to a central location in your facility, select materials, and independently transport them back to their rooms?

- How many residents reside at your facility?
- Can you guarantee a regular, accessible, first floor space for set-up?
- Can you furnish a table and two chairs for circulation of library materials?
- Can you designate a contact person who is available during our visit?
- Are you willing to promote our service through posters, calendars, and other materials we provide?
- What about the facility? Is there room to maneuver and park the vehicle? Can we get our carts into the facility? Is there space enough to provide the service?
- Can you guarantee the removal of snow and leaves from sidewalks entering your building?

It is vital that you visit each facility to ensure the information you gather is accurate. After your visit, you will know if your vehicle can reasonably maneuver and park on the grounds. You can determine if your book carts can make it past building thresholds. You will be able to determine lobby or meeting room capacity. These factors are critical to ensuring a flawless beginning to your new program.

Once a facility meets your criteria for service, you should send a letter of agreement that spells out what provisions

You Do What You Can

At Columbus Metropolitan Library, one of our eligibility requirements was that potential customers needed to reside in either retirement or independent living facilities. They had to be both mobile within the facility and capable of transporting materials to and from their rooms. Selecting sites where residents are nonmobile ran counter to the scope and ability of our program to provide adequate service. For these reasons, you will want to take great pains in choosing your sites to maximize your service without inadvertently creating barriers to customer service.

Know Your Patrons

At the start of our lobby stop program, Columbus Metropolitan Library experimented with our initial guidelines and attempted to serve a senior community center and one assisted living facility. Despite a thriving membership at the senior community center, there was no consistency to when members visited; therefore, we had no regular clientele and lower than expected circulation. This would later support the site's cancellation and the decision to forgo serving community centers with lobby stop service in the future. At the assisted living center, we actually had success, due to a dedicated staff that escorted clients to and from the lobby. This was an exception to how we normally operated; other libraries have other norms. Develop standards for eligibility and your program should flourish.

Be very selective when choosing sites. Our demographics indicated we were not meeting the needs of the people with mobility impairments within a variety of independent retirement communities. Our assumption was most senior centers provided transportation, but this was not always the case. Those who did offer transportation seldom took residents to a library, instead opting to transport them to doctor's appointments, the grocery store, and other destinations. Seniors with limited physical mobility, coupled with transportation challenges, were a group already identified and managed through our homebound service. Distinguishing the differences among senior populations helped us determine if lobby stop service was indeed the best vehicle for serving our senior population versus other outreach options.

If You Build It, They Will Come

At Columbus Metropolitan Library, we had no qualms about site staff borrowing items, but it did pose some interesting challenges. One location's staff was made up largely of non-native Hispanic employees. Incorporating them into the program meant slight enhancements to our way of doing business. We had to gear collections to their native language and spend more quality time helping them with reader's advisory. At another center, we provided service to a large senior Asian population that also required a language specific collection. They were overjoyed that we had materials in their native language and many soon became regular borrowers.

you'll make for the facility and its clients, in addition to what you expect them to provide to you. This nonbinding contract should be signed by both parties and used to enforce the agreement should procedural issues arise. The end of this chapter features a sample.

You may be surprised to find other potential customers within the facilities you elect to serve. In Ohio, subsidized senior residences provide housing to people with disabilities despite age. This holds significant weight when writing your service guidelines. For example, a younger audience may have differing reading and listening interests which could impact collection development. Another group you will need to serve is facility staff.

Setting Up for Service

Once you've identified a facility as a service candidate, you need to make sure you can set up so seniors with limited mobility and impaired vision can browse as independently as possible. This means the space must meet at least the following two criteria:

- Adequate room for people with wheelchairs and walkers to maneuver safely and easily
- Adequate lighting for browsing

Ambient noise is another factor that can impact your service. If you set up in a noisy area, it will be much more difficult to communicate with your patrons with hearing impairments, thereby reducing your effectiveness.

If the space is appropriate, you still have a responsibility to make sure your layout of carts doesn't impede traffic and hinder patron mobility. If possible, avoid shelving materials on the bottom shelf; it's just too difficult for some patrons to bend low enough to see them. You might consider using lower shelves for supplies and returned items, if you don't have a book drop or designated cart for them.

DELIVERY VEHICLES

Design

Cost is a driving force (no pun intended) behind any new initiative. In the case of mobile services there are numerous considerations when selecting your vehicle manufacturer, and deciding on a model that provides everything you need at a fair cost. Your vehicle will undoubtedly be one of your more costly expenses. However, if you fail to accurately define your needs and specifications your end product can cost more in change orders and future vehicle problems. Part of defining your plan involves wisely selecting both a vendor and a vehicle that will support all the functions of your service. There are a variety of bookmobile manufacturers in the country. For detailed information on designing a vehicle, see Chapter 14.

Lessons Learned

Columbus Metropolitan Library opted to hire a specialized bookmobile manufacturer to manage our project because they listened well, offered solid suggestions, and met our budgeting constraints. Having them in close proximity was a bonus because they could manage future preventive maintenance and warranty issues. All of these factors are important considerations when hiring a vendor.

Be precise in your explanation of how you want things done. We had concerns about the slope of our shelving when installed and wrote very specific guidelines to ensure accuracy. For example, "Install Acore shelving (of Gainesville, Florida) aluminum "rough rider" shelves with a 9" depth and a 15 degree slope and tracks on the driver's side in four sections; and on the rear of the wall in two sections with 6 shelves each section." This quality of documentation will get you closer to the vehicle you have in mind.

Working with Vendors

As you move forward with selecting a vendor and drafting specifications, it is wise to visit other libraries to evaluate their vehicles. Examining other vehicles and obtaining feedback from experienced lobby stop providers will provide you with ideas that will assist you in creating a vehicle that works for you and your customers. Generate a document listing what you want in a vehicle. Later, meet with your library's purchasing agent and transportation manager to begin finalizing your documentation and to ensure you stay within the confines of your projected budget.

When finalizing your purchase order, clearly document your vehicle's specifications and any additional contract items you deem important, such as manuals, warranty information, and deadlines. Equipment specifications relate to the engine, electrical systems, exhaust, transmission, front and rear axle, and optional equipment. Cab specifications include items such as tires, braking system, air conditioning, heater, tinted glass, audible back-up warning signal, AM/FM cassette radio, gauges, seating configuration, and mirrors. Box specifications include shelving, doors, lift, heater, flooring material, insulation factor, plywood wall covering, E-track rails, and interior and exterior lighting. Included in your documentation should be a deadline for completion. If you have a start date for implementing library services, having your vehicle delivered on time is paramount.

During the assembly phase you would be wise to make at least one site visit to the manufacturer to determine progress and to identify any potential deviations from your specifications. If you have but one opportunity to visit, do so midway through the process. Identifying issues at this point can help keep the process on schedule, so as not to delay your program's start date.

Another component to bookmobile design is carts. The number and style you'll need will be determined largely by the size of your collection and how many carts

Book Hauler

Before implementing our own lobby stop services, we visited the Topeka and Shawnee County (KS) Public Library's (TSCPL) Red Carpet lobby stop program. TSCPL's delivery vehicle was basic in its design, yet met all the functional requirements of the program. It was what one vendor called a Book Hauler, a box truck containing three components: the cab, chassis, and body. The cab was typical of most trucks of this style with a platform seat for up to three staff members. The back of the vehicle, or box, featured a platform lift used to raise and lower two book carts at a time. The carts were transported against interior walls through a fastening system comprised of E-track rails and ratcheting belts. Shelving was installed above the carts to store materials needed to replenish carts after each stop. Of particular interest were the cleverly designed vinyl cart covers used to protect materials from rain and snow!

you need to provide at each stop for patrons to browse. Fewer carts decreases loading/unloading time and can be less of a maneuvering strain on staff, but not if using fewer carts means you have to overload them. It may be wiser to provide more carts with less material to limit stress-related injuries to your staff.

When purchasing carts for your collection, consider a mixture of three-tiered and two-tiered styles. Keep in mind that you'll be transporting more than just library materials into facilities; you'll also be hauling computer equipment, paperwork such as library card applications and hold requests, and circulation supplies such as date due stamps or a receipt printer.

There is much to learn once you receive your new vehicle. Be prepared! Make prior arrangements for the vendor to spend a day or two at your library to train staff on the vehicle and answer their questions. Be certain to obtain all vehicle and equipment manuals. This will be integral to managing preventive maintenance issues in the future.

Maintenance

Routine vehicle maintenance is an often underprioritized aspect of providing mobile service. To ensure minimal down time, it is essential to schedule your vehicle and lift for regular inspections. It's a good idea to use daily preventive maintenance checklists to ensure vehicle safety by reviewing fluid levels, tire pressure, lights, and so on. All lobby stop staff should be trained to evaluate the degree of repair needed. This will aid them in referring repairs to the library's maintenance crew or a local repair shop.

Should the issue not be remedied in time to keep your appointed schedule, staff should contact the center requesting they post a sign stating service is cancelled for the day. It's also advisable that the facility phone residents as a courtesy.

The lift is another integral part of your service. If your lift is working improperly you may not be able to load or unload materials. Preventative maintenance needs associated with your particular lift, such as regular greasing, should be incorporated into your daily preventative maintenance checklist.

Carts will require simple maintenance. Periodically grease the casters to ensure they stay free from lock up. Rain, snow, dirt, dust all contribute to the demise of cart casters. Greasing them routinely will increase longevity and make steering in and out of centers much more manageable. On an average you can expect to replace your casters every three to four years.

For more information about maintaining outreach vehicles, see Chapter 16.

STAFFING

Two staff members are generally sufficient to manage lobby stops. A common staffing model is for a driver and a librarian or library assistant to divide daily responsibilities. A driver would obviously be responsible for driving and fueling, but could also take care of circulation at stops and take the lead on maneuvering carts in and out of facilities. The librarian or library assistant would be in charge of selecting materials for the carts and customer service activities like reader's advisory

A few locations may be extremely busy and in need of additional help. At those stops, a third staff person can meet lobby stop staff at the site to support circulation functions and crowd control. Volunteers are sometimes appropriate in this capacity. Even facility staff can help with nonlibrary functions, like setting up the carts and helping residents move in and out of the service area.

SCHEDULING

There are a number of issues needing thoughtful consideration when developing a lobby stop schedule. Begin by ascertaining the best times to catch seniors at home. It will be outside your ability to give everyone the time slots requested; however, attempt to manage requests as much as possible. You will want to schedule stops in close proximity to each other. This will ensure the best use of time and fuel and will limit vehicle wear and tear.

Another important consideration is the activities calendar at your service sites. Senior residential facilities usually have scheduled activities and services all day, every day. Make sure lobby stop service is not opposite popular activities like bingo, highly utilized services like the barber shop, or regularly scheduled necessities like mealtimes.

Scheduling becomes tricky as you delete and add stops over time. If you decide to maintain a waiting list of potential service sites you may find this can challenge equity. For instance, if you are determined to maintain tight territories, then those first on your waiting list may not be in the territory you are currently filling. Make it clear to centers at the start that they will be added as openings become available in their area and not according to their position on the list.

Every outreach department's service capacity differs. The number of stops your service can manage depends upon several interrelated factors. These include:

- The frequency with which you plan to visit each stop
- The length of time you spend at each stop
- The distance between stops (which determines how much time you spend driving)
- The availability of library staff, not only to work the stops, but to prepare for them

---

Special Policies for Special Patrons

At Columbus Metropolitan Library, policies within our organization are typically defined administratively; whereas procedures are generally left to individual branches or divisions to determine. For example, non-Outreach customers are limited to 20 audiovisual items checked out for two weeks. Some outreach customers receive service monthly and therefore are at a disadvantage. Administration provides an out to the Outreach division, allowing an increase in the number of audiovisual items checked out to homebound customers.

- *Collection Development Guidelines.* Clearly develop standards for collection development based on usage and any tools the library provides, such as stock turnover reports.

- *Cancellation of Service.* When inclement weather hits or vehicles are inoperable, have a mechanism in place to alert centers and their residents. Include contact information for site staff should the facility need to cancel as well.

- *Preventive Maintenance and Vehicle Breakdowns.* Be clear on defining how preventive maintenance issues and unexpected repairs are to be handled and by whom.

MARKETING

How and when you decide to market your program will be key to attracting and maintaining customers. Early in the process, employ your Communications Department to help you achieve this objective. With your brand in place, begin your marketing campaign with an initial call to a representative staff person at each facility. Take the opportunity to enlighten and excite these individuals about your new program. Since these representatives are a first link to potential customers, they need to be fully informed about the relevant aspects of the service. Work with site representatives to earmark days that library staff can drive out and preregister residents for library cards. This allows library staff to encourage registration while explaining the program's many benefits. Distribute large print calendars and letters outlining the new program to new library card holders; distribute the remainder door to door. Hang posters advertising the program in various locations within each center. Request that your schedule be posted in internal newsletters and on bulletin boards. Other forms of advertising you might try include tri-fold table top signs displayed on dining and occasional tables at each site. Library book bags highlighting a logo or brand are excellent public relations tools. Don't forget to plan for vibrant graphics on your vehicle. They are a great way to promote your library and your program. You can gain further momentum for your advertising efforts by posting lobby stop schedules on your Web site, in local news-

---

Branding

Columbus Metropolitan Library's Communications Department gave the lobby stop service an identity by creating a brand for all senior services within the division. "Words on Wheels" became our slogan, three seniors awaiting their library materials our symbol, and red and green our identifying colors. The brand was used on all marketing efforts including letterhead, posters, calendars and the graphics applied to our vehicle.

---

papers, and library brochures. Once service is up and running, consider approaching newspapers and television stations to cover your worthwhile program. Coverage of this nature conveys the wonderful work the library does while further promoting the merits of your program to future centers.

For more information about marketing outreach programs, see Chapter 1.

ADDITIONAL SERVICES

Although the intent of lobby stop service is to provide library materials to seniors with the best customer service possible, there are additional services you might consider providing. There are inherent challenges in offering options beyond the basics, so when making choices regarding the provision of additional services, be sure to reflect on the following questions. Do we have adequate staffing to manage these extra services? Do we have enough cart space to handle the storage of additional resources? Is there enough time built into the schedule to manage added functions? With these questions answered, you can experiment with a variety of offerings, such as:

- *Book Discussion Groups.* Monthly discussion groups require outreach staff to spend more time pulling reading materials, providing reading lists, and delivering materials. When discussion groups are successful, the service is worth the effort.

- *Adult Summer Reading Programs.* Participate in your library's Adult Summer Reading program. Seniors can read/listen to books and then submit an entry form with their name, facility, phone number, and titles of items read. The slips are entered into a drawing for prizes.

- *Portable Copy Service.* Offer photocopy service with a portable copier.

- *Author Visits.* Arrange for author visits in conjunction with your lobby stop schedule. These are generally well attended programs, but take extra time to plan and coordinate.

- *Book Sales.* If you have the room and the inclination, you might want to consider having book sales. If you have room on your vehicle for another cart, use it for a perpetual book sale. Try a tailgate book sale where a library van drives to a center, unloads books, and sells them to lobby stop customers. Sell book grab bags clearly marked with the genre. Customers love book sales so give them a try.

- *Computer Training.* Many seniors are interested in learning how to use computers. This could be an opportunity to have additional library staff provide training through laptop/projection equipment. Some facilities have their own computer labs, but may not have staff to do training. See if you can use their equipment if you can't provide your own.

- *Bi-Folkal Kits.* Activities directors use these to assist older adults in the art of reminiscing about a variety of subjects. Bi-Folkal kit information is available at http://www.bifolkal.org.

- *Talking Book Machines.* Provide free recorded books, magazines, and playback equipment to eligible customers.

> ### What Matters Most?
>
> At some of Columbus Metropolitan Library's centers, many people checked out few items, while at others a few people checked out an abundance of items. The question quickly became: are we more interested in higher circulation or higher user visits? We felt it prudent to give more weight to the number of user visits. It demonstrated that we impacted the lives of more people making use of the service routinely.

EVALUATING SERVICES

If your lobby stop service is a new program, your administration will want an evaluation of your new service. Often they are curious about circulation and user visits. To a significant degree your detailed statistical reports will impart the information needed to evaluate and explain your program's successes and shortcomings. However, you will want to determine what your measures of success will be, and these will often be based on the interests and concerns of your administration.

Once a year, review each site based on circulation, user visits, and compliance with your letter of agreement. Centers that meet your standards should be retained. If centers do not meet your standards, address issues with contact personnel at each center, advising them of the problem, and providing feedback for improvement. Give them a few months to rectify problems. If problems are not solved to your satisfaction, send the center a letter explaining the reasons for their cancellation.

You will also want to take stock of your collection annually to determine what is circulating and what is not. This is the time to evaluate emerging formats, especially the media formats that visually-impaired seniors rely on so much. Expect new formats to catch on slowly; this is generally a result of seniors not having immediate access to new playing devices like DVD and CD players, as well as the hesitancy of some to experiment with new technology. As more of your patrons transition to newer formats, allocate your collection budget accordingly.

Staffing patterns should also be reviewed annually. You may discover a consistent need for additional help at certain centers, which may change how you staff those sites. Reviewing staff processes and procedures is a necessary component, especially if your service is new. After working in the field for awhile, you will certainly identify practices that can be streamlined. Lobby stops are a very time-intensive service and any opportunity to save time and effort will be helpful to staff and customers.

ADVOCACY

Advocacy, simply stated, is garnering support for a cause or proposal. But advocating for a cause is seldom simple. Often you are the only person who understands the importance of your cause, and it may be solely up to you to communicate your desires to an often uninformed body. To do so you need to be informed, well prepared, and courageous in bringing your ideas forward. Experience has taught me a few things about advocacy.

- *Know your subject.* You are the expert and you must promote your ideas with authority. Be well read regarding all things in your field, keep apprised of emerging trends, gather information from those in the know, and be prepared to answer any and all question from superiors.

- *Know your community.* Understand the everchanging dynamics of the community you serve. Review demographics, conduct community assessments, focus on immigrating populations, and constantly evaluate the best mode of service delivery per dollar spent.

- *Understand your organization and make certain they understand you.* Learn all you can about your library's goals and objectives. Be a part of the process. Volunteer to provide input to the library's strategic plan. Take an active role in your organization's decision-making venues (e.g., committees, managers' meetings, focus groups). Get to know the decision-makers and communicate with them on a routine basis about your division's aspirations. Invite your Board of Trustees to shadow both staff and services. Those who take advantage of this opportunity will be much more informed and become future advocates.

- *Be prepared to give up something to get something.* Too often we become attached to particular services and the way we conduct business. Always be open-minded. Embrace change and constantly evaluate existing services. This may mean you have to give up one service to provide a better service more relevant to the community. Columbus Metropolitan Library did this when we gave up mobile collections and deposit collections to provide lobby stop service.

- *Be prepared to support your request.* Be passionate about your ideas, but ensure their feasibility with hard data. In other words, do your homework before taking your ideas forward.

- *Be confident and courageous.* For many of us, this is the hardest step of all. If you are uncomfortable with authority figures, you stand less of a chance of being heard. Develop good communication skills. Find opportunities to chat with administrators on a casual basis. You might consider taking a course on presentation skills. No matter what avenue you choose, it is vital you learn to express yourself and your goals through facts, clarity, and conviction.

- *Support library organizations.* Join library organizations, attend conferences, participate in committee work, and offer your expertise.

CONCLUSION

Should your organization elect to add lobby stop service to its roster of senior programming, know it will be a rewarding and beneficial program. You and your organization will succeed if you have the backing of your administration, if you plan accordingly, and if you are dedicated to making your new service work. You need to begin preparing yourself now for the day you need to make a case for change in your outreach program. Keep apprised of trends within your sphere of influence. Make reading library literature a priority. Support local, state, and national library organizations through membership, participation, and through attendance at conferences. Keep your supervisors and administrators aware of changes to your demographics, communicating your need for change now rather than later. Make opportunities to talk to them about your division and the dreams you have for it and your customers.

Keep an open mind. When you determine it is time to propose a change to your division or department, be conscientious about your planning. Do your research, support your case with documentation, anticipate questions from superiors and make certain your presentation is flawless.

Outreach exists to serve those unable to make use of traditional library service. The community needs us to identify emerging groups and meet their needs. Be the expert! All too often, you may be the only truly informed person on library service to the non-traditional user. These customers depend on our skills as library professionals to pave the road to outreach programming that will further enrich their lives.

ADDITIONAL RESOURCES

Sample Lobby Stop Intake Form

QUALIFICATION

Date _____ Staff _____

Is your facility located in the Anywhere School District? Yes _____ No _____

Residents in your facility need to be mobile enough to get
to a central location in your facility, select materials, and
transport them back to their rooms. Is this true of your facility? Yes _____ No _____

How many residents live at your facility? _____

Can you guarantee a regular, accessible, first-floor space for
us to set up large carts and equipment? Yes _____ No _____

Can you furnish a table and two chairs for circulation
of library materials? Yes _____ No _____

Can you guarantee a removal of snow and leaves from
sidewalks entering your facility? Yes _____ No _____

Can you designate a contact person who will be available
during our visit to your location? Yes _____ No _____

Are you willing to promote our service through posters,
calendars, and other materials we will provide? Yes _____ No _____

**Failure to meet any of the above requirements could
result in termination of service.**

INFORMATION

Facility Name _____

Contact Name _____   _____

Address _____

City _____

LOCATION

What side of town are you on? _____

What is the nearest major intersection? _____

**There is currently a waiting list for Lobby Stop service. We
will contact you when a space becomes available.**

For Lobby Stop Staff

Date service discontinued _____

Reason for cancellation _____

Figure 11.1: Sample lobby stop intake form

From *On the Road with Outreach: Mobile Library Services* by Jeannie Dilger-Hill and Erica MacCreaigh, Editors. Santa Barbara, CA: Libraries Unlimited. Copyright © 2010.

Sample Lobby Stop Letter of Agreement

Your facility has expressed an interest in becoming a Lobby Stop site receiving services from the Everywhere Public Library. In order to provide the best service for your residents and the Library's customers, the two entities agree to the following:

The Everywhere Library will:

- Provide a collection of fiction and nonfiction large print and regular print books, fiction and nonfiction audio books, music CDs, DVDs, and videos. The Library will also have two staff members deliver and circulate materials while providing a reader's advisory service.

- Provide signage and informational materials to inform potential customers of delivery dates and other library events and services.

- Issue/renew library cards to residents who do not have cards. Customers will be required to have a library card; no materials will be checked out without one.

- Enable customers to reserve materials by completing a reserve card or by placing a request through Info Line (555-READ), or online through the Library's web page (www. everywherelibrary).

Your facility agrees to:

- Provide convenient access to the facility at ground level. This must include leaf and snow removal to the access point and insuring that the loading area is clear of other vehicles.

- Post the promotional materials provided by the Library in appropriate locations in the facility.

- Provide a consistently scheduled room for set-up near the entrance that is well lit and has at least one long table and two chairs set up before arrival.

- Confirm that the vast majority of residents are sufficiently mobile to get to the Lobby Stop.

- Provide a contact person to serve as the Library's ambassador to residents at your facility.

- Promote the service to the residents.

A review of usage takes place twice a year. If the Library determines that the service is underutilized, the Library reserves the right to discontinue the program.

Location information:

Name of Facility: _____

Address: _____

Phone Number or other contact number: _____

Figure 11.2: Sample lobby stop letter of agreement

From *On the Road with Outreach: Mobile Library Services* by Jeannie Dilger-Hill and Erica MacCreaigh, Editors. Santa Barbara, CA: Libraries Unlimited. Copyright © 2010.

Name of current facility/office manager: _____

Name of resident contact: _____ Phone: _____

Facility email address (if available): _____

Entry information:

(i.e., buzzer, automatic doors, process to gain access)

_____

_____

_____

_____

Unloading/Parking location: _____ _____

_____

_____

Alternative unloading location: _____

(If regular is blocked or unavailable) _____

_____

_____

Location and directions to room for setup: _____

_____

_____

Figure 11.2: (continued)

If any of the information provided changes, *please* inform Outreach Services at 555-READ. You may contact the Outreach Manager at any time with questions you may have concerning the service.

For Office Use Only

Scheduled day for stop: _____ Time of service: _____

Staff assigned to location: _____

Figure 11.2: (continued)

Part V

Library Outreach to the Incarcerated

12

Library Services to Incarcerated Adults

By Maggie McFalls-Picher

Library services in correctional facilities serve a vital and instrumental role. For the incarcerated, libraries allow individuals to broaden their human experience through exposure to popular literature, self-help materials, and research-based texts.

—B. Gill-Tamcsu

There is an epidemic sweeping through North America. It is the mass incarceration of its population. According to a U.S. Justice Department report, the United States has the highest incarceration rate in the developed world, with one out of every 32 Americans under the jurisdiction of state or federal correctional authorities (U.S. Bureau of Justice, 2006). As incarceration rates increase, some people may be comforted by the notion that society is locking 'em up and throwing away the key. The truth of the matter is that most of the incarcerated reemerge into society to become our neighbors and coworkers. Studies show that more than 95 percent of the current prison population will be released (U.S. Bureau of Justice, 2003).

But for many of these individuals, transitioning back into the community is fraught with challenges. In order to reintegrate into society, ex-offenders are desperately in need of a variety of information resources related to housing, job searching, and life skills. Continuity between rehabilitation programming on the inside and transitional services on the outside is essential. Correctional libraries can help by meeting the information needs of incarcerated inmates and by forging relationships with the larger community to bridge their successful return to society.

This chapter explores what library service to the incarcerated involves for both correctional and public library outreach librarians, how this service benefits the population it serves, and how librarians and paraprofessionals can advocate for this service if and when it is threatened.

THE PUBLIC LIBRARY MODEL

An incarcerated person has not relinquished the right to learn and to access information, and the prison library should offer materials and services comparable to community libraries in the 'free' world.

—Vibeke Lehmann and Joanne Locke

Historically, public libraries have served as the people's university, offering educational opportunities to people who may otherwise never have had access. Library services to the incarcerated reflect the very core principles and values of public librarianship. As demonstrated in their guidelines, the ALA and other library associations around the world agree: inmates are not to be excluded from this right to information.

However, there is an inherent conflict between the mandate of a public library and that of a correctional library that make the application of public library principles within a correctional setting problematic. The very essence of public librarianship is a spirit of openness and access. In a prison, however, priority rests on security and restriction of freedoms. The underlying question becomes: as librarians, how do we advocate for freedom and equality of information to our patrons while continuing to further society's interest in security and reform?

In *Library Services to the Incarcerated* (2006), authors Sheila Clark and Erica MacCreaigh refer to three tenets of librarianship critical to correctional libraries: access and intellectual freedom, privacy and confidentiality, and social responsibility. The challenge, however, is bringing these public library values and professional ethics into a prison setting. The authors write, "the art of bringing the public library model into this environment consists of honoring the spirit of ALA's highest ideals while following the correctional facility's rules." While this may be a delicate dance requiring some creativity and persistence, it is critical to stay true to our professional ethics in order to provide the most successful correctional library services.

Service Standards

What the incarcerated person reads depends on the quality and relevance of the library collection. With a qualified staff, a collection of materials that meets the education, recreation, and rehabilitation needs of the prisoners, as well as an inviting physical space, the prison library can be an important part of prison life and offender programs.

—Vibeke Lehmann and Joanne Locke

On the whole, there has been much progress for correctional libraries in the western world over the last century. Much of this progress can be directly attributed to guidelines promoting consistency in service. The American Library Association's *Library Standards for Adult Correctional Institutions* (1992) asserts that correctional library services must adhere to the same basic tenets and values that ALA extends to all library patrons. These tenets include the "Library Bill of Rights," "Resolution on Prisoners' Rights to Read," and others. The guidelines outline qualitative and quantitative measures for correctional libraries to follow and make a compelling case for the importance of correctional library service. International guidelines laid out by the International Federation of Library Associations (IFLA) have also been fundamental in the move towards affording the incarcerated access to information (Kaiser, 1995).

The most proactive measure you can take to ensure inmates' right to information in general, and library services specifically, is to create a comprehensive document endorsed by the jail or prison administration that reflects the standards outlined by the ALA and IFLA. This document should specify:

- Services the library will provide to both the inmates and facility staff
- Resources the library will provide, including a detailed collection development policy specifying what materials will not be collected for security reasons
- Staffing
- Budget (this section should be updated annually if you are a public library providing services under contract)
- Specific and measurable goals and objectives (this should also be updated regularly)

A policy specific to library services that is accepted as part of the mandate by the corrections department can help insure against cutbacks in the future. For an example of a comprehensive service standards policy that doubles as both a state departmental regulation and interdepartmental contract, see the Colorado Department of Corrections' administration regulation on library services. (Colorado Department of Corrections, 2008)

Technology

Despite the technological opportunities possible within correctional libraries, there are some substantial challenges linked to both the nature of the users and to corrections bureaucracy. To list a few:

- Censorship
- Low literacy
- Restricted access to the library
- High demand coupled with lack of resources, staff, and funding
- Diverse population (both in terms of culture and information needs)
- Isolation of library staff within the institution and from peers in the library science field
- Low pay of staff
- Overworked/burned out staff
- Slow decision-making process

Perhaps the biggest obstacle facing correctional libraries is the widespread restriction of Internet access. While there is a clear security risk involved with providing

Ontario Correctional Institute Residents Speak Out

"When I came into the library, it was the first time I felt like a real human being since getting arrested."

"The library is a lot like a treasure chest. Within the OCI library, I have found a whole new world of opportunities and self-discovery. These treasures are priceless."

"The library is an access point to information to enjoy on the inside and to prepare for the outside."

"The library was my real place of peace and serenity here. . . . The Book Club helped me to be able to speak intellectually without being chastised."

"[Library staff] went the extra mile for me in getting titles of my interest and those surrounding those topics of interest."

Internet access, especially for those incarcerated for crimes related to Internet pornography, gambling, or fraud, the unfortunate by-product is that the entire incarcerated population remains information poor while serving their time. Imagine trying to transition into today's world, after 15 years in prison, without having been introduced to a computer, much less the Internet. Vogel (2008) sums up the problem: "By refusing to allow correctional librarians to assist their patrons in understanding Internet information-seeking strategies, correctional practice has created a greater obstacle to the assimilation of ex-offenders into the outside world. This is the legacy from twentieth-century corrections." This is an area of contention for many correctional librarians trying to hold true to their professional ethic of access and openness and a commitment to narrowing the digital divide between the haves and have-nots.

Some correctional librarians have been able to overcome this restriction through alternative solutions. For example, a CD-ROM entitled *Discovering the Internet@ Your Library*, put together by the Maryland Correctional Education Libraries, aims to promote the public library as a place ex-offenders can go to access Internet sites that will assist them in their transition back into the community (Shirley, 2002). The CD-ROM walks the viewer through some of the various Internet sites related to job, career, and education services.

Other options for providing Internet training to inmates include the use of firewalls, filters, and other software. At Red Rock Correctional in Arizona (Cramer, 2008), inmates are able to access legal information from a closed, customized LexisNexis Web site that doesn't allow navigation to the Internet. The Wisconsin Department of Corrections (Tucker, 2008) allows similar access to LexisNexis as well as firewallprotected, dedicated, and direct access to JobNet for those inmates preparing for reentry. At OCI, inmates are given a virtual Web search experience through WebWhacker, a program that allows Web sites to be copied onto a hard drive or CD.

Collections

While the physical space of the correctional library may vary and the patrons might appear unconventional, the scope of the collection and the reading interests of the incarcerated are not unlike those found in public libraries. Inmates do tend to have more challenging service needs based not only on their circumstances, but also on higher than average rates of mental health disorders, addiction issues, and low literacy. As a result of these factors, many inmates have difficulty communicating and locating the information they need. As correctional librarians, we have to respond with a more personalized service. Helpful reader advisory techniques include posting "read-alike" lists, creating displays on special topics of interest, and using genre stickers.

A core collection should include multicultural resources, legal collections, materials for the learning disabled, easy readers, and large print. Try to stock everything on the national fiction best seller lists (though budget restraints might mean you have to wait for titles to appear in paperback.) Horror and fantasy enjoy strong readership, especially in men's facilities, so core authors like Tolkein, Terry Brooks, Terry Goodkind, Robert Jordan, Clive Barker, Anne Rice, and of course, Stephen King and Dean Koontz are must-haves. Inmate patrons consistently demand Sidney Sheldon, Jackie Collins, and Harold Robbins. Female patrons will want a lot of V.C. Andrews; male patrons will want a lot of Louis L'Amour.

Urban literature (also called street lit and ghetto lit), though controversial, is enormously popular in prison, but don't limit yourself to Iceberg Slim and Donald Goines. K'wan, Nikki Turner, Zane, Teri Woods, and Relentless Aaron are in high demand. Be sure to provide the more literary street lit, too, like Nathan McCall, Sister Souljah, and Rasheed Clark. On the lighter side, Eric Jerome Dickey and Omar Tyree are staples; in some facilities, E. Lynn Harris also tops the list.

Popular nonfiction topics include self-esteem, stress and anxiety, relationships, drug and alcohol addiction, health and fitness, animals, war and history, poetry, religious material, trivia, and inspirational stories (i.e. the Chicken Soup series, which includes one book specifically for prisoners).

For emergent readers, it is helpful to provide a collection of low literacy/high interest titles that range from a second grade reading level to high school. Titles from Orca publishers and graphic novels are especially useful in attracting inmates who would otherwise not visit the library. Basic dictionaries can assist those inmates participating in literacy programs.

Don't forget to include children's and young adult titles. Materials at these reading levels catch more than emergent readers. They appeal to readers with children who want to connect with their kids through books. And many inmates express a desire to read the books they missed when they were children themselves. Classics like *Little House on the Prairie, Hatchet,* and *The Giver* can draw a lot of attention (sometimes with some helpful marketing), as do less hefty titles like *Goosebumps, Fear Street,* and *Hank the Cowdog.* Inmates sometimes feel awkward checking kid books out, so it helps if you read some of these, too, and can talk them up convincingly.

Large print serves an array of reader needs. Obviously, many patrons with visual impairments like large print. But new and struggling readers, as well as patrons with short attention spans or reading disabilities often find the large print format more accessible than regular print. The same can be said of graphic novels and nonfiction. From compendia of comic strips like Garfield and Calvin and Hobbes, contemporary spins on classic comics from Marvel, Dark Horse, and DC Comics, Japanese manga, and serious literary works like *Maus,* the graphic format captures special needs readers as well as younger offenders and long-time fans of comic book art.

The inmate population can be quite diverse. To reflect this diversity, try to carry titles for non-native English speakers. To the best of your budget abilities, carry ESL materials in print and CD. Also try to carry titles on the common countries of origin—don't make the mistake of assuming that all your Spanish speakers come from Mexico! A public library deposit collection can supplement these resources. Additionally, make an effort to have special events and displays to recognize various multicultural celebrations.

When working in a correctional library, security is always an important consideration. Each institution will have its own policy regarding acceptable materials for the library. Some institutions do not allow hard covers because of hidden contraband and some do not permit spiral or comb bindings or audio players because of their concerns about fashioning weapons and tattooing tools. Individual inmates are typically not permitted to receive books directly from outside sources. Some institutions allow donations to an individual through a vendor or publisher. For general donations to the library, it is standard process for each book to pass through main security before it comes to the library. A library staff will then inspect and process the item.

Programs

Programming can also be similar to the public library, including book clubs, literacy programs, and book talks. Mysteries, inspirational/religious books, and general fiction lend themselves well to book clubs. Another popular program is the author talk, where local poets and authors read from their works, then lead a writing workshop. Bookbinding and self-publishing classes always fill up quickly and any craft project will be well-received.

Competitions are popular, too. Trivia contests are easy if you have a whiteboard for posting questions. Copyright-free Sudoku puzzles are available online. Check with your facility administration to see if you can give out prizes. Bookmarks reinforce the library connection, are cheap, don't eat up storage space or constitute much of a security risk, and inmates love them.

Workshops on job training, career counseling, business planning, and applying for financial aid are instrumental in preparing inmates for return to their communities. Resume-writing workshops and mock interviews that focus on how to overcome and explain employment gaps help inmates gain confidence marketing themselves out in the world.

While the possibilities for programming in correctional libraries are unlimited, staffing and

Programs that Build Community

Consider activities that help connect inmates to the community. Every Christmas we have an ornament-designing competition and the ornaments are then donated to local homeless shelters.

Perhaps the most universally successful correctional library program, known by several titles like "Read-to-Your-Child," "Begin With Books," and "Read to the Children," enables an incarcerated parent to record himself or herself reading a storybook onto a cassette or CD which is then sent to their children, many times along with the book. This is a great program to offer right before the holidays and right before summer reading programs starts in the local public libraries!

resources are not. In order to have a successful program and gain the confidence of the correctional administration, it is essential to put together a well-researched and organized proposal. The proposal should include a description of the program, the goals and expectations of the program, a timeframe for planning and implementing the program, and the expected cost. Once your proposal is together, present it to your supervisor for approval. Once you have the go-ahead, inform everyone you can

Making It Work

Bringing outside experts into prison can be a challenge in a prison bureaucracy. Background security checks can scare many people who are already intimidated by setting foot inside a prison. There are ways to compromise. For example, I appealed to our local business bureau about coming to Ontario Correctional Institute (OCI) to do some workshops on writing a business plan and applying for government grants. I described the merits of OCI, explaining that OCI is a progressive institution with extremely respectful and eager-to-learn inmates. However, I wasn't able to make the sale. Despite the fact that many of the men at OCI are from the area and may visit the business bureau upon reentry, the staff were not prepared to visit.

I proposed an alternative; in exchange for literature on business plan writing, the interested residents could create their business plans and send them to the business center for edits and corrections. That plan satisfied everyone involved and has since led to a resident-led workshop. Each resident pitches his business idea and gets feedback and suggestions from the others. They can then send their drafts into the business bureau for a professional review. The business experts get to stay in their comfort zone, but through indirect interaction, the inmates still benefit from their expertise.

think of whose work flow might be affected by the program. This includes teachers, housing or recreation officers, and facility administrators. Surprises are unwelcome in corrections, so the better informed everyone is, the better everyone will cooperate with you.

Begin your internal advertising campaign as soon as you get approval. Just because you have a captive audience, it doesn't mean your patrons don't need advance notice of upcoming events.

While there is a temptation to begin many programs at once, you'll show a better commitment to quality by running only a few programs in short cycles of eight weeks or less.

REENTRY SERVICES

"The goal of transition is to ready an inmate for entry into the labor market as a law abiding, self-sufficient citizen" (Vogel 2008).

When it is time for inmates to return to their communities, their needs are great. In more cases than not, ex-offenders have no savings, housing, health care, or job opportunities. To make matters more complicated, having a criminal record limits them from certain jobs and careers, as well as housing possibilities. The gap in their employment history during their incarceration may increase their difficulty in securing a job. These needs are compounded for people plagued with a drug addiction or mental health issues. Consequently, in the first months of release, the likelihood of failure is strong.

The correctional library is an important asset to the reentering citizen only if it possesses a well-developed and current collection of resources for job searching, education, and career issues. Some examples of particularly relevant subjects are:

- Resume writing
- Interviewing
- Cover letters
- Writing business plans and grants
- Trades and practice exams
- Community resources
- College and university catalogs
- Financial aid

Of course, hand-in-hand with career and educational resources is a strong library program focusing on general reentry issues. Correctional libraries do this by providing:

- Materials and programs on parenting and relationships
- Information about finding affordable housing
- Addiction-recovery resources
- Resources on living with mental illness and surviving sexual abuse
- Materials and programs on money management
- Materials and programs on spiritual exploration

Another program that helps inmates prepare to return to society is library instruction. Library instruction can begin with a detailed orientation to the correctional library, with library staff explaining the policies and how to use the catalog to search. It is also helpful to invite a librarian from the public library in the area to explain how to obtain a library card and to demonstrate the various databases that can be used with the card to help ex-offenders help themselves to meet their basic needs. The Colorado State Library has put together a short DVD called *Out for Life!* that walks inmates through the public library experience, explaining the basics on how the public library works, what the expectations are, and so on (Colorado State Library, 2008). Some public libraries will even issue library cards to inmates before they are discharged. Obtaining a library card upon discharge is a wonderful way to bridge the gap in services between what the inmate received on the inside to what information he can access once back in the community.

While correctional libraries have a great opportunity to introduce inmates to the wonders of public libraries and the services and information they can provide, public libraries enjoy a great opportunity to reach out to ex-offenders once they are released. In a 2007 article, Brendan Dowling concludes: "Ex-offenders are a growing part of our population, and they will be visiting libraries whether librarians are prepared for them or not. By understanding their basic needs and how the public library can meet those needs, librarians can go a long way toward making ostracized members of society feel more included."

Most public libraries offer databases and classes on topics that are helpful to ex-offenders, including basic computer skills, resume writing, and job hunting. Other needs common to recently released offenders include:

- Bus schedules and transportation
- Affordable and subsidized housing
- Health care information, including addresses of clinics for the uninsured and people with low incomes
- Internet and technology training
- Legal assistance, including contact information for pro bono lawyers and information about alimony, child custody, bankruptcy, and restitution
- Educational and vocational training
- Substance abuse services

Many public libraries are recognizing the specific needs of an increasing population of ex-offenders. New York Public Library, for example, publishes a directory of local organizations that assist ex-offenders entitled *Connections*. The Albany Public Library has a similar guide entitled *On Your Own*, part of their First Stop/Next Step program for ex-offenders, and Baltimore's Enoch Pratt Free Library hosts a job fair program called "Breaking Down Barriers to Employment: Job and Career Resources for Ex-Offenders" to provide employment information to job seekers with criminal records (Dowling, 2007). Hopefully, through more partnerships between correctional and public libraries, public libraries across North America will follow suit and develop resources and programs specific to the ex-offender.

COLLABORATIONS

Within the Facility

While the programming that takes place inside the library is important, to become even more effective in aiding inmates in their transition, correctional librarians must collaborate with other departments inside the institution. Since the library is usually a removed and isolated part of the institution and often criticized as unnecessary by some staff (particularly when allocation of resources is an issue), it is always a good idea to make an effort to let the other staff know about programs happening within the library. Any steps you can take to welcome staff into the library and to participate yourself in non-library programs and committees will demonstrate your professionalism and get positive exposure for the library.

One method for getting the word out is a monthly newsletter. This should include the library schedule, policies, and new and ongoing programs. You can distribute it to staff via e-mail as well as place print copies in the units for the inmates to view. The layout and artwork should be creative and colorful, but don't worry if you're not an artist.

Many offenders are excellent artists and many prisons have graphic arts programs that would appreciate a real-world project for students to practice on.

If your facility already has a newsletter, all the better. Be sure the library has a regular column and that special events are always included. Don't forget to include local public library programs, too. Facility staff can attend them and offenders can promote them to family and friends on the outside. You'll be surprised by how many staff and offenders approach you saying that they never knew how many programs took place in the library!

The correctional library shares a similar mandate with other correctional programming within the institution, such as the school and the chaplaincy. Make every effort to collaborate with them to strengthen all of your programs. For example, the library should contain educational materials that teachers and students need to support classroom studies. Offer to assist students with research techniques that include reliable search strategies and proper citing of sources. Pay attention to chaplain-run programs on grieving and meditation and complement them with reading materials and literature. In turn, ask the teachers and chaplain to recommend titles that would be useful to the inmates. Social workers and psychologists are also wonderful resources for the library. Soliciting them for resource ideas will help you build an excellent collection of self-help books for the inmates.

Making sure the library is a relevant service for facility staff—and that they know about the service—is a great way of building productive relationships internally. An obvious way to extend the service is to set aside a physical space specifically for staff resources. If you have the space, you have the option of designating an entirely separate area for staff, complete with Internet-connected computers and books, journals, and periodicals supporting various correctional departments. The staff library could even be added to existing multipurpose space with a conference table for meetings and a comfortable lounge area for relaxing during breaks.

Invite staff to browse the resident library for recreational reading and make requests through the public library interlibrary loan. Sometimes staff (especially officers in the housing units) are tied to their work areas, so connecting the library catalog to computers throughout the institution makes it easy for staff to see what is available in the library and to place holds and request new titles. If you have the manpower to really go the extra mile, provide interlibrary loan service to staff even if you don't offer that service to residents.

Another way to connect with non-library facility staff is by joining committees. This shows your willingness to partner with other departments and it increases the visibility of the library program.

Community Collaborations

As correctional librarians, it is critical that we develop solid relationships with the outside community in order to serve as a bridge between prison life and life outside the walls. In the isolated culture of corrections, these relationships serve many purposes. Community partners open a window into the outside world for the inmates as well as library staff, make for a richer library service, help educate the public on the special needs of the ex-offender, and can be called upon as advocates in the event that the library services are threatened.

Partner with your local business bureau. Business bureaus offer many free services that may include consultations and accountant advice, business plan reviews, access to busi-

> **The Best Things in Life Are Free**
>
> OCL solicits volunteers by reaching out to local non-profit organizations whose values of reform and self-improvement are similar to those of corrections. Before a volunteer begins, he must pass a security clearance, submit three references and a written application, go through an interview process, and complete an orientation program.
>
> Some of our most popular volunteer-led programs include Toastmasters, a public speaking course, and The Bridge, which provides life skills training. At the end of each year we hold a "Volunteer Appreciation Dinner" during which the inmates make speeches, play music, and perform skits for our volunteers.

ness related databases, trade indexes and directories as well as free workshops and seminars. Partnering with these business centers not only helps to educate inmates about these resources, but it also helps to inform the business community of an emerging and growing population so that they can better tailor their resources and programming. Hosting a career day and inviting local organizations to present as well as conduct informational interviews is a great way to bring the business community together and to help inmates prepare for their future.

Reaching out to the school district also provides opportunities for collaboration. Invite teachers from the local high school to lead a book club for the inmates. Initiate GED, ESL, and literacy training programs if they do not already exist and ask teachers to lead a course. Finally, appeal to the school district to donate up-to-date educational texts, study guides, and multimedia resources that will support these programs.

Soliciting volunteers is a great way to foster a mutual understanding with the community and further the approval of the administration. Any effort to build the library program with no cost to the institution, such as recruiting volunteers or writing grants, will help build trust and encourage support for the library program.

Other invaluable resources to correctional librarians and staff are listservs and online discussion groups that provide a forum on issues as varied as how to deal with contraband to creating institution-wide policies on censorship. Through these online groups, there is a free flow of information, networking, idea sharing, and even collaboration on large-scale projects such as updating ALA standards for library services to prisoners. A fairly active listserv is the Prison Library listserv, while the networking site WebJunction offers workshops relevant to prison libraries. Blogs by correctional librarians are also a great way to get ideas for programming, find out what is happening at other institutions and get links to relevant Web sites and articles. Examples include the Prison Librarian Blog, Jail Librarian, and the Institutional Library Services blog. References to all of these and more can be found at the end of this chapter.

Public libraries, however, may be the most helpful community partner you can find, both because of your shared mission and because of public librarians' inclination to serve the disenfranchised. Their role in assisting parolees with successful reentry has already been discussed; in the next section, we look at how public libraries can reach out to the incarcerated.

The Numbers Never Lie

During my first eight months at the Ontario Correctional Institute, I put together a simple spreadsheet of circulation programs and statistics. They showed a nice trend of increasing library visits and book checkout despite a dip in total inmates in the institution. Not only was my supervisor pleased with this trend, but he was also impressed that I went to the trouble to take the daily data and to compile it to paint a picture of what was happening at the library. While he had always been supportive of the library service in principle, it was clear that he saw these spreadsheets as invaluable in proving the worth of the library to the Superintendent. Suddenly, the library rose to a professional level and became on par with the other correctional programs.

supervisor, the officer who oversees the library program, and/or public library supervisors. Be prepared with a progress report and a statistical report. An important tool for validating the role of the library in prisons, as is true in public libraries, are statistics. Statistics are a tool for measuring the popularity of a collection, a program, library usage, and more. Hard facts are often the best way to sell the merit of the library to those who would be critical. That said, be sure not to miss opportunities to share stories illustrating the library's impact. Providing inmates and guest presenters with comment cards helps capture individual impressions of the effectiveness of the library's service. Be sure to pass these on to facility administrators.

CONCLUSION

Correctional library staff and public library outreach librarians have the chance to capture the imagination of inmates for the first time and to help them develop a relationship with their public library when they return to their communities. Many inmates never visited a library before their incarceration. Once they have been exposed to the pleasures of reading, many inmates take advantage of all the correctional library has to offer. It is not surprising that user rates within prisons tend to be much higher than those in public and school libraries (Curry, 2003).

Whether you are working directly with inmates on the inside or providing outreach services from the public library, your contribution to inmates' quality of life and to their successful reintegration cannot be overstated. "By providing new and popular reading materials, literacy skills are being developed and maintained and a positive way to spend time provided. Hopefully, the maintaining of literacy skills will aid in a positive transition back into the community, and a willingness to seek out public libraries when needed" (Carreiro, 2008).

REFERENCES

Association of Specialized and Cooperative Library Agencies, *Library Standards for Adult Correctional Institutions* (Chicago: American Library Association, 1992).

Jack Canfield, ed. *Chicken Soup* series (multiple publishers).

C. Carreiro, "OCI Deposit Collection," e-mail message to Maggie McFalls-Picher, July 18, 2008.

Sheila Clark and Erica MacCreaigh, *Library Services to the Incarcerated: Applying the Public Library Model in Correctional Facility Libraries* (Westport, CT: Libraries Unlimited, 2006), 13–19.

W. Cramer, "Frequently Asked Questions," e-mail message to Maggie McFalls-Picher, December 8, 2008.

A. Curry, "Canadian Federal Prison Libraries: A National Survey," *Journal of Librarianship and Information Science,* September 2003, 141–152.

Brendan Dowling, "Public Libraries and the Ex-Offender," *Public Libraries,* November–December 2007, 44–48.

John R. Erickson, *The Original Adventures of Hank the Cowdog* (New York: Puffin Books, 1999).

I. Gilman, "Beyond Books: Restorative Librarianship in Juvenile Detention Centers," *Public Libraries,* January–February 2007, 58–66.

Lauren E. Glaze and Thomas P. Bonczar, "Probation and Parole in the United States, 2006." December 2007. Available at: http://www.ojp.usdoj.gov/bjs/pub/pdf/ppus06.pdf.

Timothy Hughes and Doris James Wilson, "Reentry Trends in the United States," United States Bureau of Justice Statistics. Available at: http://www.ojp.usdoj.gov/bjs/reentry/reentry.htm.

Institutional Library Services, "Out for Life: How your Library Can Help." (Denver: Colorado State Library, 2007). Available at: http://www.cde.state.co.us/media/cdelib/video/OutForLife/OutForLife-En.html.

F. E. Kaiser, *Guidelines for Library Services to Prisoners,* 2nd ed. (The Hague: International Federation of Library Associations and Institutions, 1995).

Vibeke Lehmann, "Planning and Implementing Prison Libraries: Strategies and Resources" (World Library and Information Congress: 69th IFLA General Conference and Council). Available at: http://www.ifla.org/IV/ifla69/papers/175-E_Lehmann.pdf.

"Library Services," in *Colorado Department of Corrections Administrative Regulations* (Colorado Department of Corrections, 2008). Available at: https://exdoc.state.co.us/userfiles/regulations/pdf/0500_02.pdf.

Lois Lowry, *The Giver* (New York: Bantam Doubleday Dell Books for Young Readers, 1999).

Gary Paulsen, *Hatchet* (New York: Simon & Schuster, 2007).

"Service to Detention Facilities and Jails," in *ALA Policy Manual (In ALA Handbook of Organization)* (Chicago: IL: American Library Association, 2008–2009), 46. Available at: http://www.ala.org/ala/aboutala/governance/policymanual/policymanual.31_3.pdf.

Glennor Shirley, *Discovering the Internet @ Your Library,* CD-ROM (Baltimore, MD: Maryland Correctional Education Libraries, 2002).

Art Spiegelman, *Maus* (New York: Pantheon Books, 1986).

R. L. Stine, *Fear Street* series (New York: Pocket Books).

R. L. Stine, *Goosebumps* series (New York: Scholastic).

P. Tucker, "Frequently Asked Questions," e-mail message to Maggie McFalls-Picher, July 31, 2008.

Brenda Vogel, "Two Million on the Wrong Side of the Digital Divide," *Interface,* Spring 2008. Available at: http://www.ala.org/ala/mgrps/divs/ascla/asclapubs/interface/archives/contentlistingby/volume30/ALA_print_layout_1_469875_469875.cfm.

Laura Ingalls Wilder, *Little House on the Prairie* (New York: Harper, 1981).

ADDITIONAL RESOURCES

Publishers and Web Sites for Graphic Formats and Urban Literature

Dark Horse Comics. www.darkhorse.com

The official site of Dark Horse Comics. *Star Wars* and *Buffy the Vampire Slayer* tie-ins can be found here, as well as less conventional takes on classic characters like Batman, and manga series *Gantz, Oh My Goddess!,* and *Berserk,* among many others.

DC Universe. www.dccomics.com

The official site of DC Comics, where you'll find Superman, Wonder Woman, Batman and Robin, and more.

Marvel. www.marvel.com

The official site of Marvel Comics, home of Spiderman, Captain America, The X-Men, The Hulk, and many others.

RAWSISTAZ. www.rawsistaz.com

With a focus on promoting literacy in the African American community, this Web site contains book reviews, support for aspiring authors, and discussion group questions for a comprehensive list of contemporary and classic titles.

TOKYOPOP. www.tokyopop.com

One of the most prolific producers of manga in the world; series include *Sailor Moon* and *Marmalade Boy*

Urban Book Source. www.theurbanbooksource.com

Describes itself as "the premiere Internet source for readers, writers, authors, publishers and vendors of urban literature." Book reviews, interviews, columnists, and exhaustive links to vendors, review sources, and fan magazines and clubs.

Viz Media. www.viz.com

Another prolific manga producer, home of the now-classic *Dragon Ball Z* series.

Web Sites for Correctional Librarians

"Connections and the Job Search." The New York Public Library. Available at: http://www.nypl.org/branch/services/connections/introduction.html. Reentry directory for prisoners and ex-offenders. While much of the information is specific to New York, it does provide a model for the kinds of information needs common to ex-offenders.

Inside: Librarians Serving Those Serving Time. Available at: jailslibrarian.blogspot.com. A blog by the Alameda (CA) County Library's jail services team.

Institutional Library Services: Where Positive Change Takes Place. Available at: http://blogs.secstate.wa.gov/ils. Blog of the Washington State Institutional Libraries.

"Library Services: Correctional and Institutional." WebJunction. Available at: http://www.webjunction.org/correctional-and-institutional/resources/overview. Resources and discussion board on correctional libraries and library outreach to correctional facilities.

Prison and Jail Librarians Discussion List (prison-l). Available at: prison-l@ala. org. Active, unmoderated listserv with over 100 members working in correctional libraries.

Prison Librarian. Available at: http://prisonlibrarian.blogspot.com. Blog for correctional librarians, maintained by Glennor Shirley, Library Coordinator for the Maryland Correctional Libraries.

Maryland Correctional Education Libraries. Available at: http://ce.msde.state. md.us/library. While much of the information is specific to offenders, this Web site also contains collection development lists, articles of interest to correctional librarians, and resources for reentry.

YALSA Lockdown. Available at http://lists.ala.org/wws/info/yalsa-lockdown. Active, unmoderated listserv specifically for librarians who work with incarcerated teens.

Many correctional facilities have written regulations that guide actions and services within the facility, and some have documents specific to the library. Familiarize yourself with these documents and learn what you absolutely can or cannot do.

SECURITY

Part of the culture shock involves security concerns. Residents are incarcerated because they have committed crimes. Just because an individual is incarcerated doesn't mean he will stop acting criminally. A criminal subculture exists in every facility and a facility librarian must learn to recognize it. Some residents favor libraries because they are ideal for passing information and congregating. The library is a prime place for transferring contraband, according to Bouchard (2002). Books are often used to pass notes or small weapons, and a facility librarian must learn to search them on a regular basis. Adopting the practice of flipping through books whenever they are checked in or out will sometimes reveal contraband. Also notice if a certain title circulates regularly, because residents may have identified it as a means to pass messages.

Monitoring activity in the library is essential for preserving safety and security. Gang affiliation and hazing occurs in prisons, so residents are discouraged from congregating and sharing information. Be aware of inmates speaking quietly and furtively. Gently split them up and direct them to other activities or areas of the library. This creates a safe, comfortable atmosphere for all residents in the library. If residents learn that the library is a safe place where they need not worry about harassment from other residents, they will be more likely to visit. Then, you can take advantage of their presence to encourage reading and learning.

Maintaining sensible security procedures also assures other facility staff that you are committed to everyone's safety first. Most security officers see the library as a security risk, and new facility librarians may be upset by what they perceive as negative attention from officers. But the library *is* a security risk. Residents have relative freedom in the library, and officers often become concerned with what they see as too much freedom. A recent study of managing conflict in a prison library included interviews of security officers about libraries and librarians in prison (Strasner, 2004). Virtually all of the interviewees expressed concern that libraries give residents too much freedom and that librarians do not pay enough attention to security. This attitude is a good one for security staff to adopt because security is their main purpose. Reacting to officer presence or concerns about library security risks in a defensive manner can create a working environment that is filled with tension. Instead, learn to appreciate the unique perspective of the officer and enlist his or her help in improving security in the library.

CHILDHOOD DEVELOPMENT

Having read about culture shock and security concerns, one might wonder where the rewards of working with incarcerated youth are to be found. As stated previously, many youth who find themselves incarcerated have already faced many challenges in their lives, including unstable homes, lack of education, and lack of opportunities. These children, while having committed criminal acts, are still children who need adult supervision and guidance. Because of your position as a service provider, you are uniquely

13

Library Services to Incarcerated Youth

By Teresa Valenti

Providing library services to children and teens is one of the most challenging and rewarding career paths to be found in librarianship. This age group is still finding its way in the world and requires much more assistance and direction than do adult library patrons. Success working with this population requires special attention to information-seeking needs and an understanding by the librarian that his job will entail much more outreach to children than to adults. Adults are more likely to seek assistance from the library than are children, who must be shown what the library has in order to determine what they might be interested in.

When you combine youth with incarceration, it becomes clear that being a librarian in a youth facility or providing outreach to incarcerated youth only magnifies the challenges of working with adolescents. Consider the population being served. It consists mostly of teenage boys, mostly from lower socio-economic backgrounds, mostly with significant socialization problems involving parents, schooling, friendships, and even gang affiliation, and all in trouble with the law. Also consider the working environment. A prison is a secure facility that controls its population and practices censorship, all contradictory to the environment of a library, which encourages freedom of access to any information one may desire. At first glance, these issues may seem to be overwhelming, and discouraging of outreach endeavors or a career working with incarcerated youth, but that would be far from the truth. Many librarians who serve incarcerated youth agree that it is one of the most rewarding challenges of their careers.

This chapter explores many issues facing children's librarians in prison and those providing outreach to incarcerated youth. These issues include culture shock, security, childhood development, meeting the special needs of incarcerated youth, and managing offender behavior. We will look at collection development, programs and services, and the importance of creating a welcoming library environment.

Incarcerated youth can be referred to in many ways. They may be called inmates, offenders, kids, or a number of other terms. For the purposes of this discussion, the term residents will be used.

Conflicts of Ethics

One of the most difficult issues I encountered as a youth prison librarian was the restriction of library services and materials. It was hard for me to resolve the conflicting professional ethics of librarianship, which asserts freedom of access to all information, with the professional ethics of correctional officer, which is to control the population and restrict access to information. As a civilian librarian, I encouraged customers to pursue any information they might seek, but as a facility librarian I was required to restrict access to certain types of information that might endanger the safety of the facility. Such information included graphic sexual content, materials that endorse hatred, or instructions for making intoxicating agents. Some books were completely banned from the facility; some were allowed with a page or two removed. For example, books about Harry Houdini had to be carefully evaluated for content, because a resident might use it to learn how to escape from handcuffs!

CULTURE SHOCK

One of the first things encountered in a facility library is culture shock. Unless you have previous experience working in a prison or jail, you will be surprised at how different it is. Brenda Vogel (1995) summarizes it nicely when she says, "As a rule in libraries, the librarian works to become one with that library's culture. This is not so in a prison and can lead to confusion and stress." Even knowing you will be working in a very different environment can't fully prepare you for the experience. In her introduction to a profile of Folsom Prison Library, Sarah Dalton writes "Libraries and prisons have opposing missions. A library represents freeing, intellectual movement—the unimpeded search for knowledge. A prison embodies closure—the radical restriction of the human impulse" (Dalton, 2003). Every activity in a facility is defined and scrutinized, including when residents are allowed to move from place to place and with how much freedom, when they attend classes, when they eat meals, when they may visit the library, and with whom they are allowed to socialize. Of course, facility staff are bound by these schedules as well. The times the library is open, what kind of programs may be held, what type of books are allowed, how much, if any, computer access is allowed, how many residents may be in the library at one time, and what they may do there are all strictly defined. Librarians working in regular libraries rarely consider these issues, instead offering services freely.

As a public librarian, you would never question a patron's request for information, but as a prison librarian you always have to think of how information might be used in a negative manner. It can be very difficult to learn to manage this role conflict, but there are tools available to help.

Read the American Library Association's Code of Ethics (2008) and the Resolution on Prisoners' Right to Read (1992), both of which can be found on the American Library Association's Web site. Section V of the Code of Ethics especially useful. It reads, "We treat co-workers and other colleagues with respect, fairness, and good faith, and advocate conditions of employment that *safeguard the rights and welfare of all employees at our institutions* (italics added)." Stevens and Usherwood (1995) say we must remember, "It's not a library with a jail around it, but a jail with a library in it." What they mean is that the security concerns of the facility come before the information needs of the residents. It isn't so hard to manage the role conflict if the facility librarian remembers that safeguarding the welfare of her co-workers is part of her code of ethics.

positioned to provide these things to children. You can monitor security more discreetly than officers, thus giving residents some relief from constant officer presence. Providing this relief gives residents a chance to practice self-control that they don't get by being closely controlled by officers so much of the time.

Childhood development is an important consideration because you must learn to evaluate whether residents' behavior is deliberately negative or disrespectful, or simply developmental. Recent brain research demonstrates that the human forebrain, which regulates impulse control, is not completely developed until about age 25. If a resident acts out in the library, maybe throwing a tantrum or even a book, you may respond more calmly if you can remember this. All children and young adults have poor impulse control, not just those who are locked up. You should not expect the same level of control from a 10-year-old as you would an 18-year-old, but do understand that impulse control is poor for all of them. Learning about childhood development may be mandated by the facility, but if it isn't, you should explore this topic on your own time.

Education is one of the most important contributors to rehabilitation, and many studies have already proven the relationship of education to improved rates of inmate success upon release. The Sentencing Project (1999) and Stojkovic and Farkas (2003) show clearly that education directly reduces recidivism. Youth in prison are still young enough to really take advantage of opportunities they are given to improve their lives. Facilities that have schools within them are already providing structured education, in which the library plays a supporting role. Curriculum support is one of the goals of a youth facility library, and if you can establish strong ties with teachers, you can provide better support to the education program. One way to develop these ties is to invite teachers to bring students into the library to teach classes.

The library is also a resource for finding information relating to personal interests and pursuits. One advantage of working with incarcerated youth is that you see the same children day after day. You can get to know your population very well and learn their likes and dislikes. This gives you a better chance of matching the right book to the right person and igniting their curiosity about the world and a desire to learn more. Many children who come to prison are very distrusting of authority, and you are just another authority figure to them. You must work to overcome this distrust and it takes time. Residents must be given clear guidelines that are applied firmly, fairly, and consistently. Once they have learned that you will monitor activities in the library, yet provide service to them, they will be more likely to seek you out for assistance.

SPECIAL NEEDS OF INCARCERATED YOUTH

Incarcerated youth tend to share some unfortunate characteristics which, at first, can be troubling or even frightening to a new librarian. Many residents come from dysfunctional homes and have family problems. Many have school problems, particularly with authority figures. Many lack much education, many have learning disabilities, and some are entirely illiterate. Some belong to gangs. Some are heavily tattooed and appear belligerent and intimidating.

As a facility librarian, you must get to know the children you work with. This is not as easy at it may seem at first. As stated previously, these children are likely to have problems with authority figures. One of your tasks will be to learn to work with recalcitrant kids. You must approach them and establish the feel of the library. Is it a welcoming place? Have you made it so? Children are not likely to approach you for reading assistance, so you must develop the rapport. Your goal is to teach children an appreciation for reading and learning. You can do this in groups or one-on-one by speaking to children about reading and books. Asking them what they like, what kinds of things they'd like to know about, and directing them to books that meet those interests can help develop a rapport. And don't give up! If a child doesn't seem interested in something you provided, you should try something else. A good tactic is to hit and run. After talking with a child about what he might like, give him some books. Set them on a table for the child to look at and then move away. If you hand books to a child he may feel obligated to take them without really wanting them. Giving the child some time to take a look, then approaching him again to see if anything piqued his interest gives the child some time to decide if he wants anything you suggested. Try to find out why or why not the child liked these books. Offer other suggestions. Do this again and again until the child learns that you really are trying to meet their needs and not trying to force them to any particular book or author. This teaches the child that reading is personal and individual. Children in a facility are strictly controlled. They are not allowed to make their own decisions about what to do, where to go and when, what to eat or even what to wear. Making a decision about what to read can be very empowering for a child and begin to teach some independence, a crucial skill for these children.

Their peers hugely influence children, and incarcerated kids probably have friends who are negative influences. During the time they are incarcerated, they are exposed to many ideas they may not have encountered before, like discipline and structured education. Learning to read and choose their own materials can teach children about other worlds and ways of living. They can begin to make their own decisions about the world and their place in it. They may begin to realize that they have the power to change their own lives. Such a simple thing as choosing what books to read can truly change these children's lives.

One reason for incarcerating children is to rehabilitate them and prevent them from returning to state supervision. Children have a much better chance of turning their lives around than do incarcerated adults, and the library, by fostering choice and independence, can add greatly to that rehabilitation.

MANAGING BEHAVIOR

Children must practice many social skills in a library. They learn that they must control their behavior to enjoy the library. If the librarian has created a safe and welcoming place, they will be motivated to do this. Perhaps most importantly, their behavior must be self-monitored. Children learn from the consequences of their behavior. If an action brings a negative response, such as burning a hand on a hot stove, they learn not to place their hand on a hot stove again. If they learn that exhibiting a certain behavior in the library brings a positive response, that behavior will be reinforced.

The librarian must be firm, fair, and consistent in his own behavior and application of rules to inspire this kind of attention to consequences in residents. Children

suggestions about which books to purchase. You may even wish to establish an advisory team that will suggest books to other residents, or develop some other method of fostering sharing of reading ideas. These types of activities will engage residents with library activities and make them more likely to take an interest in other services you might offer.

PROVIDING LIBRARY SERVICES

Collection Development

Collection development can be challenging in youth facilities. Many taxpaying citizens do not see the need to fund prison libraries because they see the prison as proper punishment for criminal acts. In their eyes, prisons should offer no perks. This attitude is very understandable. Some average citizens see that education is provided in prison, funded by taxpayer dollars, yet they cannot afford to send their own children to college. But children who come to prison are often there because of a lack of direction or opportunity in their lives, and prison offers them a chance to repair their lives. It is costly and difficult to see the long-term benefit of educating residents when the average person today is so financially burdened. However, it makes much more sense to pay less now than to pay more later, when the child we failed to rehabilitate commits more or worse crimes and we end up supporting a lifetime of imprisonment.

The reading interests of incarcerated youth are similar to those of children in the general population. As the facility librarian you may be working with girls, boys, or both. You may be working with youth as young as 10 to as old as 20. These age groups will have very different reading interests and abilities, so you will be challenged to meet a wide variety of needs. The facility will probably fund its library to some extent, but the library is not likely to have a large budget. In addition to what you may be able to purchase directly, it is a good idea to establish relationships with local school and public libraries. You should visit local libraries and get to know the children's and young adult librarians. You may be able to obtain withdrawn or extra materials from these sources. Besides reading about children's books and authors, interacting with other librarians will provide another review source and method for becoming familiar with children's materials. You may also be able to participate in interlibrary loan programs, either between youth facilities or with external libraries. Since funding may be scant, learning to stretch budget dollars to obtain the most quality materials is essential. Review sources such as Kirkus Reviews, Horn Book, or School Library Journal, while valuable, are not the only consideration. A book may have garnered all sorts of accolades, but if children won't read it, it just takes up room in a collection.

There are questions you must answer. How are books acquired? Does the library have an operating budget? Is there support from your state library, Department of Education, or other larger organizations? In Colorado, youth facility libraries currently enjoy a state-level acquisitions librarian, with support from the state library and Department of Education to provide training and materials. Do you actually make selections or are books selected and received from someone else? How do books enter the facility? Is there a library committee that approves materials coming in to the library or does the librarian perform evaluations? These questions will impact how or even if you are able to practice collection development. Either way, you must learn about children and young adult library materials. Even if someone else purchases books, the purchasing agent will appreciate input about materials that residents enjoy reading.

You must also learn what is not allowed. Some facilities have lists of books or authors that are never allowed. Find out why. Anything sexually explicit will not be allowed. But there is still the problem of defining sexually explicit materials. It's probably not the mention of kissing, but certainly the description of intercourse. Somewhere in between these two is the magic line of too explicit. What about drug use? Some people working in youth facilities believe that any mention of drugs at all is enough to disallow a title because it may make residents think about drug use. There are many excellent children and young adult authors writing about issues that real kids grapple with, involving drugs, relationships, abuse, criminal or negligent acts, foster care, and so on. Adolescence is a time of learning about these real-life issues and books talk about them. Experimentation is the natural state of the adolescent and they are curious about many things. Most have first-hand experience with abuse of many sorts, including drugs, sex, or physical violence, and reading about it in a book is more likely to help them sort these issues out than to inspire them to engage in these behaviors.

One of the most discouraging things that can happen in a youth facility occurs when an officer or other staff person confiscates a book from a resident because he or she believes that the subject matter is inappropriate. As facility librarian, you must constantly advocate for the presence of these types of materials in a facility. Rather than always reacting to these kinds of challenges, you might be more proactive about library books by sending out a regular newsletter about what books are new in the library and what they are about, which will likely reduce the number of confiscations.

Programs and Services

A facility library will not be able to offer every service a public library can, such as Internet access or computer gaming. This is where creativity and expansion of library skills can be most useful.

One goal of librarians is to teach information literacy. Since so much information today can be found online, and so much research uses electronic interfaces, how can you teach information literacy without access to the Internet? It is important to remember that information literacy isn't just about where information is found, but how it is found. The Internet is a wonderful resource, but it is still only a resource. Internet access is not necessary to teach a child how to find information in books, or how to evaluate information using books.

First, can the child read? Select an appropriate level reading material for the child's reading level. If the child can read, teach him how to use a table of contents to discover what the book broadly covers, how to use an index to locate certain kinds of information, how to use citations to find more information, and even how old the information is. Teaching information literacy is still about literacy skills. Remember that information is information, just found on different platforms. Learning to use the Internet is simply a matter of learning to use a delivery system different from paper. If children who cannot access the Internet are taught literacy skills using paper, when they are

The Power of Positive Peer Pressure

One of the most successful programs I offered at my youth facility was a Reader's Advisory by and for peers. Residents were able to suggest books for their peers. They could write a short review, conduct a brief book talk, or simply recommend a title, depending on their level of ability and comfort. This program gave residents a chance to share what they liked in a safe manner, and helped their peers discover new books and become more interested in reading. Also, as familiar as I was with children's and young adult literature, residents were more likely to know what other residents would like to read than I was. Kids are much more likely to read a book based on a friend's recommendation than they are on a librarian's. But the silver lining in this cloud is that if one child gets turned on to a book, they can and often will recommend that book to their friends and they will all read it. Everybody wins!

released from custody and do have access to other resources, they will be much better able to navigate that information environment.

Library programming also requires more creativity in a facility. A public library might have reading programs offering prizes for reading, or storytime, or after-hours tournaments or even craft programs. It is a greater challenge to offer programming in a facility library because of restrictions. Prizes often may not be offered because certain items may be used for bartering, especially if an item, such as paper, is particularly valued by residents. Problems might also arise when certain more literate or motivated children may start to be seen as the librarian's favorites. Programs must be created that teach skills while being fun, like having a scavenger hunt that involves finding material in books, or a weekly trivia contest. Awards may be nontangible, such as getting a gold star next to your name on the whiteboard for a week. Craft programs, popular in public libraries, may also be challenging because many craft materials are considered contraband. Items such as Popsicle sticks may be sharpened to use as a weapon and certain types of paint may be used as intoxicating agents. All materials must be accounted for. If a craft program requires the use of a pair of scissors, the librarian must ensure that all scissors put out are returned. It may seem discouraging at first, but a creative and caring librarian can get around these problems by offering programs that do not use contraband materials or offer prizes.

Library Environment

Another challenge in facility libraries is that one cannot simply open the door and expect children to just appear, ready to use all that the library has to offer. Some children will come of their own volition, or at the direction of a teacher, but many will need to be coerced. This is where the appearance and welcoming atmosphere are crucial. Is the library well lit and attractive? Are the books neatly lined on shelves or are they old cast-offs jumbled around the room? Are there book posters on the walls? Are the tables clean and free of papers and junk? Is the library tidy and neat? Are you wearing a smile? Are you greeting the children who come in to the library? Are you firm, fair, and consistent? Do you teach each child who visits what the library is and how to use it? Do you make an effort to get to know the children you work with? Do you make residents feel safe in the library? These are all questions that need to be answered positively to create a welcoming environment.

WORKING WITH FACILITY STAFF

Because most prison mission statements read something like, "We exist to protect the security of the public, inmates, and staff, and to provide opportunities for improvement that will help inmates lead productive lives once released from supervision," staff peers in prison are unlike coworkers in the public library. They are mostly officers, but also include administrators, teachers, custodians, groundskeepers, food service staff, and recreation staff. What they all have in common is that they are all security officers before they are their individual titles. This means the librarian is also security staff before he or she is a librarian. The better you fulfill this role, the more respected you'll be by other facility staff. And the more they respect you, the more they'll support the library's mission.

It is imperative that you take the initiative to become an integral part of the facility. How do you get your facility to value your library and your contributions to the mission of the facility? Lehmann (2000) and Vogel (1995) assert that librarians must connect with facility staff. Getting to know coworkers and the jobs they perform clarifies the purpose of a prison, and can provide the librarian with a sense of control by understanding his or her role in the organization. Librarians must bring in the security officer to assure him that the library is a secure area; they must develop relationships with all coworkers; they must have negotiating skills, management skills, and interpersonal skills, and get to know the administrators of their facilities. Spend time with teaching staff, learning what they deliver in class and how the library can support it. Invite teachers to occasionally deliver a class in the library. Visit coworkers in their work areas to learn what their roles in the facility are. Let coworkers know that they also may utilize library services. Volunteer to serve on committees and submit monthly reports of activities to supervisors and administrators. Constantly communicating library activities and services is one of the best ways to gain the support of the facility and create a positive working environment.

CONCLUSION

In a public library a librarian is limited only by his or her imagination. Find books and buy them! Think up programs and deliver them! Open the door and have patrons! This is not the case in a facility library, which is restricted in many ways and for many reasons. First and foremost, which I emphasize again, is that facilities house children who have committed criminal acts, sometimes very serious ones, and have a responsibility to protect the public, other residents, and staff. Prison librarianship demands the combination of the ability to work in a paramilitary organization, heavy with rules and control, with a creative mind to figure out how to deliver library services in such an environment. A strong desire to work with disadvantaged children also helps.

The challenges of providing library service in the midst of culture shock, strict security precautions that include censorship and restrictions on services, and the enormous social and behavioral needs of the service population, test librarians like no other specialty. The rewards that come with persistence and dedication, though, of seeing a resident succeed on the outside after learning some life skills while incarcerated, which often includes learning to read or reading for pleasure, provides unmatchable satisfaction. In the words of Brenda Vogel, outspoken champion of prison librarians, "Ask anyone who changed their life while in prison and they will say—the library did it" (Vogel, 1995).

REFERENCES

Joseph Bouchard, *Wake Up and Smell the Contraband* (Horsham, PA: LRP Productions, 2002).

"Code of Ethics of the American Library Association," American Library Association. Available at: http://www.ala.org/ala/aboutala/offices/oif/statementspols/codeofethics/codeethics.cfm.

Sarah Dalton, "Library Profile: Folsom Prison Library," *Connection,* March 2003. Available at: http://www.library.ca.gov/newsletter/2003/CSL_Connection_0303.pdf.

Vibeke Lehmann, "Prison Librarians Needed: A Challenging Career for Those with the Right Professional and Human Skills," in *65th IFLA Council and General Conference, Conference Programme and Proceedings* (International Federation of Library Associations and Institutions, 1999). Available at: http://www.ifla.org/IV/ifla65/papers/046-132e.htm.

"Resolution on Prisoners' Right to Read," American Library Association. Available at: http://www.ala.org/ala/mgrps/divs/ascla/asclaissues/prisonrights.cfm.

The Sentencing Project, "Americans Behind Bars: U.S. and International Use of Incarceration," in *The Dilemmas of Corrections: Contemporary Readings* (Prospect Heights, IL: Waveland Press, 1999).

Tony Stevens and Bob Usherwood, "The Development of the Prison Library and its Role within the Models of Rehabilitation," *Howard Journal of Criminal Justice* 34, no. 1 (1995): 45–63.

Stan Stojkovic and Mary Ann Farkas, *Correctional Leadership: A Cultural Perspective* (Belmont, CA: Wadsworth/Thomson Learning, 2003).

Teresa Strasner, "Don't let this happen to you! Or: learning to manage the prison environment: balancing the provision of library services with the need to maintain security" (unpublished essay, 2004).

Brenda Vogel, *Down for the Count: A Prison Library Handbook* (Lanham, MD: Scarecrow Press, Inc, 2002).

ADDITIONAL RESOURCES

YALSA: Young Adult Library Services Association. Available at http://www.ala.org/ala/mgrps/divs/yalsa/electronicresourcesb/websitesmailing.cfm. Comprehensive resources for librarians in public, school, and detention facility libraries serving teens and young adults.

YALSA Lockdown. Available at http://lists.ala.org/wws/info/yalsa-lockdown. Active, unmoderated listserv specifically for librarians who work with incarcerated teens.

Part VI

All about Outreach Vehicles

On the Job Experience

My library career has taken me from early experiences as a bookmobile driver while still in college to managing extension/outreach services as a department head and then on to library administration. In my 15-year library career, I have worked at four very different Midwestern libraries, of which three had an active bookmobile service. My practical knowledge of various vehicle designs comes from working on (and managing) five different bookmobile vehicles—one could say that I have learned a lot from living with the design successes and mistakes made by my predecessors!

a city library serving one municipality, or a county or district library serving a larger geographic area? Have you identified key sites where mobile library services will likely work, such as schools, neighborhoods, assisted living homes, trailer parks, outlying communities, and so forth? Is this vehicle likely to spend time serving children? Is serving children the focus or service priority of the vehicle? Will there be children in large numbers (such as schools and large daycares)? Is serving seniors also a priority? These questions are by no means an exhaustive list, but they will get you to start thinking analytically about your service. Do not forget to consider any pending shifts in your demographics and what they may mean for your service priorities. For example, the aging of the baby boom generation means that most bookmobile service plans should consider how these seniors would interact with your new vehicle.

At this stage, the easiest thing to do is create a long list of your potential service points and any known mitigating factors about the people who will utilize your services at each. It is not too early to call patrons you hope to serve at these sites. Ask many questions about the people, including their physical needs and abilities as well as their taste in library materials and services. It would also be entirely appropriate to schedule a meeting with principals/directors/representatives of schools, daycares, senior centers, and other potential service sites. If they seem receptive to your plan to offer them Bookmobile service, do not forget to ask for their support. In fact, now is a good time to gather written support from all stakeholders to help build your case for a new vehicle. Engaging these stakeholders at an early stage will insure that you are in tune with their needs and make their support for your plan more enthusiastic. Remember not to promise too much, as you are just trying to gauge what sort of service needs exist. Now save this information and move to the next step.

STEP 2: DETERMINING WHAT SERVICES YOU WILL PROVIDE

You may want to dedicate your vehicle to serving one specific community need or you may want to serve all ages and situations equally. Some of the best examples of focused mobile library services are found at the Memphis Public Library and Information Center. That library operates a mobile job and career center known as JobLINC, and a mobile training center for childcare workers known as Training Wheels. Oftentimes, these narrowly focused service vehicles are among the most successful because they have identified a need for service and they meet that need for a captive, or at least a well defined, audience.

While many bookmobiles across the nation provide specialized services, many other successful mobile library operations serve a hodge-podge of locations, attempting to bring as many of the main library services as possible out into the community. In these situations, it is quite common for a single bookmobile to carry materials for all ages and interests, just as a traditional library branch would. A typical schedule for such a vehicle may take it to a wide array of daycares, schools, and senior housing locations during the day and neighborhoods, outlying towns, mobile home communities, and the like in the evening.

So, which is right for your service area? Considering your list of potential service points in Step 1, decide if you want materials on your vehicle for all ages. If you plan to entertain visits from large groups of children, make sure you plan for enough interior space to house an entire class or group at once. Also, do not forget that such service points generate a lot of business and circulation of materials will be great. Always ensure the vehicle has plenty of room to carry enough materials to serve this level of demand. It is also not a bad idea to consider offering storytimes for children on the vehicle. If this is appealing to you, see if the manufacturer can design a space on the vehicle that feels like a storytime room in a library

What else do you need this vehicle to do? If you have a senior population to serve, you will obviously need to factor in shelving for some large print materials, and it may not hurt to explore vehicles with better than average handicap accessibility. Wheelchair lifts can be installed on many vehicle types and several manufacturers offer a line of low floor vehicles with short entry ramps to make entry/exit easier for many.

Do not forget to consider the flashier services as well. Does your community need a high tech mobile library with one or more public access computers? The King County Library System operates a mobile computer lab offering courses taught on-site in their Techlab vehicle. No matter what services you provide on your new vehicle, where practical you will want to provide some means of wireless Internet access for staff and/or public.

STEP 3: CHOOSING THE BEST-SUITED VEHICLE STYLE

Because bookmobile service is flexible and can be adapted to so many differing environments, it is not terribly hard to show a need for the service and thus make a strong case for purchasing some sort of vehicle. The crucial thing to understand here is that it is very easy to buy the wrong vehicle for its intended purpose. For example, an urban library could easily make a case for buying a bookmobile, but suggesting a tractor-trailer rig could cause the project to die in its infancy! A bookmobile purchased to serve schools will need enough space for 20 or more children to be on the vehicle at once, so a step van design may not be the best choice. A rural library district serving a huge geographic area will likely not want a gasoline-powered vehicle because gasoline engines asked to push heavy vehicles across a lot of miles do not tend to last as long as diesel engines. Therefore, it is necessary to determine the best combination of service vehicle features and service needs. Although every situation is unique and will need a good amount of your own judgment, the following may help you in determining the rough size and type of vehicle that suits your situation. Pros and cons are presented, along with ideas about the type of service each vehicle style can provide.

See Chapter 15 for specifications for each of these models.

Van

The smallest bookmobile style is a large cargo van with a raised roof, fitted with shelving. Nearly anyone can drive these highly maneuverable vehicles. This vehicle style could be the perfect setup for an urban area with extremely narrow streets or a service geared toward intermittent patron traffic (not large groups).

Conversely, because of its size, van service is the most cramped bookmobile service vehicle available. It is hard to imagine a successful bookmobile service that would not quickly outgrow this size of vehicle.

Cutaway Van/Box Truck

Just as it sounds, this is a boxy truck body attached to a small truck cab. Think of a U-Haul truck with a pass way between cab and cargo areas. These vehicles are surprisingly stout and roomier than you would think. As with the step van design, these vehicles often do not require licensing that is difficult to obtain.

These vehicles have nearly the same downsides as the step van. Small size means limited comfort and efficiency at busy service stops. Also, this style of vehicle can have floor heights that are significantly higher than what you may be comfortable with, so as with any major feature, be sure to see examples before you decide.

Step Van

Step vans are converted delivery-style trucks, often closely resembling a bread truck. Though these are popular nationwide, many fine examples of this style are found in Kentucky libraries.

These vehicles are simple and extremely durable. A Class C commercial driver's license is usually the only requirement for drivers (which is an easy license to acquire), and thus many library staff can drive step vans in a staffing pinch. Often, these vehicles have a gasoline engine which makes it convenient to find fuel and a mechanic to perform service.

On the other hand, the public space is a narrow aisle and the overall small size of these vehicles can make it a challenge to serve high attendance stops such as schools or daycares. These vehicles are often small enough to power with a gasoline engine, but large and heavy enough that the gasoline engine is expensive to run and may incur higher maintenance costs.

Bus Chassis

Bookmobiles on a commercial bus chassis feature either completely custom bodies or bus bodies with heavy modifications. These are the bread-and-butter of the book mobile world because nearly everything is customizable. You can design a vehicle that is anywhere from 20 to 40 feet in length depending on the manufacturer and the chassis used. Some vehicles even feature an RV-style slide out built into the side, which increases the floor space inside the vehicle when deployed. Most manufacturers also offer the ability to design the vehicle with a raised roof, giving interior ceiling heights approaching seven-and-a-half feet. If you want to avoid the necessity of a Class B commercial driver's license to operate the vehicle, you may choose one of the shorter lengths and ask the manufacturer to include lighter weight features (such as aluminum shelving).

The downsides of a converted bus chassis are that some people find the standard height ceilings too low or the width too narrow. Additionally, I have seen the fiberglass body on longer vehicles degrade and crack over time due to the weight and flexing of the vehicle as it moves over uneven or bumpy terrain. As a final word of warning, the immense customization available in these vehicles can also spell trouble if you choose features that are gimmicky or inappropriate to your mission.

Truck/Trailer Combo

Similar to a semi truck in that it is a hinged vehicle, a truck/trailer combo is generally smaller in every respect. Often the tow vehicle is a large pickup or flatbed truck like those used to haul fifth wheel camping trailers.

The trailer portion of this vehicle is extremely customizable. As with the semi truck option, any vehicle capable of connecting to and pulling it can move the trailer. Some feel that this is the wisest choice because if the truck wears out or goes bad you can keep the trailer and buy another tow vehicle.

The downsides of a tractor-trailer bookmobile are that they can be hard to maneuver and the floor height can make it difficult for some to enter and exit the vehicle. Additionally, driving these vehicles may also require a Class-A commercial driver's license.

Tractor Trailer

This design features a semi truck whose trailer has been converted into a mobile library. These vehicles have very high ground clearance and can generally handle any road surface conditions. In addition, you will never have more space in a bookmobile than these vehicles provide. Another benefit is that any vehicle capable of connecting to and pulling it can move the trailer. Thus if your engine breaks down you may be able to rent a tractor rig to pull your trailer to its stops while repairs are made. For many years, the Decatur Public Library operated two such tractor-trailer bookmobiles with great success. However, in recent years that library has switched to using bus chassis style vehicles. Because that library provides service to many public and private schools, it has always been worthwhile to have such a great amount of space in the vehicles.

The disadvantages of tractor trailer bookmobiles are that they can be hard to maneuver in general and most specifically in traffic congestion or narrow city streets.

Pros and Cons

Of the five vehicles I have personal experience with, four were bus chassis conversions and one was a step van. My short list of complaints includes:

The step van operated in the largest and most rural service area of all my libraries, yet it had an underpowered gasoline engine that was constantly in the shop having repairs made. Another rural area I have worked was also the hilliest and had the bumpiest roads. That library operated a converted bus chassis vehicle with a completely custom built fiberglass body. Though that bookmobile was resplendent with its oak paneling, shelving, skylights, and extra-wide body, it was also literally bounced, shaken, and cracked to pieces driving day after day in those conditions.

The other three vehicles I have worked with were all standard bus chassis conversions that operated in an urban/suburban environment. Two of these vehicles replaced aging tractor-trailer style bookmobiles that had reached the end of their useful life and were too large and unwieldy for the current service priorities. Though this change of vehicle design to reflect service needs was a positive thing, even these new vehicles had their design flaws. Chief among these was that each of these bookmobiles actually had a staff restroom fitted in the back of the vehicles! While this type of accoutrement may be appropriate for staff and vehicle traveling 100 miles a day across desolate patches of the West, it was unnecessary and wasteful of service space in vehicles that never left the city limits of a medium-sized Midwestern city!

The high ground clearance/floor height can also make it difficult for some to enter and exit the vehicle. Additionally, driving these vehicles will likely require a Class-A commercial driver's license due to the vehicle weight and length.

So, which vehicle type is right for your situation? Consider the descriptions above, talk to other bookmobilers, and talk to the vendors. Find out what people *do not* like about their vehicles and why. Most people who work on bookmobiles will be happy to share with you their vehicle joys and gripes. Your task here is to consider all vehicle styles, your patrons, and the environmental factors of your service area and then move to the next step (see Table 14.1 for comparative vehicles).

STEP 4: DETERMINING WHO WILL OPERATE YOUR BOOKMOBILE

The full scope of setting up an outreach/extension department staff to operate, support, and manage a bookmobile service is a topic too broad to address here. What you must determine now is who will actually be working on your new vehicle. Many of the following choices hinge upon what size and style of vehicle you have determined is best suited to your service priorities and environment. Whatever you do, do not make the mistake of deciding who will operate the vehicle first and then design a vehicle around their driving skills. Your vehicle's size and style should only reflect concrete service needs. Finding ways to staff and operate the vehicle must always come after.

So, will you staff your bookmobile with one person or two? For safety and efficiency reasons, two is preferable to one, but that only raises more issues and questions to address. If there will be two employees on the vehicle, do not forget to include workstations/seating for both staff members. Next, will you have a dedicated driver who only serves to move the vehicle from point to point and then someone else to conduct the library business? Since the vehicle may only change locations a few times per day, many do not like this scheme because the driver is not doing much work in a day. In addition, with only one driver, what do you do if they call in sick or leave to take another job on short notice? Successful bookmobile service relies upon consistency and missing bookmobile stops is the surest way to drive the public away.

Similarly, another popular staffing arrangement is to have one staff person designated (and licensed) as the driver and the other as the librarian. Upon reaching the service stop, the driver becomes the circulation clerk and the librarian handles the reference, directional, and reader's advisory work. This scenario is better than the first, but you still have the problem of only one licensed driver. To combat this dilemma, libraries often will pay for staff in other departments to get the necessary licensing and training in order to be able to fill in during times of need.

The most elegant solution is to provide two staff on the vehicle, both with the capability to drive and perform circulation functions, reader's advisory, and other library tasks. This ensures that either can serve as a backup to the other.

Having said all of that, based on the size and style of vehicle you are purchasing, staff/drivers may need to acquire a commercial driver's license (CDL). Now is a good time to determine if there is a CDL testing facility in your area and whether or not they have a practice/testing vehicle you can use. Many libraries opt for designing a vehicle that falls just short of the gross vehicle weight rating that necessitates a CDL driver. If a size-limited vehicle will still support your service priorities, this is indeed an option to consider. Conversely, when the service needs justify a large vehicle, considering pushing the design large enough to *require* a CDL for the drivers. With the expense of buying and operating a bookmobile as well as the liability that a rolling library incurs, requiring drivers to be good enough to pass a rigorous test is a good thing!

No matter what licensing your vehicle will require to operate, it is most advantageous for your driver(s) to be fully licensed before the arrival of your new bookmobile!

STEP 5: DETERMINING WHO WILL MAINTAIN AND SERVICE THE VEHICLE

This question, like so many others before it, opens a completely new world of difficult issues that you must face. Most bookmobiles in this country are powered by gasoline or diesel engines. Similarly, if these bookmobiles have generators (which I suspect most do), these are powered by the same fuel type as the vehicle engines. The task at hand now is to determine whether your vehicle will be driven by gasoline or diesel power (or some alternative fuel such as compressed natural gas). The reason we must go through all of this is that bookmobiles require a lot of preventative maintenance, a great deal of regular service, and yes, bookmobiles do break down!

This is the one time you should base your decision on factors other than what is ideal. For example, if you are operating a large or particularly heavy vehicle, the clear choice for longevity and low-cost operation is diesel power. If this were not the case, trucking companies would not use diesel-powered rigs. However, if your library service district happens to be a three-hour drive from the nearest reputable diesel repair shop, you may have to think twice about going with the ideal choice for your vehicle.

No matter if you choose gasoline, diesel, or some alternative, talk to the bookmobile manufacturers and determine what make and model of engines they use. Then determine if any dealerships or service shops in your area can and will service those engines. Also, do not forget that although a bookmobile's generator is powered by an engine of its own, it also has many complicated electrical components that most auto/diesel mechanics will not be trained to work on. Ideally, you need to find a generator shop in your area to perform this specialized service work.

Ask these businesses for references, and call those references to determine if the shop in question can make speedy, accurate repairs. It's not a bad idea whatsoever to establish a relationship with the folks who will be maintaining your vehicle early on in the design process, and then include them in the mechanical designs! Often times this can result in fewer problems down the road, as the full benefit of the mechanic's wisdom is brought to bear *before* there are any problems to deal with.

Another point to consider is where you will fuel your vehicle. You must consider ready availability of fuel. If it is a 30-minute drive to the nearest diesel fuel site that can handle your size of vehicle, you will soon find yourself weary of the time wasted. Again, call around ahead of time and find out where you can fuel your new vehicle and inquire about tax exempt or fuel billing accounts to make life easier down the road.

STEP 6: PLANNING VEHICLE SPECIFICATIONS

After seemingly endless brainstorming and ruminating over service priorities and vehicle styles, you are finally ready to talk about the nuts and bolts of your new bookmobile! Thus far you have determined what style of vehicle best fits your patrons and service priorities, what materials your vehicle will house, what engine/fuel type is suited to your environment, and how many people will staff your vehicle. Now you need to design and layout your bookmobile's interior. (A full discussion on developing vehicle specs can be found in Chapter 15.) Unbelievably, though this part is the most fun, it is also a lot of work.

Planning your vehicle's interior is difficult unless you are already familiar with all of the options available. Now is a good time to get some help, either from a peer at another library or by directly consulting a bookmobile vendor. In general, remember to be practical. People will be accessing your bookmobile directly from the outside in a multitude of parking situations. Depending on what area of the country you live in, expect your patrons to track snow, water, mud, and leaves inside. Plan for this by having appropriate carpeting or non-slip rubber flooring installed. You may also want to strongly consider some sort of mini-closet or storage compartment dedicated to cleaning supplies and a vacuum cleaner. Another point of practicality is your shelving. You want bookmobile shelving to be strong, durable, lightweight, and easily adjustable. Many still opt for the beauty of wood shelving, but aluminum is something to strongly consider.

Make sure there are adequate staff workstations. This should include seating that is adjustable to multiple body types and ergonomic counter heights. Nothing is more miserable than working for hours hunched over in a cramped, uncomfortable space.

Climate control is also a major factor in designing the interior of your bookmobile. Depending on your area of the country, you will likely need both heat and air conditioning. Some newer vehicle designs are revisiting the idea of centralized HVAC (heating, ventilation, and air conditioning) systems, although their abilities are questionable. For air conditioning, it is hard to beat the old standard RV-style rooftop mounted A/C (air conditioning) units. Do not forget that on longer vehicles you may need two such units, and that the unit closest to the front will have to work harder due to the heat gain coming from the sun penetrating the windshield and front windows. A retractable or sliding curtain for the windshield can greatly help A/C efficiency.

For interior heat, electric heaters with built in fans are still the norm, but consider all available options and choose accordingly. If you will be serving many small children, it is probably not a good idea to place electric heaters in places where children will likely sit as they can easily burn their fingers.

As for the rest of the interior, think about the flow of patrons you want and expect. Some vehicles that will serve extremely busy sites have two doors (an entry toward the front and exit toward the back) thus facilitating a nice flow of people through the vehicle. Also, don't forget that children cannot reach high shelves and adults rarely are happy to bend down low, so give some thought to how the materials will be arranged. I have always been a fan of drawing a mental line around the interior of the bookmobile at waist height. Everything shelved below that line is age appropriate for children and everything above is for adults. Now is the time to think about building in some sort of visual break, such as different colored shelving, to reinforce this division of materials.

Finally, avoid options that will be future maintenance headaches. For example, most bookmobiles require some form of retractable steps for patrons to enter the vehicle. All retractable step units eventually get bent from scraping curbs, crowned roads, steep driveways, and other road factors. Automatic (i.e. electric powered) steps do not do well with this inevitable rough treatment and will often die an early death. New electric step units are *very* expensive. Save yourself some headaches and request steps that retract manually with a lever or buy a low-floor model without steps.

Skylights are another unnecessary problem item in bookmobiles. They may be pretty and everyone loves the natural light they add, but it is a fact that all skylights eventually leak. Water and books do not go well together!

STEP 7: SECURING FUNDING

Buying a new bookmobile vehicle is an expensive proposition. As with so many products and services, construction costs for these vehicles has increased greatly over the past 10 years. Even though buying and operating a bookmobile is nearly always cheaper than building and operating a library building, funding is never easy to find. Generally speaking, bookmobiles are operated by public libraries and new vehicles tend to be funded in three ways: from the library budget, through grants, and through fundraising campaigns.

Ideally, your new bookmobile is something that can and will be funded via the library's regular budget. That may mean that funds were put aside for many years in a capital improvement fund or that your library budget is so large as to be able to absorb the cost of a bookmobile in a single year. In either case, it requires strong support from library administration and/or the library Board to fund such a large purchase from the library budget. In order to gather this support, you may be asked to present a funding proposal. If so, always remember to follow these tips:

- *Be prepared.* Library administrators and trustees want to hear well-prepared and heavily researched proposals. They usually have more funding requests than actual funding, so be prepared to face tough questions. If you are not prepared to fend off the naysayers with facts, you will not convince them of your need.

- *Make your case.* Remember that your idea for a new bookmobile is about serving patrons in need, so present your ideas in that framework. Include plenty of supporting statistics and compelling facts, such as it is usually cheaper per item and more efficient to circulate library materials from a bookmobile rather than an immobile library building. Stress the flexibility of a bookmobile service as compared to traditional library services.

- *Bring testimonials.* Now is the time to show how much community support there is for a new (or additional) bookmobile. If you are making a formal presentation to the library board, it is a good idea to have a couple of supportive patrons on hand to speak about the community's desire for this service. Signed petitions from neighborhoods and/or letters of support from schools, daycares, senior centers, and so forth can also be very effective.

- *Be positive and reasonable.* Accept that there is only so much money in a library budget and that the project may take a few years to bring to fruition. Be willing to work with the director and board to fundraise and plan, and be positive despite these delays.

If you are able to be patient, making the case for a bookmobile three to five (or more!) years before you plan to put it into use is ideal. (Even if you're not starting a bookmobile service from scratch, you can also successfully make a case for an additional or replacement vehicle to be purchased in just this manner.) The outreach/extension department manager (or whoever will be responsible for the bookmobile service) needs to get involved in internal library committees. Building a strong case for bookmobile service and then volunteering to work with the library director on the library's strategic or long-range plan may help you to ensure that financial planning for a future bookmobile occurs.

If funding your new bookmobile via the library budget is not an option because the budget is too small or you cannot wait that many years, then alternative funding must be sought. Grants *can* provide a means to bridge this funding need, but they should not be counted upon. For some reason, many administrators and library Board trustees labor under the delusion that there are grants galore to be had for this purpose. On the contrary, grants for any sort of construction, be it bricks and mortar or a service vehicle, are hard to come by. Having said that, every state and every region has a different set of grant makers, so do not give up on the idea.

The most likely avenue for grant funding is through private foundations and trusts. Trusts tend to include large amounts of money that are left by a wealthy person or group to aid a specific purpose (i.e., education, literacy, healthcare) in a specific city or region. Trusts are often administered through a local bank by a board of citizens or bank employees who see that the trust funds are dispersed in accordance with the wishes of the person(s) who established the trust. It can be difficult to learn what trusts exist in your area without the aid of someone on the inside, so it is wise to invite bankers into your Friends of the Library organization, onto your Library Foundation Board, or even help them to become library board trustees. Some states also maintain a database of charitable trusts, which can also help immensely.

Where trusts tend to be very local, many foundations operate at a state, regional, or even national level. Foundations are small to large organizations that exist solely to disperse money to other organizations in need of funding. Generally, foundations are created by a wealthy family or corporation to give something back to the world. Foundations will have a specific list of programs and projects for which they will or will not grant funding. Accessing a database such as the Foundation Directory Online and/or working with a certified grant writer can greatly increase your chances of finding a willing grant maker and successfully acquiring bookmobile funding. The American Grant Writer's Association is a great place to turn for assistance in locating a certified grant writer in your area who may be willing to lend assistance for very little cost.

The third option for funding a new bookmobile would be to conduct a fundraising campaign. This can be as simple as the old fashioned campaign of coffee cans on business counters around town or as complex as a major community drive similar to what the United Way does in many areas. Quite often library Foundations and/or Friends of the Library organizations contribute to fundraising campaigns. Under the best of circumstances, a group with fundraising experience (such as the Library Foundation or Friends group) will take on the operation of the campaign and bring all of their experience to bear.

Obviously, with many modern bookmobiles costing hundreds of thousands of dollars, collecting spare change is not going to do it alone. A quicker path to success is to find out where the big money is in your area. You could identify a few wealthy, philanthropic individuals or families and ask them to leave a legacy by donating funding for your bookmobile project. Another option may be that a large company in your area would be willing to donate funds to bolster its community relations and as a benefit to their employees who reside in your library service area.

As always, approaching the right people with these requests is paramount. A face-to-face meeting with potential local donors is always preferable, but to get to that point you often must first send a letter of inquiry or letter proposal. This form of cold contact is really just a very short (1–2 page) proposal. An example of a successful letter appears at the end of this chapter, together with a breakdown of costs.

Always remember, when asking for funding you must identify and answer three things in your initial contact:

- Identify the symptoms of the problem and the root causes. Why is it a problem that those people on the edge of your service area do not regularly use the library? In what ways do they suffer from this lack of service? What keeps them from visiting the library building?
- What service needs exist in the community because of these symptoms and root causes? (Tie these to any known funding preferences of the donor.)
- If a service need is determined to exist, would it be more appropriate (and cost effective) for an existing organization/program to expand its services, rather than a new organization/program meet the need?

If your idea or need for funding can pass this initial hurdle, you may well be on your way to making a full proposal either in writing or (preferably) in person.

CONCLUSION

So there you have it! You have leaped many hurdles in this chapter and should be well on your way to enjoying that new bookmobile you have worked so hard to obtain. Looking ahead, you still must write a full set of vehicle specifications, automate your vehicle, and plan/implement a maintenance program, all activities which are described in subsequent chapters. Good luck!

ADDITIONAL RESOURCES

Table 14.1. Bookmobile base vehicles, comparative table

	overall length	floor height	interior height	book capacity	service duty	service lifecycle	service types	approx. cost	maint. costs
van	20'–25'	24"–30"	69"–84"	600–900	Light	7–10 Yrs	L, D, I, H	60–80K	Low
cutaway	20'–25'	30"–33"	69"–84"	1500–2000	Light	7–10 Yrs	R, L, D, I, H	90–130K	Low
low floor	28'–32'	12"–16"	77"–84"	2000–3000	Medium	9–15 Yrs	R, U, S, E, C	180–220K	High
RV	up to 40'	42"–52"	77"–84"	2500–3000	Light	7–10 Yrs	LE, R, S	110–160K	High
step van	20'–30'	36"–42"	72"–84"	2000–4000	Medium	12–16 Yrs	R, U, S, E, C, L, D, I, H, P, LV	150–220K	Medium
truck	26'–40'	36"–44"	Up to 96"	3500–5000	Heavy	14–19 Yrs	R, U, S, C, L, D, I, LE	160–210K	Low
front-engine bus	28'–40'	42"–44"	77"–87"	3500–5000	Heavy	15–20 Yrs	R, U, S, C, LV	180–220K	Medium
rear-engine bus	32'–40'	34"–42"	77"–87"	3500–5000	Heavy	16–21 Yrs	R, U, S, C, E, LV	230–280K	Medium
trailer	20'–30'	12"–24"	Up to 96"	3500–6000	Heavy	18–25 Yrs	R, U, S, C, E, LV, P	80–150K	Low
tractor trailer	Up to 53'	30"–52"	Up to 120"	5000–7000	Heavy	18–25 Yrs	R, U, S, C, LV, P	170–300K	Low

Service Type Key: C = Children Bookmobile; D = Deposit Collections; E = Elderly Bookmobile; H = Homebound Delivery; I = Interlibrary Delivery; L = Lobby Stops; LV = Learning Vehicle; P = Programming; R = Rural Bookmobile; S = Suburban Bookmobile; U = Urban Bookmobile

Maintenance Costs: Low: 0–3 percent of purchase cost annually; Medium: 4–6 percent of purchase cost annually; High: over 6 percent of purchase cost annually.

Reproduced with permission from Specialty Vehicle Services, LLC.

Sample Request for Bookmobile Funding

Proposal to the XYZ Trust to Facilitate Public Library Services to the Aged

Overview

It is an undeniable fact that the population of our community is aging. The library recognizes that in the most recent U.S. Census report, nearly a quarter of our local population is over the age of 55, and that 15 percent are over 65 years old. We expect these numbers to increase significantly in the next decade as the baby boom generation ages. Therefore, we are asking the XYZ Trust to donate $100,000 to help us purchase a handicap-accessible bookmobile to provide our senior citizens with greater access to library materials and services.

The Benefits of a Mobile Library Visit

Our public library is the leader, and often the sole provider, of information, education, and recreation to many area senior citizens. As you may know, older adults currently visit the main library building to take advantage of our programs, collections, and various services. It is also true that the Outreach Department of the library is dedicated to making these collections and services available at the doorstep of those who can no longer leave their home to visit the library. With this proposal, we are seeking funds to provide a solution for those people who fall between these services. It is our belief that with a bit of accommodation, many older adults could still visit a bookmobile and enjoy the freedom to select their own materials.

Our Need for Better Access

Although the Great Lakes Public Library provides several options for service to those who cannot leave their homes, we have become aware that for many who still might be able to visit the library, there are a number of problems to overcome. Currently, the only public entrance to the library itself is from the main parking lot on the East side of the building. Anyone approaching from the North, West, or South (where the bus terminal is located) must use a set of concrete stairs at either the northeast or southeast corner of the library building to navigate the 3–4 foot difference in grade between the sidewalk and the library parking lot. Those who cannot navigate the stairs for whatever reason must travel almost a block to the East of the library and enter the parking lot via the automobile entrance, and then travel nearly a block back to the entrance to the library building. The difficulty of traveling this distance on foot or by wheelchair is compounded during times of inclement weather. The proposed bookmobile would alleviate these physical hurdles by bringing convenient, handicap-accessible mobile library services to where our senior residents live: their neighborhoods, apartment complexes, and assisted living facilities. For older adults with active minds and physical limitations, the ability to retain this independence is crucial to their mental well-being.

Bookmobile Purchase, Projected Costs

Purchase of bookmobile (based on estimate from Rolling Specialty Vehicles):	$160,000
Acquisition of start-up large print materials collection:	$10,000
Marketing materials and printing costs:	$5,000
Sub-total:	$175,000
Minus cash on-hand:	$75,000
Total funds needed:	$100,000

Figure 14.1: Bookmobile purchase, projected costs

Funding Required

The library has the funding to staff and operate this new bookmobile service, but it needs capital to fund start-up expenses. To make this proposal a reality we need to have a bookmobile constructed with full handicap accessibility, outfit that vehicle with appropriate materials, and market this new service to relevant service points and potential new patrons. The total project start-up costs are as follows (the library has already received donations equaling $75,000):

Conclusions

Once implemented, the increased accessibility to library services outlined in this letter has the potential to better the lives of literally thousands in our community for many years to come. With full funding, I can guarantee this project will quickly be brought to completion by a competent and experienced library staff.

For clarification of anything in this letter, or to receive a full proposal, please contact me by telephone (555-5555) or via e-mail at (spointon@greatlakeslibrary. org).

Sincerely,

Scott Pointon, Director

Resource List for Bookmobile Design and Funding

American Grant Writers Association. Available at: http://www.agwa.us.

American Library Association's Services to Bookmobile Communities. Available at: http:// www.ala.org/ala/aboutala/offices/olos/bookmobiles/bookmobiles.cfm.

Association of Bookmobile and Outreach Services. Available at: http://www.abos-outreach.org.

Foundation Center. Available at: http://fconline.fdncenter.org.

Fulton County Public Library District. Available at: http://www.fultonlibrary.com/bookmobile. htm.

JobLINC. Memphis Public Library. Available at: http://www.memphislibrary.org/linc/Joblinc. htm.

Louisville Free Public Library. Available at: http://www.lfpl.org/bookmobile.htm.

Marshall County Public Library System. Available at: http://www.marshallcolibrary.org/book mobile_program.htm.

Techlab. King County Library System. Available at: http://www.kcls.org/travelinglibrary/ techlab.

Tippecanoe County Public Library. Available at: http://www.tcpl.lib.in.us/mobile-library.

15

Writing Vehicle Specifications

By Michael Swendrowski

Writing specifications for your new outreach vehicle can be a daunting task. Your library has worked for years to secure funding for this new vehicle. They are ready to go out and purchase a beautiful new bookmobile, and have entrusted you to develop the specifications! You can do this, but many elements need to be considered during the effort to ensure it is done correctly. This chapter will highlight several of the key factors, identify a couple of no nos, and offer a few tips to make the task easier.

PRELIMINARY RESEARCH: MEASURE TWICE, CUT ONCE

Development of a new bookmobile for your library is just that, development. The process should be compared more to building a library branch than to buying a new car. Your new mobile library vehicle should be custom designed to complement and enhance your brick and mortar operations. In order to do this, you will need to write technical specifications that dictate how you need your new bookmobile to be manufactured. A bookmobile, by definition, is a specially modified vehicle that is made up of hundreds of components, some of which were never intended to be in a harsh mobile environment.

Before you write down even one letter of your new bookmobile specifications, it is important to define what it is that you need. The old carpenter's axiom of "measure twice, cut once" is useful here. The key to this is straightforward, although time consuming: research, research, research! Start taking notes. Talk to other libraries, talk with prospective vendors, search the Web, and talk with your peers. Learn as much as you can about what's available, the latest trends, what works, and what doesn't work.

Identify how your bookmobile specifications document will be used based on the purchasing protocols of your library. If you will issue the document to prospective manufacturers for a competitive bid or Request For Proposal (RFP), it needs to be written loosely enough to allow for good participation, while being comprehensive enough to ensure you get what you expect.

Get involved with peer networks like the Association of Bookmobile and Outreach Services (ABOS) and the American Library Association (ALA). They are invaluable sources of information. The ABOS annual conference, held each fall, may be the

The Importance of Good Specs

If you are able to purchase the vehicle directly from a preselected manufacturer, your life becomes a little easier, but the importance of writing your own specifications is still valid. Bookmobile manufacturers are very good at what they do, but none have the ability to read your mind. If any portion of the specification is gray or vague, it opens the opportunity for misinterpretation, many times leading to installations or modifications to your vehicle that technically meet specifications, but were not exactly as expected.

I have seen this type of scenario many times over the years; libraries taking delivery of an expensive and long-awaited new bookmobile, only to find out that a number of items were not as expected. These types of claims do not generally fall under the warranty and are typically difficult and expensive to remedy. Sometimes, the situation becomes so dire that legal proceedings are the only way to effectively mediate a solution; a no-win for everyone involved (with the exception of the lawyers).

Fortunately, most of these situations could have been avoided with a well written specification. Now is the time to write down how you expect every aspect of the vehicle and process to go. Take your time and do it right.

largest gathering of bookmobile-focused individuals and suppliers anywhere in the world, and you should attend this conference if at all possible. This type of preliminary investigation will help you narrow in on the right type of base vehicle and components.

Along with your external research, work with the folks within your library to start documenting how the unit will be used, staffed, and housed. Analyze your intended routes and budget to define the kind and quality of vehicle that will best fit your needs. Involve your mechanics, drivers, administrators, and all others who will be, even remotely, part of the bookmobile team. The more perspectives you have, the better. Establish your internal criteria such as geography, yearly climate, route distances, and number of staff typically on-board. This data will be very useful in dictating to your selected builder how the vehicle will be used once it is delivered, giving them the opportunity to offer different options you may not have considered. For example, if you will be operating in a very cold and mountainous environment, you may want your vehicle to have abundant heat and insulation, extra horsepower, and even redundant braking systems. If your routes are typically off road, you may want additional ground clearance and extra dust seals.

SELECTING THE BASE VEHICLE

You will need to select the base vehicle that will be modified into your perfect bookmobile. There are many choices, with new ones surfacing each year. The base vehicle you choose will have a direct impact on the remaining choices you make, including serviceability, overall cost, length of time to delivery, and overall vehicle lifetime.

To help jumpstart your research, the following is a quick reference list of the main bookmobile vehicle types. This list (a variation of which also appears in table format in Chapter 14) is based on a document originally published by the late Russ Topping, a respected bookmobile consultant, but has been modified and updated to reflect current offerings:

Van

Original Equipment Manufacturer (OEM) cargo van with higher headroom (including Sprinters) that can be converted into a bookmobile.

Pros: Low cost, very maneuverable
Cons: Low capacity, cramped interior space
Overall Length: 20–25 feet
Floor Height: 24"–30"
Interior Height: 69"–84"
Book Capacity: 600–900
Service Duty: Light
Service Lifecycle: 7–10 years
Service Types: Lobby stops, deposit collections delivery, interlibrary delivery, homebound delivery
Approximate Cost: $60,000–$80,000
Maintenance Costs: Low

Cutaway

OEM cargo van with a custom body installed on the rear and pass-through capabilities.

Pros: Quick delivery, straight sidewalls (typical)
Cons: Shorter service life
Overall Length: 20–25 feet
Floor Height: 30"–33"
Interior Height: 69"–84"
Book Capacity: 1500–2000
Service Duty: Light
Service Lifecycle: 7–10 years
Service Types: Rural bookmobile, lobby stops, deposit collections delivery, interlibrary delivery, homebound delivery
Approximate Cost: $90,000–$130,000
Maintenance Costs: Low

Low Floor

OEM truck that has been modified to allow a low entry threshold and wheelchair ramp. Typically, this type of vehicle is converted to a front wheel drive, with the OEM frame rails removed and replaced with a custom body.

Pros: Ease of entry for elderly and children
Cons: High service costs, low ground clearance
Overall Length: 28–32 feet
Floor Height: 12"–16"
Interior Height: 77"–84"
Book Capacity: 2000–3000
Service Duty: Medium

Service Lifecycle: 9–15 years
Service Types: Bookmobile (rural, urban, suburban, elderly, children)
Approximate Cost: $180,000–$220,000
Maintenance Costs: High

RV

A vehicle originally designed as a recreational vehicle that has been converted into a bookmobile.

Pros: Low cost to space ratio
Cons: High floor height, light duty construction
Overall Length: Up to 40 feet
Floor Height: 42"–52"
Interior Height: 77"–84"
Book Capacity: 2500–3000
Service Duty: Light
Service Lifecycle: 7–10 years
Service Types: Learning vehicle, bookmobile (rural or suburban)
Approximate Cost: $110,000–$160,000
Maintenance Costs: High

Step Van

Delivery type vehicle with aluminum body on a commercial chassis.

Pros: Low corrosion factor, straight sidewalls
Cons: Noisy, prone to roof leaks
Overall Length: 20–30 feet
Floor Height: 36"–42"
Interior Height: 72"–84"
Book Capacity: 2000–4000
Service Duty: Medium
Service Lifecycle: 12–16 years
Service Types: Bookmobile (rural, urban, suburban, elderly, children), lobby stops, deposit collections delivery, interlibrary delivery, homebound delivery, programming, learning vehicle
Approximate Cost: $150,000–$220,000
Maintenance Costs: Medium

Truck

Commercial cab and chassis with custom body installed on the rear. These can include pass-through capabilities if desired.

Pros: Ease of service, very durable
Cons: Front seats cannot swivel to desk(s)
Overall Length: 26–40 feet
Floor Height: 36"–44"

Interior Height: up to 96" (without modification)
Book Capacity: 3500–5000
Service Duty: Heavy
Service Lifecycle: 14–19 years
Service Types: Bookmobile (rural, urban, suburban, children), lobby stops, deposit collections delivery, interlibrary delivery, learning vehicle
Approximate Cost: $160,000–$210,000
Maintenance Costs: Low

Front Engine Bus

Commercial-duty bus (typically school type) with the engine mounted in the front of the vehicle, including cowl nose type (with protruding hood).

Pros: Very durable, solid construction
Cons: Curved roof structure, high cab noise
Overall Length: 28–40 feet
Floor Height: 42"–44"
Interior Height: 77"–87" (with modification)
Book Capacity: 3500–5000
Service Duty: Heavy
Service Lifecycle: 15–20 years
Service Types: Bookmobile (rural, urban, suburban, children), learning vehicle
Approximate Cost: $180,000–$220,000
Maintenance Costs: Medium

Rear Engine Bus

Commercial-duty bus (typically school type) with the engine mounted in the rear of the vehicle.

Pros: Very durable, solid construction, low cab noise
Cons: Curved roof structure, cost
Overall Length: 32–40 feet
Floor Height: 34"–42"
Interior Height: 77"–87" (with modification)
Book Capacity: 3500–5000
Service Duty: Heavy
Service Lifecycle: 16–21 years
Service Types: Bookmobile (rural, urban, suburban, children, elderly), learning vehicle
Approximate Cost: $230,000–$280,000
Maintenance Costs: Medium

Trailer

A pull behind, fifth-wheel or gooseneck trailer (excludes semi-trailers) that has been converted to a bookmobile.

Pros: Low entry height, very long life cycle
Cons: Requires tow vehicle and trailer skills
Overall Length: 20–30 feet (plus tow vehicle)
Floor Height: 12"–24"
Interior Height: up to 96"
Book Capacity: 3500–6000
Service Duty: Heavy
Service Lifecycle: 18–25 years (minus lifecycle of tow vehicle)
Service Types: Bookmobile (rural, urban, suburban, children, elderly), learning vehicle, programming
Approximate Cost: $80,000–$150,000
Maintenance Costs: Low

Tractor Trailer (Semi-Trailer)

Pros: Large space, very long life cycle
Cons: Requires tractor and special licensing
Overall Length: Up to 53 feet (plus tractor)
Floor Height: 30"–52"
Interior Height: Up to 120"
Book Capacity: 5000–7000
Service Duty: Heavy
Service Lifecycle: 18–25 years (minus lifecycle of tractor)
Service Types: Bookmobile (rural, urban, suburban, children, elderly), learning vehicle, programming
Approximate Cost: $170,000–$300,000
Maintenance Costs: Low

GETTING VENDOR INPUT

It's best to try to make contact with a number of prospective bookmobile manufacturers. If you don't get a chance to talk with them in person at a conference (such as Association of Bookmobile and Outreach Services or Public Library Association conferences), you should call them and ask them questions. Beyond making suggestions about which type of bookmobile they feel might suit you best, they are a good source of information for your specifications. Feel free to ask them for rep-

A Special Consideration

One item sometimes forgotten is local serviceability of the vehicle. The vehicle being specified will actually drive up to your door one day and at some point need to be serviced. How far away is the nearest service center? Do they have a good reputation? Have they worked on similar types of vehicles in the past? Depending on the type of base vehicle that you're gravitating toward, this may be an element that can be improved by brand choice. For example, if you're specifying a cutaway-type bookmobile, the base vehicle can be either Chevrolet or Ford. With a truck-type bookmobile, the base vehicle choices are even greater. Personal preference aside, most brand choices will offer comparable features, leaving serviceability of the unit as a weighted decision factor.

resentative specifications on particular models they offer. Be mindful, however, that manufacturers may have a base vehicle brand preference, allegiance, or affiliation. If you need to write competitive specifications, the direct use of manufacturer provided specifications within your RFP may result in a proprietary process. Feel free to use their specifications as a reference, but supplement this information with research data obtained through independent sources, such as the base vehicle and component manufacturers. If you're not set on receiving specific brands or models, the use of the phrase "or equivalent" opens the RFP for a more competitive response.

Alright, let's assume you've done your research. You're ready to put pen to paper, right? Not quite yet. Review your research carefully one more time. Confirm the selection parameters you used to make your decision. (Remember, "Measure twice, cut once.") This allows you to make sure you're choosing the best options for your library's needs and have taken into account that the vehicle, once delivered, will be with you (and possibly your successors) for a very long time.

WRITING THE SPECIFICATIONS DOCUMENT

Now we're ready to start writing. Let's talk a little about the document itself. There are three basic types of vehicle specifications, or specs. Your specifications may be primarily one type or encompass elements of each. The National Association of Fleet Administrators (NAFA) defines the following three basic spec types:

- *Performance Specifications.* A description of a vehicle's operating requirements, such as gross weight, speed, acceleration, maximum grade negotiability, weight and volume-carrying capacity, fuel economy, emissions levels, axle loads and distribution, and compliance with industrial or governmental standards and/or statutes such as SAE (Society of Automotive Engineers), OSHA (Occupational Safety and Health Administration), or DOT (Department of Transportation).

- *Design Specifications.* A description of a vehicle's physical dimensions, structural properties (e.g., moments of inertia, resistance to bending, tensile or yield strengths) or other engineering parameters (e.g., power or torque).

- *Proprietary Specifications.* A description of a vehicle's required equipment specific to a particular manufacturer, such as a Caterpillar engine, Allison transmission, or Eaton rear axle.

A word of caution. There are two extremes to avoid when writing vehicle specifications. Vague, two-page

---

Mix and Match

Feel free to mix and match the elements as you establish the most critical aspects of each selection. Just ensure that elements do not conflict with each other. For example; "there shall be one (1) Duo Therm Penquin, or equivalent, 13,500BTU low-profile air conditioner installed per drawings," and "air conditioning shall be sufficient to cool the cabin interior to 72°F at an external ambient temperature of 98°F." Unless you have done the proper BTU calculations, factoring insulation values and frequency of door openings, the Proprietary Specification will most likely conflict with the Performance Specification. Choose the one specification that will be more critical to your intended use of the vehicle.

specifications that list only basics, such as "Bookmobile; capacity for 3,000 volumes," will make bidders wary because it gives them no clear idea of what you really need. Be specific.

On the other hand, potential bidders may balk when they see a 52-page specification that tells them what color the caulk should be and the type of fasteners to use to attach the body exterior to the frame. This detailed approach forces them to repeatedly ask the library's permission for approved equals (substitutions that do not alter the vehicle significantly, but satisfy the performance requirements). You don't want to eliminate vendors unnecessarily. Having to repeatedly seek approved equals permission can transform a bookmobile purchase into a long, tedious affair for everyone involved. Try to find a happy medium that covers the important elements, but does not go into extensive detail. For an example of what a specifications document looks like, see Appendix B.

Begin the specifications with a statement on how the vehicle will be used and housed (based on your internal research). I usually begin with something like this:

> The Bookmobile described herein is intended to provide contemporary mobile library services to a broad mix of patrons including the elderly and children in an operationally efficient manner. The unit will operate within a suburban environment in northeastern Illinois and shall be designed and equipped to safely operate in an environment of relatively flat, paved roadways. Expected routes for this vehicle are an average of 3000 miles annually on a 30–35 hour weekly schedule. The unit will be kept in the library garage when not in service. The approximate temperature range of this area is 12°F to 85°F, with occasional winter temperatures falling to -5°F to -20°F.

Beyond your base vehicle selection, there are many additional items that need to be specified to ensure you receive what you need. Items include: door and interior configurations, finish selections, HVAC systems, electrical systems, communications systems, paint colors, graphics scheme, and on and on. In order to not miss important items, you should use a checklist similar to the preconstruction questionnaire featured in Appendix C.

SHOPPING YOUR PROJECT TO PROSPECTIVE VENDORS

After your specifications have been completed, reviewed and authorized by your library, it's time to go shopping. The technical specifications you've just completed need to be joined with additional specifications for the actual Request For Proposal (RFP) process. The RFP specifications are more or less instructions, written to prospective manufacturers to dictate what is expected in their response. These specifications should detail, at a minimum: contact information (who should be contacted with any questions), response deadline and format (i.e. paper or e-mail), and pricing breakouts desired (i.e. any options you're considering), payment terms desired, and any vehicle delivery deadline or desire you may have. Additionally, these specifications can spell out: evaluation criteria (how you will analyze the responses), any indemnification or infringement clauses, and insurance requirements required of the successful vendor. This specification will supplement the technical specification and typically become part of your overall contract with the successful vendor.

Finding prospective manufacturers to send your completed package to may involve a bit more research. If you've been working with some of them during your development phase, you may simply need to ask them who their competitors are. If you haven't, some internet research or inquiries to other libraries may be very helpful. You may want to check with your administration as well; some require that the solicitation be posted in your local newspaper.

Because there are relatively few companies in the U.S. that specialize in bookmobiles, it's very typical to have only three or four prospective companies on your list. Contact each of your prospects prior to release of your package to make sure you are sending it to the correct person and gauge their interest in your project. Once your package is released, follow up a couple days later to ensure they have received the package and are comfortable with the response deadline.

Generally speaking, it is courteous to allow a minimum of three weeks for all prospective manufacturers to submit their proposal. Depending on their current workload and/or the complexity of your project, they may need additional time, but should formally request an extension as part of the response procedure.

ANALYZING THE PROPOSALS

You've now received several responses/proposals from prospective vendors, and you need to determine which will receive your award. At this point, simple logic would say the lowest cost wins, right? Unfortunately, it may not be quite that easy. What if the price is right, but that respondent's delivery time is four months longer than the others? What if the company is on shaky ground and ready to fold up shop? What if they've proposed wood shelving in lieu of your desired aluminum? It's important at this point to carefully analyze each response, and for that matter, the company that has authored it. Yes, it's time for some due diligence.

Depending on the response format you requested, the first task is to go through each to look for notable exceptions—generally starting with the low bid first. Have they agreed to provide a vehicle with all features and options you've requested? Have they stated that they would prefer to provide alternates to your specifications? If so, are these deviations significant? Each manufacturer prefers to do things slightly differently than their competitors, either to set themselves apart or because of unique supplier relationships. For example, if they've stated that they can fabricate your desired shelving but with an alternate finish, it's entirely acceptable to overlook this minor deviation if you're comfortable with the alternate and the overall vehicle will meet your needs. If they've stated that that the shelving will be fabricated from wood, when you specified aluminum, it may have far-ranging implications that should be heavily factored in your analysis. Ask yourself: what are the long-term impacts of this deviation on your program? Will the deviation have an impact on your annual operations budget? Is there an effect on the happiness and safety of your patrons? The significance of the deviation will be based on your unique needs and makeup. It's up to you to determine if the deviation is acceptable, and at what cost, monetarily or otherwise. If you're unclear about any of the response, feel free to contact the company and request clarification(s).

Along with your response analysis, it's just as important to investigate the company behind it. You may be working closely with them for many months, entrusting them with significant information, and most importantly, conducting a sizable financial transaction! Find out as much as you can about their history and makeup. How long have they been in business? Who are the key players? How will they support you and the bookmobile in the years to come?

Feel free to contact company references and get their opinions about the company and product they received. Contact the Better Business Bureau (BBB) to see if there have been any issues with the company. Do they have a Dun and Bradstreet (D&B) rating? Will they share company financials for analysis by your administrators? Feel free also to conduct a Web search under the company (or key personnel) names to see what turns up. It's important to conduct as much research as possible to feel comfortable with the company you might do business with, before you enter into contract.

CONCLUSION

It's been a lot of work, but take heart that you've done things right. You've determined which type of bookmobile is best, written the specifications to detail what you want, and made sure you awarded the construction project to a secure and capable builder. You can now breathe a little easier. The next phases are more enjoyable as you work with your chosen vendor to refine interior finishes, exterior graphics, and the final layout of your new bookmobile.

Though a challenging task, keep in mind that you are creating an enduring vehicle that will deliver the joys of reading and education to typically underserved individuals and groups within your community for many years to come. This should be a labor of love, one done with perseverance and diligence in hopes that is appreciated by all those it touches.

16

Vehicle Maintenance

By Jeremy Andrykowski

With all of the wonderful books on automotive technology, maintenance, and care, why would any more need to be written on maintaining a vehicle? One answer to this question lies in the fact that many librarians are not that interested in the technical aspects of a bookmobile. You are primarily concerned that the vehicle works consistently to serve your beloved patrons. The knowledge and tips conveyed in this chapter are to lead you in setting a regimen to minimize the difficulties that inevitably arise in the day-to-day service of a bookmobile.

For simplicity the term bookmobile is used for all Outreach Services vehicles, forgoing the plethora of other terms like mobile library, Tech-mobile, Bucher Buss, and so on. The term librarian is used to mean any person delivering library services via such a vehicle. And for the sake of grammatical, if not political, correctness, mechanics and other automotive specialists are referred to as "he."

This is not a technical manual, but an approach to vehicle maintenance that will help keep your bookmobile rolling beyond the typical expected life of a bookmobile and your accountant's full depreciation with as few problems as possible. (The National Bookmobile Guidelines recommend budgeting for vehicle replacement after 10 years, with some vehicles remaining in service for 15–20 years [Sec. 1.2.2.1.1].) Some assumptions are made in this chapter, primarily that you, the reader, are not a mechanic but an intelligent person capable of reading and thinking, taking what you find written, and making it work for you. The technicality of the information provided is minimized for those of you who would prefer to be reading a good mystery.

WORKING WITH A MECHANIC

One of the key aspects of servicing any vehicle lies in the challenging relationship you may have with a trained mechanic. Considering that repairing and performing preventive maintenance on vehicles such as yours is all they do, they should be qualified to answer any detailed question and solve any issues that arise with your vehicle's performance. These mechanics are not concerned with how much to charge a small child for damaging a book when they cannot afford it or how to find a title for a patron who cannot remember anything more than the color of the cover. This dichotomy of directives can lead to communication problems between you and your mechanic

A Mechanic You Can Trust

When I was having generator problems on the 32-foot-long vehicle I supervised, I sought our local mechanic to work on it. I had some faith in his abilities and familiarity with our vehicle, but I knew a generator is a different matter. I was happy when the mechanic warned me I would be paying him to learn. He could probably fix it, but he would need more time than someone who worked only with generators. I ended up taking my bookmobile 30 miles away to a specialist who only worked on generators. I had even more faith in my mechanic for telling me that. He did continue to service the vehicle and even to perform regular maintenance on it, but not delve into the generator repairs. Now some of you may not have an option and will have to pay someone to learn your vehicle. Just make sure you are paying a good mechanic to be better at maintaining your vehicle, but avoid this altogether if possible.

Another clue to a good mechanic is proper facilities. Good tools make an enormous difference in a service call, whether it's balancing tires or rebuilding a rotator on a generator. When I started working as Bookmobile Supervisor, I was told we used a certain facility often, but I shied away from this shop in search of a closer mechanic. After about five years, I decided to go back and give them a try for a simple repair. I was amazed that my bookmobile didn't even fit in their garage. All of the previous repairs had to have been done in their cluttered lot. I later found out that the reason we used them before is that they were cheap. I didn't go back again. Your customers depend on your vehicle too much to go cheap.

and may be one of the most difficult interactions you have.

The mechanic's experience should be an asset to you in maintaining your vehicle. It should not feel as if you are negotiating with a hostage taker or extortionist. His experience should guide you, but you remain in control of the situation with respect to the necessary and realistic limitations of the mechanical beast. It is easy to feel foolish when asking a question or asking about qualifications, just as when you are dealing with a medical doctor or technology person.

Often this feeling is exacerbated by professionals, but usually this is a signal that they are unsure themselves and do not want to be questioned to a fault. Ask your questions anyway. If he is professional and knows his stuff (i.e. your vehicle and its needs), he should be willing to answer a few questions about it.

Some questions to ask your mechanic at the very beginning of your relationship include:

- How familiar are you with working on a generator (or diesel, specialty vehicle, or other specifics to your own vehicle) such as this?
- What maintenance are you comfortable doing on our bookmobile?
- What aspects of service are you *not* comfortable performing? Where would you recommend taking it for other service work?
- Our library and the people who use the bookmobile depend on our schedule. What kind of scheduling can we work out to minimize our time out for service?
- What are your priorities in your shop? What kind of work will bump ours?
- Do you have facilities to perform all the maintenance required in your shop?
- Will you work with us in building a preventive maintenance program for our bookmobile?
- What other advice would you give us?

Questioning can lead to important conclusions and minimize great expectations. If a mechanic is familiar with diesel engines but does not regularly work on them, you may want to find another mechanic to perform your maintenance and repairs. Most trained and experienced mechanics know enough to troubleshoot and install a new alternator or battery, but nothing replaces experience on a particular vehicle. Considering the cost of bookmobiles today, it pays to have an expert. This is why you do not see many Ferraris getting their oil changes at a local gas station. They are special vehicles, as is your bookmobile, and many exotic cars cost half as much as your bookmobile. So treat your vehicle right.

MANAGING A PREVENTIVE MAINTENANCE PROGRAM

Getting Staff and Administrators on Board

Most everything in life revolves around relationships. Managing a preventive maintenance (PM) program definitely requires as many soft skills as hard, from dealing with the vehicle manufacturer and mechanics to bookmobile staff and administrative staff. Some of these relationships will be easier than others and some will be rather challenging. And, yes, you even have to develop a relationship with your bookmobile! Relationships can be a love-hate sort of marriage as you challenge each other in difficult situations. Machines have varying characteristics, quirks, and preferences like people, but these may well be the simplest relationships with which you have to deal.

All relationships require delicate and effective listening and communicating skills. The better you are at your soft skills, knowing when to be passive, assertive, and aggressive, the longer your vehicle will remain on the road with fewer problems along the way.

Things really begin with your vehicle's manufacturer. Even if you've inherited your bookmobile, you may need a solid relationship with the manufacturer for information on the construction of the vehicle, wiring diagrams, parts, and various other information. They may or may not be able to help you, but it's a good place to start if your predecessor did not maintain any manuals and handbooks properly. If you're purchasing a new vehicle, you have a great opportunity to gather this information in total. The detailed information you gather, from how the electrical box is wired to how the generator was installed, can be immensely helpful to a service technician. An electrical problem can be repaired much more easily if all the paperwork is complete and maintained from the start. Good records and a complete wiring diagram can also help get your relationship with your mechanic off to a good start. A qualified mechanic can troubleshoot via the diagram, as opposed to doing a sort of exploratory surgery, which saves him time and you money.

Pre-trip and post-trip inspection reports are key in maintaining a vehicle, although getting staff to perform these simple routine inspections can be a frustrating task. Too often drivers can get comfortable just getting in and driving off. With time constraints, lack of training, and reliance on others to perform inspections, a driver can easily skip inspections and overlook signs of needed service. Make sure your staff are held accountable for performing the vehicle inspection, and gather support from your administrators. Here too, soft skills and management skills will be put to the test. You must make sure staff understand that routine inspections catch problems and maintain vehicle performance and safety. There is a reason tire tread wear is on the Commercial Driver's License (CDL) exam. An inspection can bring to light a nail in a tire that could lose air slowly and become inconvenient or even disastrous. A generator running low on coolant could cost thousands of dollars and months out of service, when simply checking and filling it to the proper level could have prevented overheating.

Administrators need to understand not only the value of the service the bookmobile delivers, but the great responsibility of keeping the vehicle in top performance. Time spent on inspections and maintenance tasks will pay off in reliability and repairs. Administrators also need to know that a 15-ton vehicle can become a great liability if not cared for properly. A small accident can cost millions of dollars or even the bookmobile itself. Careful maintenance and continual training can help reduce chances of problems on the road and minimize accidents.

Scheduling Preventive Maintenance

The soft skills needed in managing a PM program for your vehicle(s) cannot alone satisfy the requirements needed. Hard skills are needed in planning, organizing, implementing, and evaluating your maintenance needs. Effective planning begins by defining your needs. How many days off for maintenance do you expect? Do you plan off days for maintenance?

There are a few different methods by which to schedule your maintenance; mileage and time are the two most common, but you need to consider the maintenance needs of both the driving engine and the generator. If you have a relatively short range, but your generator will be running most of the day, you shouldn't schedule maintenance based upon mileage.

Keep track of hours of service on the generator and follow manufacturer recommendations. By maintaining a repair/maintenance log, you will be able to adjust your maintenance schedule to the bookmobile services calendar. Your professional mechanic can be a great help in generating an effective PM schedule. Including him in the scheduling process helps bring him on board in maintaining the vehicle.

Know Your Vehicle

Use your mechanic and your manuals, but also educate yourself. Remember, we work in libraries, so we have access to a large number of resources. Use them to learn about your vehicle and understand its needs. Become knowledgeable about basic vehicle functions. You don't need to know what size alternator your generator needs,

Minimize Down-Time

In my bookmobile program, we strived to minimize days out of service for PM. We would schedule maintenance in the early mornings when we had afternoon routes, and we even found a really good repair facility that had 24-hour service. Though the mechanic wasn't always available, we were able to drop the vehicle off late at night so he could begin working on it as soon as he came in the next morning. By eliminating down-time for PM, we were better able to handle down-time due to the inevitable mechanical failure.

but do learn the basic theory of an internal combustion engine and its major parts. This goes for the generator as well. There are plenty of simple books on the subjects and, of course, the Internet. You need to be able to talk to your mechanic about basic

> **Frequency Is Key**
>
> Much of our PM was performed quarterly. This coincided with the recommended generator hours of service for oil/filter changes, but ran the mileage on the engine short (i.e. before it was recommended). More frequent PM on the vehicle engine proved helpful as the detergent-rich oils that cool, seal, lubricate, and protect the engine degrade over time. Here the cost of changing the engine oil and filter a little more frequently than needed was offset both by benefits to the engine and by not disrupting the bookmobile service schedule.

components. This not only will help in troubleshooting problems, but will help build valuable rapport with him. Your vehicle manufacturer can help here, too. Follow the recommendations for service, especially where warranties may be concerned. Use their professional knowledge to build your vehicle knowledge. Some of the basics about your vehicle you should know include: Gross Vehicle Weight Ratio (GVWR); engine model, make, and design; generator model, make, and design; braking system used; and fuel type used for both the generator and the engine. If you have one, be familiar with your inverter power system and any maintenance requirements it has.

Know what your gauges should read so you can tell when oil pressure is low, the temperature is hot, or the voltage is low or high. Check with your mechanic or the manufacturer to know what the running temperature, oil pressure, and voltage should be on your engine and generator. Make note of any changes that occur over time, as this could indicate potential problems.

If you are lucky enough to have a hand in purchasing a new vehicle, or replacing a major component such as a generator, do your homework. Find out what manufacturers are closest to you and which have local service centers. I've heard of bookmobiles being driven to another state for a seemingly simple repair. This has a negative effect on your bookmobile service financially; it can also negatively impact patrons' perception of the reliability of the service. Once a patron's confidence in your reliability is lost, it may take a long time to regain their trust. During that time your customer may find an equally effective source of information or books from a competitor, such as other libraries, bookstores, or the Internet.

If you are purchasing components for your vehicle, whether large or small, talk to your mechanic. Here he can provide invaluable advice on which components are easier to maintain, work on, and which are more prone to problems. Working closely with your mechanic will also give you a chance to relay to him the importance of offering reliable service to your patrons.

Customizing an Inspection Report

Create an inspection report using your own talent and style (see Additional Resources at the end of the chapter for a sample.). Whether you're more likely to write out a report or utilize a checklist to mark off inspection points, tailor your inspection report to your liking. You will be more apt to complete the inspection and more likely to maintain an effective PM program. Although your manufacturer should supply a comprehensive inspection and PM service schedule, take their form and make it your own. Get samples from books or other manufacturers and work up your own form, including all the points you need to cover a complete inspection. Borrow from other bookmobilers as well. One of the greatest things about bookmobile librarians is their willingness and enthusiasm to share information and ideas. Tap into this wealth of knowledge and experience to fill your own needs. Once you get a form (you may need one for daily inspections and one for longer periodic maintenance points), show your mechanic and ask if he has any advice or if anything is missing. Like most team projects, including him in the process will further improve his support of your vehicle's maintenance. Finally, continue to maintain a log of repairs. This will help you analyze and evaluate your program and adjust your inspections to maximize efficiency and effectiveness.

Disaster Planning

No amount of maintenance will prevent all mechanical failure. Though most vehicles today are much more reliable than earlier makes, they are still complicated machines with a large number of moving parts. The processes involved in an internal combustion engine, generator set, and indeed any vehicle on the road, are prone to simple failure that can lead to a complicated problem. With this in mind, have a disaster plan in place for dealing with these unforeseen events.

Having a disaster plan or a set of procedures in place will also enable you to recover service more quickly. For example, in our service, we began maintaining a list of patrons and the bookmobile stop they usually come to. We use this list to notify patrons when our service is down. We also notify all of our service points, post on our Web site that the bookmobile is out of service and what patrons need to do with their material, and call any of our usual patrons to let them know we won't be there. As with most bookmobile services, we broadcast to our patrons that fines are waived and that we will return service as soon as possible. Work with your mechanic to find out an estimated time for return. You don't want to tell your customers you will be out for a week only to find the vehicle repaired and ready for service after two days. This may be the point where the quote most often attributed to Winston Churchill becomes valid. "Plans are worthless, planning is invaluable." Be ready to adjust and adapt, improvise and overcome, but be ready.

TREAT THE VEHICLE WITH *C.A.R.E.*

A few key aspects come into view when you begin evaluating an effective approach to an automotive/bookmobile maintenance program (and yes, this should be useful for any automobile). One can easily see and understand what it takes to maintain a vehicle, and that is *C.A.R.E.* Like most things we face in life, caring for something stands as the master ingredient in maintaining anything, whether it is a relationship, a neighborhood, or a vehicle. You begin with *cleaning* your vehicle. Much more than aesthetics depends upon keeping your vehicle clean. In performing a maintenance program, you must be *attentive*. You must learn which areas to keep an eye on for signs of problems and pay attention to details as you inspect your vehicle. Continuing further, you must develop a *routine* to build in consistent checks and make these as efficient as possible.

There are many words that could easily be used to represent the final "e" of the acronym *C.A.R.E.*: efficient, economical, and extensive, but the most important characteristic to develop in your maintenance program and routine inspections must be *effectiveness.* You must take action on the questions that are raised during your inspections and you must follow through with a regimented maintenance program. If you do not have the staff to do all of the maintenance required, you may have to hire out. For example, in keeping your vehicle clean, you can take it to an auto detailer or even have trained volunteers help out if they are available. Though drivers are always responsible for pre- and post-trip inspections, ultimately the manager must make sure all aspects of the preventive maintenance schedule are completed. You must take *C.A.R.E.* of your vehicle's needs promptly in order to maximize service time for your patrons and minimize your time dealing with your vehicle.

Keeping Your Bookmobile Clean

Advantage of a Clean Vehicle

Cleaning your vehicle should be much more than running it through a car/truck wash or having someone performing delegated community service hose your vehicle down. (In some cases, these approaches can actually damage your vehicle.) Have a plan for cleaning your vehicle and make it part of your scheduled maintenance. The interior must be cleaned as well as the exterior, including the undercarriage of the vehicle and the engine compartments. Attention to these details will extend the life of your vehicle.

Paint left uncared for will oxidize and lose its protective value, as well as its looks. As paint oxidizes, it allows moisture to penetrate to the metal, and along with chips and scratches, will lead to rust. Rust is the natural deterioration of metal and is a major cause of putting a vehicle to rest, that is, out of service permanently.

Your vehicle is a breathing machine too. Like lungs, as air filters become clogged your engines will at best lose performance and at worst cough and choke to a stall.

Dirt and grime on the vehicle can lead to greater problems when dirt gets inside the engine. This greatly wears the internal components and may cause expensive mechanical failure. Dirty and rusty bolts and locked threads can make a simple repair a monster job. Keeping your vehicle clean will not only allow you to detect potential areas that need to be attended to, but it makes it much easier and pleasant for your mechanic to work on. Grime built up on nuts and bolts makes for the classic busted knuckles of mechanics. This does not make a mechanic like your vehicle, which will affect the work he does on it to a greater or lesser degree.

Dirt can hide problems. A grimy engine can hide the fact that a gasket is leaking oil. Some leaks can be minor and the cost of rebuilding an engine not worth the repair, but even this can be watched more closely if the area is kept clean and the leak wiped up during inspections. Not only will this minimize potential problems, but it will allow you to see if the problem is growing to a point where it must be attended to.

Cleaning the Interior

Interior care is important in any PM program. Maintain the driver's area and keep the windshield and gauges clean and clear. Avoid spraying your window cleaner directly onto the gauges as the overspray can make unattractive streaks on areas you have already cleaned with a protectant. Better to spray on a cleaning towel and clean only the glass.

You can include cleaning your computers in an interior schedule. Use compressed air to blow dust and particles from the keyboard and keep the area around and behind the computers clean. This will help your computer's cooling and can improve performance. Your computer manual should have specifics on cleaners to use and routine maintenance to perform.

Your shelving, whether metal or wood, needs to be cared for and protected to keep your vehicle looking in top shape for your patrons. Maintaining your woodwork with a quality wood care product will help your vehicle looking new for many years of service. Use a clean cloth for application to avoid excessive residue that could damage your library material.

Keep your flooring clean. Shampooing the carpet and cleaning commercial flooring will make an impact in your patrons' image of your bookmobile service. Note that you should not use a rubber/vinyl protectant on hard flooring as it can leave a very slick surface that can lead to slips and falls.

Follow your vehicle manufacturer's recommendations for maintaining your vehicle's interior to keep your bookmobile looking its best and lasting the life of the vehicle.

Cleaning the Exterior

The exterior cleaning should also be completed with care. Washing by hand, with a bucket, will save a lot of water. Using a bucket with a good auto shampoo or cleaner will leave your vehicle protected and beautiful as you deliver your service in the community. Using a power-wash can be a simple way to get a quick wash, but the high pressure of the spray can force water into areas that are unprotected and speed up oxidation. A power-wash can also force dirt particles into the paint and damage your finish. If you must use a sprayer, try to avoid direct spray against the paint and into seams. You can use a power sprayer to reach the undercarriage of your vehicle. This can help remove salt and dirt and help minimize rust underneath. Again, care must be taken to avoid forcing water into unprotected areas that can trap the water and speed up oxidation.

Begin with clean water, sponges, or cloths. Clean problem spots such as bugs, tar, and bird droppings before your full wash. Use a good tar and bug cleaner to remove the debris and try to lift the dirt away from the paint. Avoid using regular soaps, such as dish soap, as it will strip your wax and leave your paint bare. Using a good automotive soap or shampoo will clean the dirt from your vehicle and leave the wax to protect from the elements. Keep your sponge clean and get a fresh bucket of clean water as needed.

Do not scrub spots or rub debris as this can also scratch your finish. Once the problem areas are cleaned, begin by wetting the surface to soften and lift the dirt and dust.

The idea is to lift the dirt away from the paint without scrubbing it; scrubbing causes scratches that build over time. You can see swirl marks on the finish of many cars that are run through commercial car washes, often on very expensive cars. The swirl marks are from using dirty towels repeatedly. Detailers recommend using a sweeping motion in the direction the wind flows over your vehicle. Rinse the vehicle and dry with a chamois or synthetic cloth to avoid unsightly water spots.

Polish can be applied to revive paint color and bring back a shine. Care must be taken as a polish removes the surface of the paint. Ideally you will remove the oxidized layer and reveal the paint's true color beneath. Power buffers can be used with care but are not necessarily needed. A buffer can easily remove paint to the underlying primer or even the metal. Polishing by hand can be just as effective and safer. Make sure to apply a good coat of wax after polishing to protect the paint and maintain the shine. If your wheels are painted, maintain a good coat of wax on them. If your wheels are chrome, use a chrome polish to protect the finish.

Maintaining a good wax coat will extend the protective properties of the paint and make a beautiful shine on your bookmobile. Waxing can be done with a carnauba wax or a synthetic compound. Again make sure your cloth is very clean. You also want to apply the wax in small areas that can be removed within a few minutes of application. Waxing is best done when the vehicle surface is cool to touch and in the shade. If the sun bakes the wax into the surface, the marks can be permanent. Avoid getting wax on the rubber trim or in seams and cracks. This leaves an unsightly buildup and looks shabby. Wax can discolor rubber and plastic and be very difficult to remove. Use a soft bristled paint brush to remove wax buildup from seams and crevices, and then go over the area to remove any brush marks in the wax coating. With such a large vehicle you can even do your waxing in sections over time. If you do this, make sure to note what has been waxed to ensure full coverage over a month of so of service. A good wax coating will protect your paint's finish, keep your paint from oxidizing, and give your bookmobile a lustrous shine when washed.

Some detailers recommend washing and waxing every two to four weeks. This can depend upon local climatic conditions and whether or not your vehicle is garaged. Living near the ocean, the salty sea spraying in the air can exacerbate rust. Living in a rainy area can also speed up the oxidation process and this will shorten the periods between washing and waxing. Good lubrication of pivoting joints can also protect moving parts. This can be done by your mechanic during periodic visits for PM.

A lot of vehicles are using vinyl wraps with graphics for exterior decorations advertising. There are many companies that offer vinyl wrap application and removal. If you do get this work done, make sure to follow their recommendations, especially if the wrap is warranted. There are kits available with cleaning products for keeping wraps in good condition. You will also want to keep watch for peeling edges and cracks in the vinyl. Early maintenance can extend the life of your graphics.

Use a quality rubber/vinyl protectant on wheels and other rubber trim. This will protect the rubber from ultraviolet damage and will help your rubber stay flexible and keep it from cracking. Spray the conditioner onto a rag and apply to rubber or vinyl door seals, tires, and interior trim. Take care to use it sparingly on knobs and your steering wheel as some cleaning solutions can leave a slick surface. You may leave it on your dashboard to soak into the vinyl, but a towel run over will give an even, clean surface, protected and attractive.

While you are cleaning your vehicle make sure to keep moisture from accumulating in areas that will trap it. Protect your seals with a conditioner, and lube hinges and latches periodically to keep them working in top form. Check with your manufacturer and your mechanic to make sure what is best for your vehicle's configuration. Don't forget the small stuff: door and window seals, vents, disabled lift door jam, wheel wells, and hood. Your vehicle will look great and you will be better able to maintain it for a long life of service to your community.

Cleaning the Engine, Generator, and Other Moving Parts

There are some other areas of a vehicle to keep clean that managers often overlook. The engine and generator compartments need to be kept clean for these engines to run in top condition. As mentioned previously, keeping air intake clean and free of debris can be crucial to an engine running properly, but cleaning your engine compartments can also help you notice other potential problems. Some generators can run approximately 20 degrees cooler with a clean radiator. As a sort of lint builds up on the radiator, the air-flow diminishes, reducing the cooling and increasing the operating temperature.

During your inspection you should be looking for leaks from shocks, hoses, and under the vehicle. Having a clean engine compartment will allow you to see if there is a leak somewhere. A water-pump has a weep hole that will begin seeping coolant when it is wearing out. This is a signal that the water-pump should be replaced. If

Keeping It Clean Saves Repair Money

The generator on our bookmobile slides out on a tray like a drawer. This makes getting to the components of the generator much easier, but requires a flexible exhaust pipe to be mounted from the generator engine. This pipe had become rusty, and as the pipe flexed when the tray was pulled out, it cracked inside the generator compartment. As the crack grew, exhaust was being breathed directly into the compartment feeding the air needed to run the generator. The air filter clogged with diesel soot and stalled the generator engine. Our Maintenance Department thought this was just an old filter and replaced it, only to find it soon stalled again from a clogged air filter. Though this was a component failure, care in sliding out the generator for service and improved inspections could have avoided this problem.

Another time when failure to keep an area clean can lead to mechanical failure is trouble with a simple fan belt. Again, in the generator on our bookmobile, a tube was cracked and leaked oil very slightly near the cooling fan. As this small amount of oil was blown by the fan back onto the fan belt, the belt's gripping ability diminished to the point where it created enough friction to heat up and fail. As this belt powers the cooling fan, which is key in maintaining operating temperature, the generator overheated and shut down. The bookmobile clerk failed to carefully inspect the generator before getting it running again, and ran it until it shut down again. This caused immense heat in the generator engine and had the potential to completely destroy the generator. A few drops of oil left unattended led to great cost in dollars and in service. What could have been repaired for under $100.00 cost twice that much and a day out of service, and could have been disastrous. All of this could have been avoided by a proactive mechanic and attentive inspections. I learned a valuable lesson the hard way.

your vehicle is coated with dirt and grime, you may not be able to see this and can end up with expensive towing and days out of service.

While you are keeping compartments clean, make sure to maintain your electrical boxes, inverter compartment, and wheelchair lift. Electricity and water do not mix well. Keep these areas clean and dry. Keeping your wheelchair lift lubricated will keep it ready for use anytime. If you do not use your wheelchair lift often, make sure to include it in your maintenance schedule and run it through an exercise periodically to keep it in top working order. The same can be said of awnings and RV slide-out compartments.

Use a shop rag to clean up in your engine compartment. You can use degreaser, but again avoid spraying directly on the engine or compartment. Overspray can damage your paint and rubber coated components. Spray the rag with the cleaner and wipe up excess gunk from the engine compartments. Make sure to wear protective gloves, as engine degreaser can be hard on your skin. If your engine is very dirty, let your mechanic steam clean it so he can cover electricals and avoid starting and running problems.

Being Attentive

Often in our daily grind we get busy and begin to cut corners. A pre-trip inspection becomes an easy target as the departure time comes quickly, but this is also where poor habits can develop and oversights can be made. The devil is in the details, and details left unattended are breeding grounds for gremlins, ghosts in the machine, and many other folkloric causes of mechanical failure. Many of these problems will be reduced or eliminated with an attentive program. The checklist should include enough detail to ensure you are checking all the right spots, such as that hoses are not cracked, lights are working, and there are no leaks on the ground or leaking shocks. An attentive approach ties directly in with cleaning. While you are performing your cleaning procedures, stay attentive to the details, and you will easily spot issues that can be corrected to save money and improve service reliability to your patrons. If you are attentive when washing your vehicle, you will spot the cracks in the paint that can be touched up before rust takes hold. Rubber seals on lights or cracks in seams in the bodywork can be replaced or repaired before a larger problem develops.

You must stay awake and aware during your inspection. Use a narrow-beamed flashlight during your inspections. This enables you to focus the light on specific components when checking under the vehicle. Focusing on the details, plus effort and practice at doing inspections, will help you notice subtle

---

Pay Close Attention . . .

On our vehicle, the staff reported driving over something on a side street. They thought it was a muffler that had fallen off another vehicle. There were no driving problems or noticeable differences in vehicle performance. During my inspection, I noticed something different. The rear spring brake cap was missing. It had become rusted and finally had become weak enough that the pressure of the compressed spring shot it off under the vehicle while driving. This was the right rear, so when the parking brakes were used, or if the air pressure had become low enough to activate the spring brakes, only the left rear brake would apply. Fortunately we live in an area with few steep hills and we park on level ground. Without an attentive inspection, this could have been easily overlooked.

changes such as a slight drop in voltage, slight increase in running temperature, a few drops of something beneath the rear axle, or a broken bolt.

Creating a Routine

As time runs short before you hop in your bookmobile and start it up, rushing to make your first stop on time, how do you know you have everything you need with you? Much of what we do on a daily, weekly, or monthly basis involves routines we follow to keep systems working and make sure nothing is overlooked. Build a complete routine for your inspection. This will help build efficiency into the inspection and you will be confident that nothing is left unchecked. The more you perform your routine, making adjustments and improvements in your procedures, the easier and faster it will become. A complete inspection can be finished in 5 to 10 minutes, checking fluid levels, compartments, lights, and so forth. If you find something failed and you didn't catch it, learn from it and adjust your inspection routine.

Now, that said, many of the most exciting things in life are the variations in our routine. Don't worry about getting too monotonous, just make it complete. The variations will come in the mechanical changes you'll notice. What you are looking for are these changes, no matter how slight. This way you will at least be able to bring these to the attention of your mechanic. He will be able to tell you to let it go, keep an eye on it, or repair it promptly. He will also be impressed that you noticed it. This will further your rapport with your mechanic and you'll learn more about your vehicle.

Making It Effective

In designing a PM program, keeping your vehicle clean, being attentive to details, and having a solid routine, the final aspect of the process must be focused on effect. All of your time, planning, work, and effort must be evaluated on how effective your program is. You must follow through on the things you notice. Keep track of the slight changes, talk to your mechanic, and make sure repairs are made. Inspect your vehicle after a service has been completed. Check that the fluid is clean and the filters have been changed. Check that a replaced hose is not leaking and that replaced headlamps are adjusted correctly. Make adjustments in your procedures as needed to cover things that were missed. Make staff realize the importance of follow-through and that the vehicle's safety, reliability, and comfort depend upon how effective their efforts are in maintaining your bookmobile.

CONCLUSION

We human beings have unique relationships with our vehicles. That's probably why many people throughout history have named vehicles of all sorts. (Think of Herbie, KITT, and The Eliminator, just to name a few.) And like any relationship, to really work well it requires, first and foremost, care. If you care for your vehicle, you will do your best to maintain it properly, and it in turn will do its best to perform for you with comfort, reliability, and efficiency. Developing an effective preventive maintenance program for your bookmobile will minimize frustrations, and you may also find that taking care of your vehicle can be fun and rewarding.

Sample Bookmobile Pre-Trip Inspection Report

Month/Year:	1	2	3	4	5	6	7	8	9	10	11	12	13	14	15	16	17	18	19	20	21	22	23	24	25	26	27	28	29	30	31
1. Approach Vehicle - Look for Leaks																															
Overall condition, clear of obstructions																															
Clear of fuel, oil, or water leaks																															
2. Check Under Hood (engine & generator)																															
Engine oil level																															
Coolant level and condition of hoses																															
Power steering fluid																															
Transmission fluid																															
Battery connections, wiring insulation																															
No evidence of leaks																															
Generator compartment clean & no leaks, check oil																															
3. Start Engine and Check Inside Cab																															
Windshield & mirrors																															
Washer fluid																															
Emergency equipment																															
Oil pressure & temp																															
Ammeter																															
Warning lights, buzzers																															
Steering wheel, horn, wipers, washers																															

Figure 16.1: Sample bookmobile pre-trip inspection report

Month/Year:	1	2	3	4	5	6	7	8	9	10	11	12	13	14	15	16	17	18	19	20	21	22	23	24	25	26	27	28	29	30	31
4. Check Headlights and Warning Lights																															
Lights, flashers, markers all working																															
5. Conduct Walk-around Inspection																															
Left front tire, tread, wheel lugs																															
Left rear tire, tread, wheel lugs																															
Right rear tire, tread, wheel lugs																															
Right front tire, tread, wheel lugs																															
6. Check Signal Lights																															
Turn signals on & flashing normally																															
7. Check Air Brake System																															
Test low pressure warning signal																															
Check that spring brakes come on automatically																															
Check rate of air pressure buildup																															
Test air leakage rate																															
Check compressor governor cut in and cut out press																															
w Final Check																															
Disconnect electric cable and exhaust hose																															

Notes:

U   Check completed OK

X   Problem noted, explain further as needed

R   Repaired

_____

_____

_____

Figure 16.1: (continued)

17

Automating Your Bookmobile with Telecommunications Technologies

By Tom Walker

Because of the complexity and the relative newness of telecommunications technologies, coupled with rapidly shifting ILS (Integrated Library System) platforms, the framing up of a one size fits all or universal step-by-step plan for bookmobile automation is not possible. However, every bookmobile can be automated—maybe not with a perfect solution, but with one that is functional and practical. The interesting processes involved in delivering the advantages of connectivity to bookmobile staff and patrons are well worth the effort.

The objective of this chapter is to describe some of the most practical methods for connecting to the wired Internet wirelessly from a vehicle. For convenience, such a vehicle is referred to by the obviously too restrictive term, bookmobile. Also highlighted throughout the chapter are some of the industry trends that should be of interest to us as we face the important challenge of applying mobile communication technologies to our evolving library circulation system software platforms. To help you make sense of the technical terminology throughout this chapter, words appearing in italics are defined in the Automation Glossary at the end of this chapter.

TELECOMMUNICATIONS TECHNOLOGIES

Currently there are three modes of wireless connectivity worth discussing—cellular, *satellite*, and WiFi.

Cellular

The most practical way to connect to the Internet from a bookmobile is via a cellular modem attached to a laptop computer. (The term laptop is used as a catchall to include notebooks, laptops, tablets and such, and it will be presumed that it has an available PC, *ExpressCard* or *USB* port.) The cost of a cellular solution is very modest.

At the time of this writing, the monthly fee for unlimited service is only about $40. The initial outlay for the *aircard* (cellular modem) ranges from free to about $250. The term aircard actually comes from a registered trademark (Aircard) of Sierra Wireless, a leading communications equipment company and producer of excellent cellular modems. (For contact information for Sierra Wireless and other companies listed throughout this chapter, see the automation vendor contact list at the end of this chapter.) Now the term aircard is generally applied to all cellular modems that can be installed in a laptop through either a *PCMCIA* slot or a USB port. Installation is easy and the data *throughput* rates are usually good.

Testing the Signal

Most cellular carriers offer a free 30-day evaluation period, so it's pretty hard to go wrong. A logical first step in considering cellular is to travel by car to all the stops and see if you can complete a cell phone call. While aircards are not used for voice communications, they do use the same cell tower signals as regular cell phones. If a cell phone won't work from a stop, an aircard probably won't either.

If the cell phone test results are promising, the next step is to contact a cellular carrier such as Verizon or AT&T and order a new cellular account and aircard.

Selecting an Aircard

When you are ready to order an aircard, there are a few features to keep in mind. Some bookmobile staff find that they have stops that are located in signal-challenged areas where they may need an external antenna to boost the signal. If you, too, ever decide that you want to attach an external antenna, you'll need to have an aircard with an external antenna connection port. Many do not.

Also, there are two generations of *cellular transmission protocols* available, each associated with a different data throughput speed. Not surprisingly, the newer one brings faster speeds. Which protocol or speed you acquire will depend on your geographical area and the cell tower signal within range of each stop. Since each of the protocols offers a different *data-rate*, you will want an aircard that can gracefully flip-flop between each protocol—not all aircards do. I'll talk more about antenna options and those data-rate protocols later. Staying with the subject of aircards, at the time of this writing, one good and reasonably priced one which will address both the external antenna and dual speed issues is the Kyocera KCP650 which sells for about $200. Your *carrier* should be able to sell you one with your cellular service account if that is your preference, although most cellular carriers routinely deliver their own branded aircard with new accounts. Despite the favorable review of the quality of the Kyocera modem card, it's advisable to accept and install

Choosing a Cellular Provider

At our library, the Charleston County Public Library (CCPL), we use Verizon for our bookmobile cellular connectivity. I also use Verizon for my personal Blackberry account. I think they have very good coverage and services but my direct experiences are also limited to them. I recommend using that carrier with which you or the library already have a satisfactory relationship.

the aircard provided by your carrier, especially if it's free. That keeps things simpler and you'll probably thrive with it. If not, you can change aircards later.

Installation

Once you receive your cellular account and aircard and are ready to set up the laptop, keep in mind that you can set everything up in an office and then just try the laptop from a car as you drive from stop to stop. It will be less hassle to troubleshoot, if necessary, from an office or car than the bookmobile. The aircard installation process is pretty straightforward and includes the following steps:

- Load the software that comes on a CD onto the laptop and answer "yes" to the question about putting an icon on the desktop.
- Run the software from the desktop icon.
- After responding to a few prompts, you'll be instructed to attach the aircard.
- During the remaining setup process, you'll be given a lot of operational preferences such as automatically launching a *VPN client* or a Web browser. Those preferences can be changed later if you find any settings you selected to be sub-optimal.

Connection Speed

Once you have connected to the Internet, you can check the connection speed and throughput statistics via the *on-screen network management software display*. (For Verizon, it's called VZAccess Manager and you simply click on the "Statistics" tab of the *Session Information Window*.)

It was mentioned earlier that there are two aircard connection speed possibilities. The faster connection speeds are the result of the development of better *data compression* technologies. The more compressed that data is, the faster it can travel over radio waves. There are two classes of speeds available, depending on the technology deployed. The slower is roughly equivalent to a *DSL* connection or around 60 *KBPs*. That is sufficient throughput speed to support one computer surfing the Web. What the service is called depends on both the technology deployed and the marketing department of the carrier. The most common term used is the acronym *CDMA* (Code Division Multiple Access). (Verizon calls their CDMA service National Access Network Services. AT&T uses a technology termed GMS and calls it Edge.) Speed claims by the carriers for these services are varied, and so are the actual customer observations of those speeds. The service names are numerous but CDMA seems to be the most common name for the slower of the cellular Internet services.

The most prevalent higher speed service is *EV-DO* (Evolution Data Optimized) and is roughly equivalent to half a *T1* or around 600 Kbps. (Verizon calls their EV-DO service Broadband Access. AT&T uses a technology called HSDPA and calls it 3G for Third Generation.) The topic of throughput speeds, the various technologies used, and the associated nomenclature outstrips both the scope of this chapter and the author's know-how, and what you've just read is a gross oversimplification. However, most of us can get by with knowing that there are two levels of service, the nearly ubiquitous and slower CDMA and the considerably faster and increasingly available EV-DO. It's common to encounter each of the two services depending on where you are located within a market area. Carriers are gradually supplanting the slower services with the faster EV-DO, *HSPDA,* or such. Older aircards continue to function in the EV-DO areas, just at the slower speed. (To view the current EV-DO coverage for Verizon, point your browser to http://b2b.vzw.com/broadband/coveragearea.html.)

Boosting the Signal

If you find that some of your stops are located in signal-challenged areas, attaching an *external antenna* may be a solution. In order to attach such an antenna, your aircard needs to have an external antenna connection port. As mentioned earlier, not all cards do. Some external antennas can be sited inside the bookmobile on the dashboard area. A more effective antenna location is high and outside. You could also clamp the antenna to the passenger side rear view mirror. A magnetic antenna that can be temporarily slapped onto the bookmobile's roof with the connecting cable running through a slightly opened window is a good approach, too. The problem with mounting an antenna permanently on the roof is that it will be vulnerable to being sheared off by low-hanging branches. When purchasing an antenna, the following are the specifications that should suit your bookmobile

- *Dual band.* Operates on both 800 MHz and 1900 MHz
- *Tri-Mode.* Operates at both 800 and 1900 MHz and at 800 MHz analog
- *3dB gain.* Best signal coverage
- *Ground plane.* Uses the metal roof as a ground or has a built-in ground for glass mount or mirror attachment

Dual band and Tri-Mode are the signal types and frequencies within which cell phones operate. Gain is a quantifier of signal amplification and is usually expressed in decibels. For our purposes, we can think in terms of an antenna as transmitting and receiving signals in all directions. If we deployed a *6dB* (6 decibels) antenna, the signal amplification pattern would resemble a huge horizontal baseball bat, being weaker at the close and far ends but extending a great distance. The 6dB gain antenna would be better in a desert. A 0dB antenna would form a signal pattern resembling a basketball. The signal amplification pattern would extend high in the air but not very far to the sides. This might be suitable for use in mountain valleys or amid the skyscrapers of Manhattan. The recommended 3dB gain antenna would have an amplification pattern resembling a horizontal rugby ball, with high signal strength at the business ends, yet extending pretty far in distance—just right for most bookmobiles. One of the larger suppliers of antennas is Wilson Electronics.

Satellite

If your bookmobile route includes areas not covered by cellular signal, you may want to investigate the very interesting technology of mobile satellite broadband. Historically, the primary focus of the communications satellite industry has been to serve large enterprises that include television broadcasting, global positioning systems, large computer networks, telephone systems, and the military. The capabilities available through satellite systems are vast and include voice transmission, card payment protocols, imaging systems, and a host of other sophisticated applications that far outstrip the relatively basic needs of bookmobile automation. However, a fairly recent industry development has been the offering of scaled down products aimed toward the residential consumer and small businesses. An even newer industry development has been the entry into a much narrower market to address the communications demand from mobile users such as RV owners, boaters, truckers, and so on. It is within this market niche that bookmobiles fit. However, because of the inherent technical sophistication of those foundational large systems, the smaller ones still tend to pass along an unwelcome, albeit manageable, amount of complexity. Don't let that scare you off, though.

The general steps involved in using a functional satellite system for Internet access include the following:

How Satellite Technology Works

- The bookmobile parks in a spot that allows a rooftop dish a view to the south.
- A command is given to a *controller box* that directs the rooftop antenna (dish) to search for and lock onto the satellite.
- After receiving notice that the antenna and satellite are synced, the bookmobile staff use the Web browser to send a data request out to the Internet.
- A modem converts that data request from *digital* to *analog* and sends it via cable to the rooftop antenna and on up to the satellite.
- The satellite redirects that received data request down a *Network Operations Center* (NOC) on Earth.
- The NOC converts the analog signal to digital, sends the request out to the wired Internet and receives back the reply data.
- The NOC then converts the reply data back into analog and transmits it up to the satellite.
- The satellite redirects the reply data back down to the bookmobile dish.
- The cable from the dish carries the signal back to the modem, where it is converted back into digital, and ultimately the computer displays the reply.

Common Challenges

While the scenario can be and should be as simple as just outlined, in trying to get to that point, bookmobile customers can encounter some unforgiving barriers. Because mobile satellite systems involve electromechanical devices that are applying some precise laws of physics, physical obstructions can present some first order problems. A few of those show stoppers are described below.

PARKING

If you must park your bookmobile in a garage, you will need about two feet of available clearance from the top of the entryway before installing a rooftop antenna. In the stowed or collapsed position, the dish can be from 14 to 20 inches high, depending on the model. You also need to account for differences in tire pressure, heat expansion, and the like, and perhaps a build-up of ice or snow at the threshold. Take a very close look at the garage door clearance situation if you're in a severe weather climate. Charleston County Public Library has parked its bookmobile outside since having a dish attached, but in coastal South Carolina where the weather rarely gets cold, this has not been a problem.

BOOKMOBILE ROOF

Another thing to consider is that your bookmobile's roof will need to permanently support up to 200 pounds and occasionally a person or two standing on it. Currently, the lightest antennas weigh about 100 pounds. The roof will also need a clear area of about eight feet in diameter to allow the antenna to rotate 360 degrees and also lie flat in a stowed position. Once an antenna has been considered for purchase, its physical dimensions need to be evaluated in terms of requisite clearance space from other rooftop structures on the bookmobile such as vents, TV and radio antennas, AC units, skylights, and so forth. By the time you read this, smaller and lighter antennas may be available, but that does not appear to be the current trend. In any case, the physical placement issues need to be addressed at the very beginning of your evaluation process.

SATELLITE POSITION

As you shop for satellite systems you will, in a sense, also be shopping for a particular *satellite*. There are lots of satellites or birds in orbit. Each network service provider leases space on one or a group of satellites. The satellites are launched by private companies, usually under government contract, from various launch facilities around the world. They stay in *geostationary orbit* around the equator at a distance of 22,000 miles or so. Geostationary means that the satellite maintains the same position relative to the rotation of the Earth, so that its view angle from the Earth remains the same. Since the satellites are in orbit at various spots around the equator, the signals they beam down to Earth form different footprints. That is, they are stronger in some areas directly below, weaker around the margins and nonexistent on the opposite hemisphere. If you are located in southwest Texas, for instance, the signal strength from the satellite Charleston County Public Library's bookmobile points to may be weaker or stronger depending on the distance and severity of the angle between the satellite and each rooftop antenna. Those differing view angles are what form the *signal footprint*. When you sign on with a network service provider, they should assign you to the satellite with the most favorable footprint for your location.

ENVIRONMENTAL BARRIERS

Obviously, if you are attempting to point your bookmobile dish at a particular satellite,

Signal Footprint

At CCPL, we point to a satellite named Satmex 5. If you link to www.lyngsat-maps.com/sm5.html, you can see an image depiction of the Satmex 5 footprint.

you need to park somewhere where there is a *view angle* to that satellite. On our bookmobile route, we have some stops where there are trees or a building blocking the view angle and we cannot use the system. We also have stops with low hanging live oak branches that prevent the lifting of the dish. Another thing that can cause problems are parking lots that are severely sloped for drainage purposes. Dishes lock onto satellites through a combination of vertical, horizontal, and tilted positioning.

Our Satellite Systems

In late 1999, I was tasked with the project of automating our soon-to-be-delivered bookmobile. At that time, the only company I could find that could provide an affordable and technically accessible mobile satellite system was C-Com Satellite Systems (www.c-comsat.com) in Ottawa, Ontario. By today's standards, that system was a clunky arrangement. The system used a MotoSat DataStorm antenna to acquire the downlink from the satellite. The uplink was provided by a large Sierra Wireless standalone modem utilizing a 1200 *baud* regular cell phone number to dial into a Mindspring Internet account. The service was provided by Hughes and was called DirecPC. That original system provided Internet access to six public computers as well as the DRA text-based circ client at two staff computers. Eventually, Hughes developed a two-way system called DirecWay (now HughesNet) and C-Com developed an antenna called the iNetVu. We replaced the MotoSat with a larger iNetVu antenna and switched over to the DirecWay system, eliminating the need for the large and expensive Sierra Wireless modem and Mindspring account. We also acquired a Verizon cellular broadband account and a Kyocera KCP650 aircard to work around those instances where we had no satellite view angle. Several years ago we also migrated our ILS from DRA to Sirsi Unicorn. That's still the configuration that we use today. The system, at five years old, is actually getting a little long in the tooth.

Sloped drives can make dish positioning very difficult. Some vehicles can have trouble keeping a connection because of the bouncing caused by patron entry and egression. If all those hassles aren't discouraging enough, there is also the occasional problem of rain attenuation, when a severe storm will shield the signal for a while. Yet somehow it's still an interesting and worthwhile technology.

Provisioning Hierarchy

While shopping for satellite systems, it's important to understand the several layers within the satellite system *provisioning hierarchy* because a lot of vexing problems for shoppers are caused by the considerable overlap among those layers. Figuring out where to establish the best point of contact when you are interested in evaluating systems can be difficult. The explanation that follows should clear away some of the fuzziness. For our purposes, there's no need to be concerned with those who manufacture and launch the satellites, but the important layers below them deserve some attention. They are:

- Network service providers
- Satellite network gear manufacturers
- Mobile antenna manufacturers
- System integrators and resellers
- Installers and support providers

Network service providers are those who lease space on the satellites; establish a network operations center for relaying signals from the satellite to the wired Internet and back; and probably those to whom you will pay a monthly access fee. How do they lease satellite space? Envision a satellite to be sort of dragonfly shaped. Each of those two long extended rectangular wings is subdivided into rectangles called transponders. The service providers lease those transponders. The satellite to which our bookmobile dish points, Satmex 5, carries 24 transponders and Hughes Network Systems leases 8 of them for HughesNet customers. Hughes also leases transponders on other satellites, as do competitors such as iDirect and WildBlue. In fact, one of the factors relating to the quality of service is how many customers are assigned to each transponder, the fewer the better from the customer's perspective. This is called the *contention ratio*. It is better to have a lower contention ratio because of the more stringent steps that the network service providers must take in order to be sure that your signal transmissions back to the satellite will not interfere with the signals of other customers. With a higher contention ratio the network service provider must impose a more exact pointing of your antenna (dish) before they can turn on the transmission capability during the initial searching and locking-on process. To mention a specific example, one of the reasons that an iDirect service is more expensive and considered better than HughesNet is that it has a much lower contention ratio. When buying a system, ask for a comparison of contention ratios for the network service providers under consideration.

Many of the companies that make satellite modems, routers, and hubs also provide network services. This is where a lot of the confusing overlap begins. For instance, one of the leading high-end network gear manufactures, iDirect, also provides network services. Likewise, Hughes manufactures its own line of modems and leases satellite space. Gilat Network Systems and their SkyEdge products is another example of a company that can jump in and address customer needs at various levels. If you're in North America, regardless of where or how you buy a mobile satellite system, the network services and modem will likely be provided by Hughes, iDirect or SkyEdge.

There are lots of fixed satellite antennas on the market but far fewer mobile (self-pointing) ones. The mobile antennas are complex, consisting of a servomotor with software driven gears and levers operating in response to readings from a built-in compass. Of course, they also need to have controller software that can be updated with the relative location of a host of satellites. Those are the reasons that the price jumps from a few hundred dollars for a fixed antenna to a range of a few thousand to several thousand dollars for a mobile one. Some examples of *mobile satellite antenna* manufacturers are C-Com, MotoSat, TracStar, and AVL. C-Com and TracStar manufacture mobile antennas as well as also set up and sell accounts to the network services. With satellite antennas, size matters and bigger is better. Currently, for bookmobile applications the sizes range from a diameter of .75 meters to 1.2 meters. The premium network services usually require the larger antennas. The price for an antenna will be based on the convenience factors and sophistication built into the controller box, the diameter of the antenna pan and various performance measures such as transmission power.

All pieces considered, a complete system (network account setup, modem, antenna, controller box and installation) will cost between $6,000 and $20,000. You may be able to get by with less than $6000 and you can certainly spend more than $20,000. Monthly connection charges will range from around $100 to $300. When signing up for a new service, I suggest beginning with a base rate charge for data throughput and change to a faster (and more expensive) service later if you find that to be necessary.

This is rather expensive when compared to the initial outlay of $0 to $200 for an aircard and monthly fees of around $50 for cellular broadband services. Using WiFi is basically free, presuming that you have a wireless capable notebook or laptop. The equipment used with cellular broadband and WiFi should last a very long time, especially when compared to the more damage vulnerable electro-mechanical mobile satellite antennas.

The *integrators and resellers* are the ones with whom you will probably deal when purchasing a system. Again, here there is plenty of overlap with the other categories. Among the companies already mentioned from whom you can buy a complete system as well as ongoing support are C-Com, iDirect, TracStar, and SkyEdge. One example of a company that is an integrator and reseller but not a manufacturer is MobilSat. Like the others, MobilSat can give you a quote on a service, configure a modem and antenna setup, arrange for installation, authorize the commissioning of your new account with the service NOC, and then offer ongoing support.

Installation

Regardless of how you acquire your satellite system, someone will need to climb onto the roof of your bookmobile, mount the antenna on the sheet metal, run cables inside to the circ station computer, run a wire to the power source (probably a 12-volt battery) and connect everything up and test the equipment. Most resellers have installers under contract who will come to your site. You could also choose to hire a local installer. A few words of warning are in order here: you need to be careful that whatever you do to the roof of your bookmobile does NOT compromise a warranty you may have in place with your bookmobile vendor. You need to check that out first. Also, some installers have only had experience with installing mobile antennas on RVs. Installing on a bookmobile is usually much more difficult because of the shelving and attendant support structures. Lastly, a few installers have tried to morph into a reseller's role and have gotten in over their heads. A few rogues have given the business some black eyes. I urge caution and suggest working with the larger, proven companies.

Bookmobile vendors such as Farber Specialty Vehicles, Matthews Specialty Vehicles, and OBS, Inc. are continually working with satellite system vendors and by now have seen track records develop. The bookmobile vendors can also install equipment on the roof more easily, especially if they are in the process of building your bookmobile. I suggest talking to them about satellite systems even if your bookmobile is far from new. Satellite systems can be a great investment and will provide needed services to patrons and staff, but unlike cellular aircards, they represent a large investment in both money and overhead. Get some advice from the bookmobile vendors and others on the bookmobile online forums before making the decision to purchase.

WiFi

Unlike the cellular or satellite technologies that allow virtually limitless mobility, WiFi requires you to be at least within 500 feet from a WiFi access point. The WiFi access point connects wirelessly to a laptop but that access point itself is wired to a data network. Considering the distance restriction, there are only a few ways to use WiFi. You can park the bookmobile near an unsecured hotspot and use wireless equipped devices to surf the Web or perhaps use your circ client software. However, there would be a number of ethical, security, and performance issues to evaluate within that scenario, but it could work nicely. If your route includes schools, nursing homes or other institutions that deploy WiFi, and if they would permit or encourage you to use their secured WiFi access points and provide passwords, that would be an ideal situation.

Another way to use WiFi would be to get Internet connectivity through cellular or satellite and then set up a wireless hotspot from the bookmobile. A $50 wireless router would suffice for that. A bookmobile-based hotspot could be used by staff or patrons sitting in or near the bookmobile. Staff could also take a wireless device such as the SirsiDynix Pocket Circ PDA or a wireless-capable laptop into a lobby stop and log circulation transactions.

Some communities are providing WiFi access throughout their towns. Bookmobiles in those areas could obviously utilize the hotspots. As WiFi hotspots proliferate, they will become more useful for bookmobiles, but for now WiFi does not represent a first line connectivity solution.

TROUBLESHOOTING THE CIRCULATION CLIENT

Unfortunately, many find that access to the Internet does not guarantee use of the ILS circulation client. Three conditions cause most of the problems—security blocks, signal latency, and slow connection speeds.

In terms of both physical distance and network circuitry, the bookmobile is usually very far away from the ILS production server. Many libraries house their servers off-site within a city or county IT department. Even where the library system houses and maintains its servers and security appliances, the bookmobile is still outside the protected network. An important task of network security is to keep out intrusions—access very similar in properties to what you are attempting from a bookmobile. The ports used for Web traffic (the HTTP stuff) are routinely opened by the firewall in order to allow Web site and catalog access. However, the ports used by the circ clients need to be closed to all but those with permission to launch the proprietary ILS circ client software. Most network administrators consider that opening those ports to the outside and simply relying on password protection to be unreasonably risky.

One possible workaround is to acquire a *Static IP* address from your cellular or satellite service provider. Without arranging for a static IP assignment, at each login you will be given the next available IP address from a pool of valid addresses. You should be able to acquire a static address for a modest fee. Once you arrange to receive a static IP address, the network administrator will be able to add that specific IP address to the security appliance access-list and thereby grant the bookmobile computer use of the necessary ports and protocols.

Setting up a *VPN* (Virtual Private Network) client on the bookmobile computer is another option. A VPN establishes an encrypted tunnel from a distant computer to a designated server inside a protected network. This is the system used by many telecommuting business people as they submit sales reports or access company databases while on the road. Cisco, which holds a huge share of the network gear market, offers free VPN clients. By synching a VPN client on the remote computer with the appropriately configured security features on the host network, a safe connection can be established. There are also convenient browser-based VPNs, where no client software needs to be loaded on the remote computer.

Using a *remote desktop control program* such as LogMeIn (www.LogMeIn.com) or Norton pcAnywhere (www.symantec.com) will allow you to remotely take over the desktop of an office computer at the library that is actively running the circ client. If the dedicated office computer is left running, a bookmobile computer making the remote connection can scan barcodes and do database lookups just as if it were using that computer located in the office. This approach may deliver some payoff from a security standpoint. However, the primary advantage of using a remote desktop control connection is that the remote computer does not need to download and maintain all the workstation configuration, data, and help files that are pushed from the host server at login. Some find that the bookmobile connection just cannot support the data transfer overhead associated with running the ILS circulation client. For what it's worth, at CCPL we use the SirsiDynix Unicorn C Client without any performance problems.

Another practical way to deal with both security issues and the rather bandwidth-hungry demands of running a remote circ client is to deploy a version of *Citrix* and/or *Terminal Services*. In this setting, the application software resides on a secure central server and the terminal services run on the bookmobile computer. The remote computer does not need a high-speed connection because it is mostly sending keystrokes to the central server and receiving only appropriate screen-shots in response.

Others have reported that they can log in with the circ client but that maintaining a consistent connection is difficult. One reason may be that some circ systems establish a socket connection at login whereby the connection identifier is a combination of IP address and port number. In dormant situations, the socket's port number may get reassigned, causing a network conflict. Running a persistent PING command from the bookmobile computer to the host can keep the connection alive and intact. To run a persistent PING you can use the command "ping -t (server name or IP address)" as in ping -t 192.162.249.235 or ping -t web2.ccpl.org. To stop the persistent PING, use the command "Ctrl/c" (push the Control and C keys simultaneously). You can enter the ping command by clicking on Start, then Run, and entering it in the dialogue box after Open or enter command in that same dialogue box and use the resultant DOS command line for entering it. Since PING displays the round-trip time in milliseconds, it will also provide a continuous glimpse of the connection speed.

Within satellite technology there is phenomenon known as *signal latency* that is caused by the very long distances that the signal travels from Earth to the satellite and back. If this seems to be causing problems, ask the network technician to check the various keep-alive time settings. Adjusting them gradually to longer periods may solve the problem.

Let's talk now about connection slowness. If you can latch up to your host computer from the bookmobile but the connection speed is just too slow at times to run the circulation client effectively, you can use a *SIP2*-based product called MobileCirc, sold by Integrated Technology Group for about $1,000. MobileCirc will allow you to log real-time transactions, trap holds, invoke circulation policies, and so on. There will be no need to upload transactions at the end of the day, as one does with the standalone backup systems or with some of the handheld devices. MobileCirc utilizes the ITG self-check software to pass barcode numbers via the SIP2 protocol. Network overhead is minimal and MobileCirc can be used with the slowest possible connection. A few years ago, we used it at 1200 baud. These days you would never connect at a speed that slow. In order to use MobileCirc, however, your library will need to already possess or purchase a SIP2 license from your ILS vendor. If your library uses a self-check, PC reservation, or print management system, then you already have a SIP2 license. In any case, an additional SIP2 port will need to be configured for the MobileCirc application.

CONCLUSION

As for the future, it's difficult to talk about ILS circulation systems in terms of connection handshakes, security, and data transferring in a contemporaneous fashion because while I'm composing this chapter several ILS vendors are rolling out browser-based circulation clients. That is a trend that troubles some network administrators because of its inherent security weaknesses. Interestingly, those weaknesses may turn out to be allies to those wishing to connect from bookmobiles. Additionally, some ILS vendors are offering, cajoling, or forcing customers into a hosted services arrangement, which could end up shifting the security burdens I have been talking about over to the ILS networking and IT staff.

If those developments don't confuse the issues sufficiently, there is also a significant move by the major operating system producers toward a programming model that distributes the processing loads differently from the desktop-centric models we see while using more familiar systems like SirsiDynix Unicorn. The development of Microsoft .Net (or Dot Net) is just one example of this trend. To the extent that the ILS vendors develop circulation software around these new models, there will be changes in the security and data transfer parameters for remote users. Let's hope that those trends make life easier for bookmobile and library system IT staff.

In closing, I hope these pages will provide some help to those considering automation or prove to be interesting reading to those who have already done so. Good luck with your future connectivity projects.

ADDITIONAL RESOURCES

Automation Glossary

Aircard: A device that uses an available USB port, PCMCIA card slot or ExpressCard slot on a portable computer in order to provide Internet access via cellular signal.

Analog: A signal type that is characterized by a series of waves. The radio waves used in mobile communications are analog signals. Analog signals can be contrasted with digital signals that are the pulse-like signals used by computers.

Baud rate: The speed at which a modem communicates, usually expressed in bits per second, as in kilobits or 1000 bits per second.

Carrier: A cellular/mobile network operator or wireless service provider. It is a company that transmits cell phone calls, signals and data through radio frequency signals to wireless device users. Verizon and AT&T are examples of carriers.

CDMA: An acronym for Code Division Multiple Access. It is a communication standard used by many carriers and in the context of this chapter, it represents a second generation technology which delivers speeds up to 115 Kbps.

Cellular Transmission Protocol: Sets of standard rules for the data representation, signaling, authentication, and error detection required to send information via radio waves within the cellular spectrum. The later generation protocols are more streamlined and reliable.

Citrix: Software designed to facilitate secure access to applications and content located on a central server.

Contention Ratio: A measure of the number of users assigned to a specific satellite transponder. Lower contention ratios generally result in superior user satisfaction.

Controller Box: The housing for the processors and main circuitry used to control a roof-mounted satellite antenna for operations such as searching, locking on, and stowing.

Data Compression: A technology that maximizes bandwidth and increases throughput speed by reducing the data element size and thereby allowing more data to be transferred in a given amount of time. The various data compression schemes are accomplished by applying complicated algorithms for breaking down and later reassembling data frames.

Data Rate: The rate of data transmission, usually expressed in kilobits per second; also referred to as line speed.

dB: The abbreviation of decibel. In the context of this chapter, decibel is used as a measure of the signal amplification factor expressed in an antenna's gain rating.

Digital: Describes electronic technology that generates, stores, and processes data in terms of two electronic states: positive and non-positive, expressed as a string of 0s and 1s. These state digits are referred to as bits.

DSL: An acronym for Digital Subscriber Line, a type of high-speed Internet connection using standard telephone wires.

EVDO: An acronym for Evolution-Data Optimized. EVDO is a third generation wireless radio broadband data standard that enables faster speeds than those available in CDMA and other second generation or "2G" services. EVDO users can expect 400 to 700 Kbps speeds.

ExpressCard: A technology designed to deliver wireless communications and other features to a suitable laptop, notebook, or desktop computer. The card differs from a regular PC card by being smaller and generally delivering improved performance.

External Antenna: A specialized device that converts radio-frequency fields into alternating current or vice-versa. In the context of this chapter, it refers to a device placed outside the vehicle for the purpose of boosting the signal to and from a cellular modem.

Geostationary Orbit: A geostationary satellite is an earth-orbiting satellite, placed at an altitude of approximately 22,300 miles directly over the equator, that revolves in the same direction the earth rotates. The term geostationary comes from the fact that such a satellite appears nearly stationary in the sky as seen by a ground-based observer.

HSDPA: An acronym for High-Speed Downlink Packet Access and is a third generation mobile telephony protocol that delivers throughput speeds of 400–700 Kbps.

Integrators and Resellers: Companies that contract with satellite equipment manufacturers and service providers to repackage, configure, and sell a composite but complete system capable of acquiring Internet access.

Kbps: Kilobits per second, a measure of data throughput or line speed.

Mobile Satellite Antenna: A self-pointing, roof-mounted dish that locks onto a communications satellite by deploying software loaded on an onboard computer or controller box.

Network Operations Center (NOC):   A place from which administrators supervise, monitor, and maintain a telecommunications network. For satellite service providers the NOC is the hub that receives signals from the satellite and relays them on to the wired Internet and then reverses the process for the reply.

Network Service Providers: A company that provides Internet backbone services to cellular and satellite broadband customers.

Onscreen Network Management Software: The proprietary graphical user interface that Verizon supplies to customers of cellular broadband service. By using it, Verizon customers can configure and monitor their Internet connections.

PCMCIA: An acronym for Personal Computer Memory Card International Association. It is a removable device, approximately the size of a credit card, that can be plugged into the card slot of a portable computer. PCMCIA devices can include modems, network cards, and hard disks.

Provisioning Hierarchy: A listing of the various suppliers of goods and services that pertain to the acquisition, installation, and ongoing use of a mobile satellite broadband setup.

Remote Desktop Control Program: A product designed for secure communications in networks using programs such as LogMeIn or PCAnywhere. With such a product one can remotely take over the desktop of a distant computer.

Satellite: In the context of this chapter, a satellite is a specialized wireless receiver/transmitter that is launched by a rocket and placed in orbit around the Earth.

Session Information Window: A tab on the desktop display of the Verizon onscreen network management screen that will give users information regarding the current speed of the network connection.

Signal Latency: A satellite signal traveling 22,300 miles up and down and then back up from the NOC and down to the bookmobile takes about 480 milliseconds. This is called signal latency.

SIP2:   An acronym for Standard Interface Protocol, Version 2. It is a protocol that was developed by 3M, Inc. in order to pass barcode information from a self-check station to a circulation system server and back.

Signal Footprint: The geographic area on Earth toward which the satellite directs its signal.

Static IP: An address that is assigned to a computer by an Internet service provider to be its permanent address on the Internet.

T1:   The most commonly used digital transmission service in the United States and Canada. It consists of 24 separate channels at an overall rate of 1.544 million bits per second.

Terminal Services: A feature of the Microsoft Windows Terminal Server program that allows remote users to access applications running on a central server.

Throughput: In data transmission, throughput is the amount of data moved successfully from one place to another in a given time period.

USB: An acronym for Universal Serial Bus, a connection port that supports Plug and Play installation. Using USB, you can connect and disconnect devices without shutting down or restarting your computer. A USB port is usually located on the back of your computer near the serial or parallel port.

View Angle: An unobstructed line of sight view from a satellite antenna to its designated satellite that will allow for the proper elevation, azimuth, and skew of the antenna in order to successfully lock onto the satellite.

VPN Client: An acronym for Virtual Private Network, a private network that encompasses encrypted and authenticated links across public networks. VPN connections can provide access and routed connections to private networks over the Internet.

Automation Vendor Contact List

AT&T Wireless
866-429-7222
www.wireless.att.com

AVL Technologies
130 Roberts Street
Asheville, NC 28801
828-250-9950
www.avltech.com

C-Com Satellite Systems, Inc.
2574 Sheffield Road
Ottawa, Ontario K1B 3V7
Attn: Jim Ferris
877-463-8886 Ext. 4975
jferris@c-comsat.com
www.c-comsat.com

Farber Specialty Vehicles
7052 American Parkway

Columbus, Ohio 43068
Attn: Martin Marek
800-331-3188
mmarek@farberspecialty.com
www.farberspecialty.com

Gilat Satellite Networks
www.gilat.com

HughesNet
888-667-5537
www.hughesnet.com

iDirect, Inc.
13865 Sunrise Valley Drive
Herndon, Virginia 20171
Attn: Genevieve Gwei
703-648-8051
ggwei@idirect.net
www.idirect.net

Integrated Technology Group
500 Miller Court East
Norcross, Georgia 30071
Attn: Scott Hackstadt
800-207-3127
scott@integratedtek.com
www.integratedtek.com

Kyocera
10300 Campus Point Drive
San Diego, CA 92121
800-349-4188
www.kyocera-wireless.com/wireless

Matthews Specialty Vehicles, Inc.
101 South Swing Road
Greensboro, North Carolina 27409
Attn: Dennis Hoag
www.msvehicles.com

MobilSat Satellite Technologies
1500 Technology Drive, Suite 102
Chesapeake, Virginia 23320
Attn: Walter Sims
757-312-8300 Ext. 307
wsims@mobilsat.com
www.mobilsat.com

MotoSat
1955 South Milestone Drive
Salt Lake City, Utah 84104
800-247-7486
www.motosat.com

OBS, Inc.
1324 West Tuscarawas Street
PO Box 6210
Canton, Ohio 44706
Attn: Barb Ferne
barbferne@obcinc.net
www.obsinc.net

Sierra Wireless
2290 Cosmos Court
Carlsbad, CA 92011
760-476-8700
www.sierrawireless.com

TracStar Systems
2400 North Orange Blossom Trail
Orlando, Florida 32808
www.tracstar.net

Verizon Wireless
800-899-4249
www.verizonwireless.com

Wilson Electronics
3301 E. Deseret Drive
St. George, Utah 84790
800-204-4104
sales@wilsonelectronics.com
www.wilsonelectronics.com

ADDITIONAL READINGS

Richard Charpentier, *Digital RV* (Morrisville, NC: LuLu.com, 2007).

E. Phil Haley, *Over-the-Road Wireless for Dummies* (Hoboken, NJ: Wiley, 2006).

Michael J. O'Farrell, *Mobile Internet for Dummies* (Hoboken, NJ: Wiley, 2008).

Appendix A

Association of Bookmobile and Outreach Services Guidelines (2008)

PART I. BOOKMOBILE/OUTREACH SERVICES PROGRAM GUIDELINES

Section 1. Administration of the Bookmobile/Outreach Services Program

1.1 Management: The Bookmobile/Outreach Services program is managed with criteria equivalent to branch or other library program management criteria.

The bookmobile/outreach services program meets this guideline if:

1.1.1 Proper planning for bookmobile/outreach services, including the development of the library mission statement, goals, objectives and procedures, is done to identify community needs and includes the various roles which the bookmobile/outreach services can effectively play in meeting these needs.

1.1.2 Bookmobile/outreach services staff members are included in all library planning activities.

1.1.3 Bookmobile/outreach services planning, both initial and ongoing, is based on such factors as monitoring demographics and use patterns, levels of need and public demand, as well as utilizing cooperative partnerships with local agencies and schools to determine underserved areas and populations with special needs who would be best served by bookmobile/outreach services.

1.2 Funding: Bookmobile/outreach services should be adequately funded.

A library meets this guideline if:

1.2.1 Bookmobile/outreach services program has an operating and materials budget adequate to meet the needs of targeted service populations.

1.2.2.1 Bookmobile/outreach services costs are documented, as are other system costs, and included in long-range library planning.

ABOS
ASSOCIATION OF BOOKMOBILE
AND OUTREACH SERVICES

1.2.2.1.1   A vehicle replacement fund is part of the library budget. The fund should be no less than 10 percent of the cost of a suitably sized vehicle. Because the cost of maintenance increases and vehicle reliability diminishes annually, 12 years is a reasonable life span.

1.2.3   Appropriate physical facilities to house the bookmobile/outreach services program are provided. A library meets this guideline if:

1.2.3.1   Office space, not including space for collections, and equipment provided for each bookmobile/outreach services staff member, is equivalent to the space and equipment provided to other library staff.

1.2.3.2   Bookmobile/outreach services vehicle parking facilities meet federal OSHA (Occupational Safety and Health Act), state, or Canadian/provincial, and other applicable standards. Parking facilities allow staff to carry out bookmobile/outreach services tasks without interference from or to other library activities.

1.2.3.3.1   Garage doors are of adequate height, preferably at least 14 feet, automatic and secure. A heated, covered, well-drained drive-through garage that is large enough for easy docking and loading of vehicles and facilities for washing, cleaning and maintenance of bookmobile/outreach services vehicles is optimal.

1.2.4   Funding is adequate to include bookmobile/outreach services in major library-wide programming and provide circulation systems equivalent to those in library branches.

1.3   Staffing and Supervision: The bookmobile/outreach services staffing is organized to provide personnel adequate to carry out the objectives of the program.

A library meets this guideline if:

1.3.1   Requirements for the employment and training of bookmobile/outreach services staff are comparable to those of other departments with similar responsibilities.

1.3.1.1   A current written job description for each position is provided.

1.3.1.2   At least one staff member per vehicle has a post high school education, [four year college degree] and a minimum of one year of public library experience.

1.3.1.3   A librarian with a master's degree from a program accredited by the American Library Association, or its equivalent in experience in bookmobile/outreach services, is advisable at the administrative level.

1.3.2   A minimum of two staff members work on the bookmobile during all service hours.

1.3.3   All bookmobile/outreach staff are trained in basic reference work and readers advisory, along with necessary clerical duties.

1.3.4   Administrative staff makes on site visits and uses the same criteria for program and staff evaluation used in other departments.

1.4   Stops: Criteria for establishing and maintaining bookmobile stops.

A bookmobile schedule reflects the bookmobile service program and is designed to place the bookmobile where convenience, location, and time will potentially maximize use by customers.

The bookmobile schedule meets this guideline if the following factors have been considered:

1.4.1   Appropriate service hours are provided for each segment of the targeted service area, e.g., after-school hours for children, evening and/or weekend hours for most adults, senior facilities and day cares.

1.4.2   Stops are scheduled, as often as feasible, with a minimum duration of one half-hour, to provide continuity and establish a use pattern.

1.4.3   Evaluation of bookmobile stops is essential and ongoing.

1.4.3.1   Schedule changes are made in response to changes in circulation and customer usage, seasonal stops, etc.

1.5   Collection development: The collection development and materials access policy for bookmobile/outreach services operations meets the needs determined in the bookmobile/outreach services program mission statement and is consistent with the written board-approved goals of the library. The bookmobile/outreach services collection development policy serves as a guideline for the selection, ordering, and retention of materials and provides for access to materials not immediately available on the bookmobile.

1.5.1   An attractive, available collection of high interest materials in a variety of formats (books, large-print books, books-on-tape, videos, DVDs, compact discs (CDs), periodicals, etc.) for both current and retrospective materials for both recreational and informational needs of the bookmobile/outreach services customers is provided.

        1.5.1.1   The collection consists of a dedicated core collection, supplemented by reserve services from other library collections and interloans, or is supplied and restocked primarily from other library collections.

    1.5.2   Person(s)/position(s) responsible for selection and maintenance of materials are clearly identified, and decisions are based on expressed bookmobile/outreach services customer interests and professional selection criteria.

        1.5.2.1   Provision is made for input into the selection process by bookmobile/outreach services staff having personal contact with the public. Liberal request/reserve policies are strongly encouraged.

    1.5.3   A separate bookmobile collection is preferred for reasons such as ease of access during restocking and filling of requests.

        1.5.3.1   Where a separate collection is not utilized, sufficient staff time should be allotted for restocking and filling of requests.

1.6   Marketing/Public Relations: The marketing and publicizing of the bookmobile/outreach services program is a part of the overall library program and is designed to reach potential customers throughout the library services area.

    1.6.1   Bookmobile schedules are made available in all libraries and at all library-sponsored programming.

    1.6.2   All library brochures, newsletters, bookmarks, and any other library publications include bookmobile/outreach services information.

    1.6.3   Bookmobile/outreach services information is included on the library website.

    1.6.4   Bookmobile/outreach services programs are included in any cooperative community information distribution. (e.g. radio and television programs, church and school bulletins, government agencies, service clubs, etc.)

1.7   Bookmobile/outreach services programming may include story hours, public speaking, community events, parades, book talks, etc.

Section 2. Bookmobile Public Service

2.1   Bookmobile circulation services are comparable to services at branches.

    2.1.1   Bookmobile/outreach services statistics are maintained which are comparable to library wide statistics.

2.1.2   All library collections, including books, audiovisual materials, software, realia, and other items are available to bookmobile patrons on a comparable basis as to all other customers.

2.1.3   Circulation rules and procedures are comparable for all library customers.

2.1.4   Bookmobile/outreach services customer requests and reserves are given the same priority as other requests and reserves.

Section 3. Bookmobile Emergency Procedures

3.1   Bookmobile emergency procedures are comparable to emergency procedures at the main library.

PART II: BOOKMOBILE/OUTREACH SERVICES VEHICLE CONSTRUCTION AND MAINTENANCE GUIDELINES

Section 1. Bookmobile/Outreach Services Vehicle Construction Guidelines

This section provides broad guidelines for the construction of a bookmobile/outreach services vehicle. The intent is to provide advice for those designing a vehicle to meet local needs for service. Where United States requirements are cited, Canadian users should reference appropriate Canadian standards. Specific citations are to current and successor government or industry standards.

Construction of a bookmobile/outreach services vehicle is comparable to that of a fixed library facility. A similar planning process should be followed. This section is not intended to be comprehensive. There are too many variations in vehicle design and chassis for such an approach. Relevant codes or regulations, such as the National Electric Code (NEC), Occupational Safety and Health Agency (OSHA), the Department of Transportation (DOT), state motor vehicle codes, Federal Motor Vehicle Safety Standards (FMVSS) in the United States or the Canadian Motor Vehicle Safety Standards (CMVS) in Canada, Underwriters Laboratory (UL), etc., should be followed whether or not they are specifically cited in these guidelines. New standards and amendments, routinely issued by the National Highway Traffic Safety Administration in the United States, will appear in the *Federal Register*. In Canada, the library's provincial ministry of transportation should be contacted for up-to-date information. Where questions arise, it is strongly recommended that a professional engineer who has bookmobile or similar expertise and who is a member of the Society of Automotive Engineers be contacted.

1.1   A bookmobile/outreach services vehicle should be of a size and configuration designed to facilitate its proposed specific use as determined by the bookmobile/outreach services program for which it is being designed. Program variables include intended customers, proposed numbers and types of materials, access, collection, desired storage space, automation, etc. Most added features, also, have an impact on vehicle size or holdings.

1.2 The following components are determined in relation to the bookmobile's intended function:

    1.2.1 Chassis. The chassis must be adequate to support vehicle weight and to support features made necessary by law, good engineering practice, standard specifications, ease of accessibility for maintenance and to meet program objectives.

    1.2.2 Payload weight. One pound per book is standard for estimating payload weight.

    1.2.3 Gross vehicle weight. Determine loaded weight by adding the estimated payload weight to the proposed vehicle weight.

    1.2.4 Wheelbase. It is preferable that at least 55 to 60 percent of the total vehicle length is covered by wheelbase.

    1.2.5 Axle-front.

    1.2.6 Axle-rear.

    1.2.7 Brakes. All braking systems must comply with FMVS- I05 or 121 and manufacturers recommendations for design, including air brakes.

    1.2.8 Alternator. Sized to meet the vehicle needs.

    1.2.9 Engine.

    1.2.10 Fuel tank.

    1.2.11 Fuel. The type of fuel used should be selected relative to its availability. Use of the same fuel for the engine and generator is recommended.

    1.2.12 Steering Power. Assisted/integral power steering is recommended.

    1.2.13 Transmission. Automatic 3-4 speed is recommended.

    1.2.14 Tires. Steel belted, sized and rated to match chassis weight and axle ratings are recommended.

    1.2.15 Battery(s). Sized to meet the vehicle and generator needs.

    1.2.16 Springs/Suspension. Must conform to chassis gross vehicle weight (GVW) ratings.

    1.2.17 Tow hooks. Front and rear tow hooks are recommended.

    1.2.18 Vehicle frame. Seamless box channel, carbon-steel channel or their equivalent are recommended.

    1.2.20 Radiator/Cooling. Must be adequate for climate and terrain.

    1.2.21 Horn.

1.2.22   Wiring. Wires should be bundled and labeled and be of a continuous color their full length to conform to or exceed current standards of the Society of Automotive Engineers or Underwriters Laboratories, Inc. *National Electrical Code* as required. A diagram should be provided to the purchaser.

1.2.23   Undercoating. The entire underside of the body, including floor components, sides and panels below floor level and exterior compartments, should be coated with fire-resistant rubber base, or other approved material applied by spray method.

1.3   A bookmobile/outreach services vehicle must have a body coordinated with above chassis selection, designed to meet program needs and be durable, attractive, functional and comfortable for staff and customers.

A bookmobile/outreach services vehicle body/shell meets this guideline if, with program-related exceptions, it responds to the following:

1.3.1   Dimensions maximize usable space.

1.3.2   Inside height is maximized.

1.3.3   Inside width meets program needs.

1.3.4   Space from the rear of the vehicle to driver's seat is maximized.

1.3.5   Exterior side panels are made of aluminum, steel, or fiberglass with structurally sound wood or metal framing.

1.3.6   Floor is protected from dust, dirt and road deterioration.

1.3.7   Roof is leak proof.

1.3.8   Doors are customized to meet program and safety needs.

1.3.9   Windows are placed and sized to meet program and safety needs.

1.3.10   Steps/ramps are built-in, added-on or provided in size and configuration to safely meet program needs.

1.3.11   Wheelchair lift or other accessibility equipment meets the regulations of the Americans with Disabilities Act or the Canadian equivalent, if it is applicable to the program.

1.3.12   Handrails are strategically located both inside and out to meet needs of all customers.

1.3.13   Warning signals are provided to alert the driver when the steps are down, shoreline cables are in use, satellite antennas are deployed, etc.

1.3.14   All doors, exterior compartments, and wheel wells are tightly sealed against dust.

1.3.15   A minimum of two inches of insulation, fiberglass or equivalent, are applied to roof, floor and wall panels to meet insulation needs relevant to climate.

1.3.16   Exterior lettering and painting reflect a quality library image.

1.3.17   Exterior lighting includes, at a minimum, lighting at each door.

1.4   Interior furnishings and floor plan must reflect program needs.

A bookmobile/outreach services' interior design meets this guideline if it responds to the following:

1.4.1   Floor plan reflects program needs, maximizing use of the interior space available.

1.4.2   Shelving design fully utilizes available wall space.

1.4.2.1   Standard shelving can be either fixed or adjustable with a minimum of 10″ between shelves attached at a 15-degree angle for sidewall shelves and a 20-degree angle for rear shelves.

1.4.2.2   Special shelving needs (e.g., periodicals, AV, pamphlets, etc.) are included in shelving design.

1.4.3   Special features such as bulletin boards, closets, added storage space, screen, seats, etc., and their location are included in the interior design.

1.4.4   Workstations in the vehicle are designed to accommodate all anticipated circulation, staff and customer needs.

1.4.5   Lighting must be provided, preferably by two banks of fluorescent lighting running lengthwise.

1.4.5.1   Auxiliary 12 volt back-up lighting is included in the interior design.

1.5   Provide heating and air conditioning. The vehicle must have a heating, ventilation and air-conditioning system adequate to maintain a comfortable temperature year-round with the doors in use. Technical details will vary significantly with vehicle design, size and program. A vehicle meets this guideline if it responds to the following:

1.5.1   Climate control systems are designed to meet anticipated heating and/or cooling needs and for ease of maintenance.

1.5.1.1   Heaters

1.5.1.2   Air conditioners

1.5.2   Auxiliary systems for auxiliary temperature control are provided where applicable in the vehicle design (e.g., heat strips, cab heater and air conditioner, etc.).

1.6   Provide an appropriately installed power supply to meet current and anticipated electrical needs for lighting, heating, air conditioning, outlets for computers and other equipment, etc. This requirement may be met through a combination of "on vehicle equipment" and "off vehicle" power. The power supply meets this guideline if:

    1.6.1   On-vehicle power supply (solar panels, LP gas, diesel and gasoline powered generators, etc.) are properly sized to meet design requirements program needs.

        1.6.1.1   An adequately sized and accessible generator storage compartment, preferably with a slide out tray, is provided.

    1.6.2   Off-vehicle power is supplied using a properly sized shoreline power cord up to 35 feet in length, plugged into an appropriate electrical supply.

        1.6.2.1   An adequately sized shoreline storage compartment is included in vehicle design.

1.7   Provide a safe, comfortable driver's area, have necessary instruments, and equipment to meet all federal and state motor vehicle codes and regulations and be capable of utilization for public service as needed. The cab meets this guideline if:

    1.7.1   The driver and passenger seats are fully adjustable.

    1.7.2   Required safety equipment is provided (e.g. fire extinguishers, first aid kits, safety triangles, etc.).

    1.7.3   A two-way communication device is provided (e.g. cell phones, etc).

1.8   Consider optional equipment, to enhance the service program. Options listed below are among those utilized for specific programs and should be considered:

    1.8.1   Inside and outside speakers for radio/tapes/CDs.

    1.8.2   Engine block heaters on diesels.

    1.8.3   Low water/oil alarm.

    1.8.4   Wheel chair lift or ramp, as appropriate and feasible.

    1.8.5   Side mirrors adjustable from cab interior.

    1.8.6   Cruise control.

    1.8.7   Cross over switch to allow engine battery to start generator and vice versa.

    1.8.8   Floodlights on street side.

    1.8.9   Storage for toolbox containing minor tools.

1.8.10   Rear closed circuit TV.

1.9   Important miscellaneous items are addressed:

    1.9.1   Terms of pick up or delivery of the vehicle are agreed upon in advance to the satisfaction of both buyer and vendor.

    1.9.2   Vendor provides warranties of a standard nature. At delivery, written and verbal instructions on operation and maintenance of vehicle and components are provided.

    1.9.3   Inspections of the vehicle on an agreed-upon schedule by library staff or representatives throughout the construction of the vehicle. Appropriate times for inspection by the purchaser are:

        1.9.3.1   At chassis delivery.

        1.9.3.2   During floor and wall framing.

        1.9.3.3   During interior completion.

        1.9.3.4   Before delivery (final inspection).

        1.9.4.5   Areas for special consideration at inspection.

            1.9.4.5.1   Seals at openings and body seals for leakage.

            1.9.4.5.2   All functioning equipment, outlets and instruments.

            1.9.4.5.3   Exhaust system.

            1.9.4.5.4   Proper door and window function.

            1.9.4.5.5   Shelving.

            1.9.4.5.6   Generator/auxiliary power supply.

            1.9.4.5.7   Furnishings.

        1.9.4.6   Final payment is not made before all specifications are met.

Section 2. Bookmobile/Outreach Services Vehicle Maintenance is essential to a reliable bookmobile program.

2.1   All maintenance and warranty documents should be followed.

2.2   A schedule of maintenance for the vehicle and generator is developed and followed.

    2.2.1   Daily vehicle maintenance.

        2.2.1.1   Check the vehicle for safety items such as the brakes, tires, horn, windshield wipers and lights as well as the recommended fluids.

2.2.2   Periodic vehicle maintenance.

    2.2.2.1   A convenient garage and reliable mechanics able to work on the bookmobile should be assured.

    2.2.2.2   Manufacturers' documents that spell out recommended periodic maintenance checkpoints must be followed.

    2.2.2.3   Drivers are required to note and report unusual noises or variances from the vehicle's normal operation.

2.2.3   Generator maintenance.

    2.2.3.1   A convenient garage and reliable mechanics able to work on the generator should be assured.

    2.2.3.2   The generator will have maintenance recommendations similar to the vehicle. These recommendations should be followed scrupulously.

Appendix B

Sample Bookmobile Specifications

YOUR LIBRARY

Bookmobile Specifications (for a 34' rear engine bus style unit)

Version 1.0

Released: Date

Project #: Number

Prepared for: Outreach Manager
Your Library
Any Town, USA

© **Specialty Vehicle Services, LLC. 2008**

W196 S8406 Plum Creek Blvd.
Muskego WI 53150
P: 262.679.9096
F: 262.679.2066
www.vehiclesuccess.com

1. GENERAL SPECIFICATIONS

1.1 Scope

1.1.1   The intent of this specification is to describe the construction of one (1) 34–35 foot (approximate) long, heavy duty, rear engine transit style bus into a Bookmobile for use by Your Library ("Library"). The unit shall be built on a 36,200 lb. GVWR chassis for adequate support of the body, conversion, and diversified collection of approximately 4,000 items.

1.1.2   The Bookmobile described herein is intended to provide contemporary mobile library services to a broad mix of patrons, including the elderly and children, in an operationally efficient manner. The unit will operate within a suburban environment in northeastern Illinois and shall be designed and equipped to operate safely in an environment of relatively flat, paved roadways. Expected routes for this vehicle are an average of 3000 miles annually on a 30–35 hour weekly schedule. The unit will be kept in the Library garage when not in service. The approximate temperature range of this area is 12°F to 85°F, with occasional winter temperatures falling to -5°F to -20°F.

1.1.3   It is the Library's utmost goal to ensure that the Bookmobile is well-equipped to operate efficiently and safely in this environment.

1.1.4   The successful vendor shall furnish all materials not specifically denoted as "customer supplied," as well as the labor to complete the conversion of the Bookmobile specified herein, as shown on the attached drawings, or as required to complete and/or exceed the general intent of these specifications.

1.1.5   These specifications have been developed by Specialty Vehicle Services, LLC ("SVS"), under contract with the Library.

1.2 Brand Names

1.2.1   Any reference to a specific manufacturer or make or model of product not followed by "or equivalent" or "or equal" may not be substituted. The particulars listed within this specification shall be considered minimal, and the vendor is expected to increase them where necessary to meet or exceed the general intent.

1.3 Contacts

1.3.1   All *contractual* correspondence shall be directed to:

Your Library
Attn: Outreach Manager
Any Town, USA
Phone:

Fax:
Email:
Web:

1.3.2   All *technical* correspondence shall be directed to:

Specialty Vehicle Services, LLC.
Attn: Michael Swendrowski
W196 S8406 Plum Creek Blvd.
Muskego, WI 53150
Phone: 262.679.9096
Fax: 262.679.2066
Email: mswendrowski@vehiclesuccess.com
Web: http://www.vehiclesuccess.com

1.4   Manuals and Documentation

1.4.1   The following shall be provided for each unit at the time the equipment is delivered:

1.4.1.1   Two (2) each technical service manual sets for the chassis, body, generator, and each component installed. Vendor shall include all manufacturer updates for the first year of service.

1.4.1.2   Two (2) each visual parts books or two (2) CD ROM sets if books are not available for the body, chassis, and generator.

1.4.1.3   One (1) line set for chassis.

1.4.1.4   Two (2) complete sets of conversion electrical schematics "as delivered".

1.4.1.4.1   *Electrical schematics shall be provided for review prior to scheduling of final inspection.*

1.4.1.5   One (1) certified IL weight ticket issued at point of entry; front, rear and total.

1.4.1.6   Five (5) complete key sets (ignition, doors, auxiliary locks, compartments, fuel); maximum keys per set shall be five (5).

1.4.1.7   One (1) complete dimensional layout drawing of interior front, rear, and both sides.

1.5   New Equipment

1.5.1   Equipment shall be new (unused), and of manufacturer's current model year production, and shall comply with all applicable Federal environmental, motor vehicle, and safety regulations. The conversion shall be equipped with all features and accessories considered standard for the make and model vehicle/equipment provided as well as those specifically detailed within this specification.

1.6   Quality & Standards

1.6.1   Conversion accessories shall be built and assembled in accordance with the specifications and shall conform to the best standard practices in the industry at the time of construction. All dimensions, weight, and performance values shall be in accordance to SAE J732c and J742b, as last revised. The vendor will provide all systems integration and testing. All electronics will be installed, fully operational, and tested by the vendor. The vehicle shall be equipped with all features and accessories considered standard for the make and model vehicle/equipment provided.

1.6.2   All equipment and construction methods shall meet all applicable regulations of the Occupational Safety and Health Act (OSHA), Federal Motor Vehicle Safety Standards (FMVSS), Department of Transportation (DOT), National Electrical Code (NEC), Federal and State noise and pollution control restrictions, and all other applicable local, state and/or federal regulations in effect at the time of execution.

1.6.3   All workmanship, welding, and construction shall be in the best manner of the trade. Workmanship shall be subject to inspection and approval by the Library.

1.6.4   Welding fillets shall have good penetration, good fusion, good appearance, and shall show no cracks or undercutting.

1.7   Guarantee

1.7.1   The successful vendor shall furnish a warranty stating that the equipment is suitable for the service intended in accordance with the specifications. The vendor shall also furnish the Library with a minimum FULL ONE (1) YEAR WARRANTY and shall agree to replace and install without charge, within the warranty, any defective part or parts not suitable for the service intended or found to be defective due to poor workmanship. The proposal will be weighted toward longer warranties and vendor is encouraged to offer, as an option, any available extended warranties with related literature and their costs. Warranty period shall start on the date the unit is put into service by the Library.

1.7.2   All warranty work shall be repaired by the vendor at the Library facility or preauthorized service facility. The Library reserves the right to schedule and complete warranty work at a local facility of its choice if requests for resolution are not satisfied in a reasonable time frame. Vendor shall be given proper notice of such intent prior to execution and an invoice shall be forwarded to the vendor for payment.

1.7.3   That the Library may be assured of being able to maintain and repair equipment purchased, there shall be a local service facility with a stock of repair parts identified with the vendor's proposal. These specifications also require that common wear parts such as filters and hoses be available within 24 hours and all other parts within 48 hours.

1.7.4   Proposal shall list names, locations, and contact information for the nearest authorized service, parts, and warranty facilities. This list shall include facilities related to bus/chassis, generator, conversion, etc.

1.7.5   Any and all extended warranty options applicable to this vehicle and its components shall be listed within vendor's proposal with associated costs.

1.8   Inspections

1.8.1   The Library may make inspection visits during the vehicle conversion to help ensure specification compliance and trouble-free delivery. If the equipment/vehicle(s) is inspected after delivery and rejected because of deficiencies, it shall be the vendor's responsibility to pick up the vehicle, make the necessary corrections, and redeliver the vehicle for inspection and acceptance. Payment and/or the commencement of a discount period (if applicable) will not be made until the defects are corrected and the vehicle

1.8.1.1   SVS Inspections. Equipment/vehicle(s) shall be inspected at vendor's place of business once before delivery by an authorized representative of SVS for workmanship, appearance, proper functioning of all equipment and systems, and conformance to all other requirements of this specification. If deficiencies are detected, the vehicle will be rejected and the vendor will be required to make the necessary repairs, adjustments, or replacements. The costs of this trip shall be the responsibility of SVS.

1.8.1.2   Library Inspection. Equipment/vehicle(s) shall be inspected at vendor's place of business at any time during the conversion process by authorized representative(s) of the Library. These inspection(s) may or may not be in conjunction with SVS inspections. The cost of these trips shall be the responsibility of the Library.

1.9   Training

    1.9.1   Vendor shall provide in-service training and familiarization for operators and maintenance personnel. Training shall be conducted by factory-trained personnel and shall be comprehensive enough to allow Library staff to operate and maintain the equipment provided with maximum safety and design efficiencies.

        1.9.1.1   Training shall occur at the Library facilities at the time of delivery and last approximately 8 hours.

2. VEHICLE SPECIFICATIONS

2.1   Intent

    2.1.1   It is the intent of the following section to describe the type of vehicle that shall be used for the Bookmobile. Accessories and construction techniques not specifically mentioned herein, but necessary to furnish a complete unit ready for immediate use shall also be included.

2.2   Type

    2.2.1   The chassis shall be a 2008 or current model year Thomas Built Buses, Blue Bird, or equivalent heavy duty forward control rear engine transit type bus. The chassis, body and accessories shall be built and assembled in accordance with the specifications and shall conform to the best standard practices in the industry at the time of construction.

2.3   Capacities/Dimensions

2.3.1	Overall exterior length:	34' 3"–35' 5" (approximate).
2.3.2	Overall exterior width:	94"–96" (excluding mirrors).
2.3.3	Overall exterior height:	12' 6" (including rooftop ACs).
2.3.4	Interior height:	84" minimum.
2.3.5	Interior width:	92".
2.3.6	Wheelbase:	209"–217".
2.3.7	Ground Clearance:	12" (minimum).
2.3.8	Fuel tank capacity:	60.00 gallons.
2.3.9	GVWR:	36,200 lbs. (approximate).

2.4   Chassis

    2.4.1   Engine

        2.4.1.1   Cummins ISB-220 or equivalent, in-line six-cylinder, 4-cycle, 220HP @ 2600 rpm, 520 lb.vft. torque @ 1600 rpm.

2.4.1.2   Engine shall be capable of running on #2 diesel or ultra low sulfur diesel, or bio-diesel fuel (B20) at user's discretion with no modifications.

2.4.1.3   2007 EPA/CARB emission certification.

2.4.1.4   Electronic cruise control.

2.4.1.5   Engine oil drain plug, magnetic.

2.4.1.6   Engine shutdown system.

2.4.1.7   Fuel/water separator and fuel filter in single assembly; with water-in-fuel sensor mounted on engine.

2.4.1.8   Air cleaner restriction indicator, air cleaner mounted.

2.4.1.9   Electronic road speed governor; set to 65MPH max.

2.4.1.10   Engine oil filter, spin-on type.

2.4.1.11   Wct type cylinder sleeves.

2.4.1.12   28" diameter, 8-blade fan.

2.4.1.13   Aluminum radiator, 814 sq. in., CAC 381 sq. in. Radiator shall be accessible through hinged service door.

2.4.1.14   Single element paper type air cleaner.

2.4.1.15   High-idle engine speed control, dash mounted.

2.4.1.16   Denso starting motor without thermal over crank protection.

2.4.1.17   Single, horizontal exhaust system with after-treatment device.

> 2.4.1.17.1   *System shall be modified to merge the generator exhaust and exit through a vertical stack, rear corner of the body on the street side of the unit.*

2.4.2   Transmission and Equipment

2.4.2.1   Allison 2500 PTS or equivalent, 5-speed automatic.

2.4.2.2   5-speed automatic, non-fire emergency.

2.4.2.3   No PTO provisions.

2.4.2.4   No retarder.

2.4.2.5   Transmission-mounted oil filter and magnet in oil pan.

2.4.2.6   Allison push-button type shift control.

2.4.3   Front Axle, Suspension and Equipment

2.4.3.1   13,200 lb. rated heavy duty I-beam, integral steer axle.

2.4.3.2   Single stage, taper leaf front spring suspension, 14,000lb. capacity.

2.4.3.3   Two (2) front shock absorbers.

2.4.3.4   Tilt and telescoping steering column.

2.4.3.5   2-spoke, 18″ diameter steering wheel.

2.4.3.6   Ross TAS65 or equivalent power steering gear, 20.4 to 1 ratio.

2.4.4   Rear Axle, Suspension and equipment

2.4.4.1   23,000 lb. rated single reduction rear axle.

2.4.4.2   Rear axle drain plug; magnetic.

2.4.4.3   Variable rate rear spring rear suspension, 23,000 lb. capacity.

2.4.4.4   Two (2) rear shock absorbers.

2.4.4.5   Spicer 100 series or equivalent driveline, dynamically balanced with coated slip section and drive shaft guards.

2.4.5   Air System

2.4.5.1   Wabco dual airflow air compressor, 18.7 CFM capacity.

2.4.5.2   Four (4) air reservoirs with total capacity of 6470 cu. in.

2.4.5.2.1   One (1) shall be dedicated for air-operated accessories only.

2.4.5.3   SAE standard J884 air line system, color-coded for easy identification.

2.4.5.4   Automatic air tank drains, heated, in addition to manual drains.

2.4.5.5   Bendix AD-9 or equivalent air dryer with heater.

2.4.6   Brake System

2.4.6.1   Meritor-Wabco 4S/4M ABS or equivalent dual air s-cam air brake system, with indicator light on dash.

2.4.6.2   Spring set air release parking brake, 30 sq. in. chambers, dash-mounted control.

2.4.6.3   Parking brake lever located right of driver.

2.4.6.4   Engaged parking brake indicator light.

2.4.6.5   Parking brake alarm to sound horn if ignition is turned off with park brake not set.

2.4.6.6   Front pads–16 ½″ x 6″ x 0.85″, 378 sq. in. lining area.

2.4.6.7   Rear pads–16 ½″ x 8 5/8″ x 0.85″, 542 sq. in. lining area.

2.4.7   Frame and Equipment

    2.4.7.1   9 5/8" x 3" x ¼" high strength low alloy steel frame rails (50,000 PSI yield), with drop frame at rear engine location.

    2.4.7.2   Full width front and rear bumpers, FMVSS approved.

    2.4.7.3   Front and rear tow hooks (4 total), frame-mounted.

2.4.8   Fuel Tank and Equipment

    2.4.8.1   60-gallon top draw, rectangular steel fuel tank, center mounted, with access plate.

    2.4.8.2   Fuel filter/water separator with temperature controlled electric heater and filter restriction/change indicator.

    2.4.8.3   Reinforced nylon fuel hose throughout.

2.4.9   Front Tires, Hubs & Wheels

    2.4.9.1   Two (2) 22.5" x 8 ¼" steel, 10-stud, hub-piloted wheels.

    2.4.9.2   Two (2) Goodyear 11R22.5, 14-ply G159A tires.

    2.4.9.3   International oil-lubricated wheel bearings and seals.

    2.4.9.4   Stainless steel wheel liners with valve extensions shall be installed.

2.4.10   Rear Tires, Hubs & Wheels

    2.4.10.1   Four (4) 22.5" x 8 ¼" steel, 10-stud, hub-piloted wheels.

    2.4.10.2   Four (4) Goodyear 11R22.5, 14-ply G159A tires.

    2.4.10.3   Oil lubricated rear seals and wheel bearings.

    2.4.10.4   Stainless steel wheel liners with valve extensions shall be installed to the outboard wheels.

2.4.11   Spare Tire

    2.4.11.1   One (1) complete wheel and tire set shall be provided. *Ship loose with completed vehicle.*

2.4.12   Electrical System

    2.4.12.1   12-volt, negative grounded.

    2.4.12.2   Leece-Neville 175A minimum, with internal regulator, self-diagnostic system, aluminum housing and heavy-duty bearings.

        2.4.12.2.1   Alternator shall have a minimum idle output of 110A.

    2.4.12.3   Two (2) group 31, maintenance free 12-volt batteries, 1,520 CCA total.

2.4.12.4   Battery box, skirt mounted with slide-out tray.

2.4.12.5   SAE blade type electrical fuses.

2.4.12.6   Headlight dimmer switch integral with turn signal switch.

2.4.12.7   Dual electric horn.

2.4.12.8   Air horn, black, single trumpet, air solenoid operated, mounted behind bumper on right rail.

2.4.12.9   Parking light integral with front turn signal and rear tail light.

2.4.12.10 Halogen headlights, composite aero design for two-light system, including daytime running lights.

2.4.12.11 Electric starter switch, key-operated.

2.4.12.12 Self-canceling turn signal switch with headlight dimmer and "flash to pass" feature.

2.4.12.13 Dual motor windshield wipers with intermittent feature.

2.4.12.14 Front heater and defrosting system, 90,000 BTU, with integrated ductwork and controls.

2.4.12.15 One (1) cigar lighter.

2.4.12.16 Back up alarm, electric, 102 dBA.

2.4.12.17 Manual reset SAE type III circuit breakers with trip indicators.

2.4.12.18 Chassis wiring shall be color coded and continuously numbered.

2.4.13   Instruments and Controls

2.4.13.1   Gauge cluster (English).

2.4.13.2   Electronic speedometer.

2.4.13.3   Electronic engine oil pressure.

2.4.13.4   Electronic water temperature.

2.4.13.5   Electronic fuel.

2.4.13.6   Electronic tachometer.

2.4.13.7   Hour meter.

2.4.13.8   Odometer display; miles, trip miles, engine hours, trip hours, fault code readout.

2.4.13.9   Warning system; low fuel, low oil pressure, high engine coolant temperature, low battery voltage (visual and audible).

2.4.13.10   Allison transmission oil temperature gauge.

2.4.13.11   On-board diagnostics display of fault coded in gauge cluster.

2.4.13.12   Two (2) air gauges with low air audible indicator.

2.5   Body

2.5.1   Thomas Built Bus, Blue Bird, or Library approved equivalent.

2.5.2   34′ 3″–35′ 5″ overall length.

2.5.3   94″–96″ overall width (excluding mirrors).

2.5.4   *84″ interior height minimum.*

2.5.5   14 gauge rolled channel steel roof bows extending to bottom of skirting, 29″ OC.

2.5.6   14 gauge "C" channel steel welded floor structure.

2.5.7   20 gauge, double lapped, zinc coated steel roof sheeting, with integral drip rails and superior rust-proofing.

2.5.8   16 gauge, smooth, zinc coated steel side sheeting with superior rust-proofing.

2.5.9   2″ nominal thickness polyurethane foam insulation in ceiling and sidewalls—R14 insulation value.

2.5.10   3″ nominal thickness polyurethane foam insulation under floor—R21 insulation value. Entire underbody shall be undercoated with rubberized automotive undercoating after conversion and under floor insulation is complete.

2.5.11   Engine compartment, rear-mounted, with heat and noise barrier to interior cabin area.

2.5.12   Engine access door, top hinged, locking.

2.5.13   Front and rear mud flaps with anti-sail devices.

2.5.14   Four (4) rubber fenderettes shall be provided, one at each wheel opening.

2.5.15   Two-piece continuous curved safety plate laminated windshield. 3185 sq. in. minimum surface area with 5″ glare resistant band at top.

2.5.15.1   Windshield shall have LLumar UVShield or equivalent clear window film professionally applied to the interior surface. Film shall provide 99.9% UVA and UVB protection without distortion.

2.5.15.2   Windshield shall include two (2) 6" x 30" (approximate) tinted lexan double-articulating sun visors; one (1) mounted on each side.

2.5.15.3   Two (2) defroster/auxiliary fans with multi-speed motors and ball joint adjustment shall be provided: one (1) mounted on each side.

2.5.16   Two (2) "half-slide" windows shall be provided; one (1) each on the driver and passenger side of cockpit.

2.5.16.1   *Windows shall be emergency egress type.*

2.5.16.2   Windows shall have LLumar UVShield or equivalent clear window film professionally applied to the interior surface. Film shall provide 99.9% UVA and UVB protection without distortion.

2.5.17   FMVSS 108 lights and reflectors, *LED at all locations available*

2.5.17.1   Two (2) halogen sealed beam headlights.

2.5.17.2   Two (2) 7" LED round white back-up lights.

2.5.17.3   Four (4) 7" LED round amber directional lights; two (2) front and two (2) rear.

2.5.17.4   Two (2) LED sealed side directional lights.

2.5.17.5   LED clearance/market lights with intermediate side marker lights.

2.5.17.6   Two (2) 7" LED round red stop/tail lights.

2.5.18   Rosco integrated style heated remote-control mirrors or equivalent, with flat and convex assemblies.

2.5.19   One (1) 24,000 BTU, engine-driven dash/cab air conditioner system shall be installed and incorporated into the existing defroster ducting system.

2.5.20   Wiring shall consist of modular chassis wiring harnesses. The harnesses shall utilize sealed style connectors to provide optimal electrical connection. There shall be a harness for dash electrical, the printed circuit board connectors, and for various other systems inside the front electrical compartment. There shall be a main chassis harness connecting the front and rear of the bus. A junction box located in the engine compartment will utilize a sealed connector and a vehicle electrical center for rear circuit breakers, gauges and switches to control ignition, compartment lights and rear starting.

Multiple wiring harnesses aid in troubleshooting and provide access to the electrical system.

2.5.21   All chassis wiring is to be color coded and numbered according to a logical and intuitive wire numbering system. For extra protection, exterior (outside) harnesses are routed through convoluted tubing.

2.5.22   All cockpit switches shall be rated for 125% of load, clearly labeled and illuminated for ease of nighttime operations.

3. CONVERSION SPECIFICATIONS

3.1   Exterior

3.1.1   Two (2) 31" x 80" (approximate) passenger side "sedan type" mid entry (patron) doors placed per drawings. Doors shall be of double-wall commercial quality aluminum construction and internally insulated between inner and outer skins.

3.1.1.1   *The leading edge of the front door **must** be placed 43.5" from the centerline of the front axle for alignment with the Library's loading dock. Additionally, the centerline of the front axle shall not be further than 112" from the front bumper of the vehicle.*

3.1.1.2   Doors shall be fitted with one (1) Yale 5100 series or equivalent door closer each to control the movement of the door.

3.1.1.3   Doors shall be equipped with one (1) positive hold-open device each.

3.1.1.4   Door interiors shall be finished to complement interior.

3.1.1.5   Doors shall have deep tinted safety glass upper horizontal sliding window and deep tinted safety lower fixed-pane window.

3.1.1.6   Doors shall utilize continuous stainless steel, aluminum or similar noncorrosive type vertically-mounted hinges.

3.1.1.7   One (1) Yale push-bar "classroom" or equivalent entrance latch shall be installed on each door.

3.1.1.8   One (1) Yale 112 series or equivalent heavy-duty latch bolt shall be installed on each door, in addition to the main latch.

3.1.1.9   Step wells shall be a two-step configuration with 12" deep (approximate) treads and 9" high (approximate) risers. Each step shall incorporate heavy-duty, slip resistant commercial rubber step tread reinforced with aluminum back. The front edge of each tread shall incorporate a 2" safety yellow or white edge. Step wells shall contain 12VDC lighting to assist with entry/egress, controlled at the driver's switch panel.

3.1.1.10   Door/step well areas shall be outfitted with a total of four (4) 1.25" diameter stainless steel handrails each to provide solid entry/egress assistance.

    3.1.1.10.1   One (1) 36" approximate length handrail shall be installed vertically on the exterior, just aft of the door.

    3.1.1.10.2   Two (2) angle-mounted handrails shall be installed one each side of the step well.

    3.1.1.10.3   One (1) angle-mounted handrail shall be installed to the interior of the door below the upper window.

3.1.2   One (1) 42" x 60" (approximate) passenger side "ADA access" door shall be placed per drawings. Door shall be of double-wall commercial quality aluminum construction and internally insulated between inner and outer skins.

    3.1.2.1   Door shall be equipped with one (1) positive hold-open device each.

    3.1.2.2   Door shall have no windows.

    3.1.2.3   Door shall utilize continuous stainless steel, aluminum or similar non-corrosive type vertically-mounted hinge.

3.1.3   One (1) 26"T x 24"W (approximate) "half-slide" window shall be installed in the side wall, near the rear desk.

    3.1.3.1   Window shall be *emergency egress type*.

    3.1.3.2   Window shall be dark tinted with fiberglass screens.

3.1.4   One (1) 26"T x 24"W (approximate) "solid" window shall be installed in the rear wall.

    3.1.4.1   Window shall be an *emergency egress type*.

    3.1.4.2   Window shall be dark tinted.

3.1.5   Four (4) 14" x 22" single dome white acrylic skylights shall be installed with white PVC interior trim.

3.1.6   One (1) 24"x24" minimum Transpec or equivalent escape hatch shall be provided to allow emergency escape by personnel as well as fresh air ventilation. Hatch must conform to FMVSS 217 regarding emergency exit, window retention, and release.

3.1.7 Two (2) electric-operated, single auxiliary steps or equivalent shall be installed, one each at the entry doorways. Steps shall be finished with a non-skid surface. Steps shall utilize a single dash-mounted control switch (not door controlled).

3.1.7.1 Steps shall be modified to provide a 10-12″ step run.

3.1.7.2 Height of step shall be consistent with the overall staircase run—for smooth patron entry/egress.

3.1.7.3 Steps shall be finished with a non-skid surface and a safety yellow, non-skid front strip.

3.1.7.4 Steps shall include an audible/visual indicator system to warn the driver that the step is extended when the ignition key is activated.

3.1.7.5 Two (2) additional step assemblies shall be provided and shipped loose with the completed vehicle as "spares." These assemblies shall be identically configured to the installed units for rapid field replacement by Library staff.

3.1.7.6 *"Manually Operated" auxiliary step detail and costs, if available, shall be included in proposal for Library consideration.*

3.1.8 One (1) generator compartment shall be fabricated to mount and enclose the generator. Generator mounting shall be configured to allow easy access to the generator for service, as well as easy removal of the unit for overhauls. This compartment shall be located forward of the rear axle, driver side. *This compartment MUST maintain a minimum 12″ ground clearance.*

3.1.8.1 Compartment shall be constructed of 12-gauge galvanized steel, aluminum, or equivalent materials.

3.1.8.2 Doors shall be constructed of aluminum and vertically hinged with ¼″ pin stainless steel continuous hinges.

3.1.8.3 Doors shall have positive "compression" style, "slam latch", or equivalent latches.

3.1.8.4 Compartment and door(s), shall be insulated with Glacier Bay Barrier Ultra dB Flex and Panel or equivalent 2″ nominal thickness acoustical insulation.

3.1.8.4.1 Reference: http://www.glacierbay.com/insulation_ultradb.asp.

3.1.8.5 Generator compartment door shall be ventilated to allow ambient heat escape.

3.1.9 Two (2) general storage compartments shall be installed to house additional Library materials. Compartments shall be of maximum size available and located based on final design. These compartments shall be sealed to prevent moisture penetration.

    3.1.9.1   Compartments shall be constructed of aluminum or equivalent materials.

    3.1.9.2   Doors shall be constructed of aluminum and vertically hinged with 1/4" pin stainless steel continuous hinges.

    3.1.9.3   Doors shall have positive "compression" style, "slam latch", or equivalent latches

    3.1.9.4   *One (1) of the compartments shall be adequately sized to house winter related equipment including a snow shovel.*

3.1.10   One (1) underbody shore cord/mechanical compartment shall be installed to house the transfer switch and shore cord. This compartment shall contain provisions for resecuring the aluminum door if the shore cord is deployed.

    3.1.10.1   Compartment shall be constructed of aluminum or equivalent materials.

    3.1.10.2   Door(s) shall be constructed of aluminum and vertically hinged with 1/4" pin stainless steel continuous hinges.

    3.1.10.3   Door(s) shall have positive "compression" style, "slam latch", or equivalent latches.

3.1.11   One (1) auxiliary battery compartment shall be installed to house the auxiliary battery bank. Compartment shall contain a slide tray with positive latch and hold downs for ease of battery maintenance. Tray shall be lined with an isolation material to help prevent battery corrosion.

    3.1.11.1   Compartment shall be constructed of aluminum or equivalent materials.

    3.1.11.2   Door shall be constructed of aluminum and vertically hinged with ¼" pin stainless steel continuous hinges.

    3.1.11.3   Door shall have positive "compression" style, "slam latch", or equivalent latches.

3.1.12   Vehicle underbody shall be fully undercoated with rubberized spray to provide additional sound resonance dampening and underbody insulation protection.

3.1.13   Two (2) Yarder Manufacturing series SS-418 ad-card frame shall be installed; one (1) on the rear exterior and one (1) on the curb side exterior.

3.1.13.1 Approximate size of the rear frame shall be 28″ x 70″, subject to final overall exterior graphics design and Library approval.

3.1.13.2 Approximate size of the curb side frame shall be 28″ x 35″, subject to final overall exterior graphics design and Library approval.

3.1.14 Vehicle shall be painted dual colors per specification.

3.1.14.1 Where the vehicle is cut or modified, or additional fabricated components are added to the exterior, exposed metal shall be properly prepared and painted to match vehicle exterior color.

3.1.14.2 Panels shall be properly cleaned and prepared for paint application in accordance with standard commercial practice and to requirements of the construction materials involved. Surfaces shall be properly cleaned and inspected before cover materials are applied.

3.1.14.3 The prepared surfaces shall be spray primed with synthetic base primer, which contains corrosion resistant pigments and resins. Extra coats shall be applied around moisture catching moldings, etc. *All hidden areas such as overlapping metal, underside of moldings, underside or rubber extrusions at windows shall be cleaned and primed and where necessary caulked with sealing compound during construction.*

3.1.14.4 DuPont or equivalent basecoat/clearcoat paint shall be applied to all areas of the metal. Each coat shall be properly dried and evenly sanded before the following coat is applied. "Orange peel" surfacing will not be acceptable.

3.1.14.5 Paint colors TBD by Library after award of contract.

3.1.15 Vehicle shall have a "moderate" level vinyl graphics package in addition to the base paint. Vendor shall indicate organization or persons that the Library will work with in the development of this graphics scheme.

3.1.15.1 Vendor shall include a *$4,000 allowance* for the development, printing and installation of this graphics package within their proposal.

3.2 Interior

3.2.1 The Bookmobile interior shall be designed to accommodate a collection of approximately 4,000 items, which includes but is not limited to: books of various sizes, DVDs, CDs, books on disc, oversized materials of odd shapes, magazines, etc.

3.2.2   Since a bookmobile is a mobile library, and a quiet environment is most important in the successful operation of any library, all interior finishes shall contribute to absorbing ambient sounds. Appropriate panels, ceiling, and flooring shall have superior acoustic qualities in addition to durability and aesthetics. Sound control measures shall comply with the Occupational Safety and Health Act (OSHA) sound level (dbA) requirement in effect at time of award of contract, for an eight (8) hour maximum operator exposure time; measured at operator's ear with engine at governed RPM.

3.2.3   Floor covering shall be Heuga 6090000004, "super floor" carpet squares.

    3.2.3.1   Sub-flooring shall be properly prepared prior to installation of the floor covering.

    3.2.3.2   Carpeting shall be installed in a manner consistent with the manufacturer's recommendations.

    3.2.3.3   Any carpet remnants remaining from the carpet installation shall be shipped loose with the completed vehicle.

    3.2.3.4   The Library will select the exact color and pattern of carpet based on other interior color choices.

    3.2.3.5   Reference: http://www.heuga.com/HomePage/uk

3.2.4   Carpet runners shall be provided to apply over the main flooring. Two (2) sets of runners shall be provided, with two (2) runners per set (4 total runners) to cover as much of the main floor as feasible.

    3.2.4.1   Runners shall be of a commercial quality and have sufficient backing to prevent sliding during normal operations.

    3.2.4.2   The Library shall select color of carpet from vendor's offerings.

3.2.5   Ceiling shall be finished with a 1/2" padded fabric headliner or equivalent. Completed headliner shall have a minimal amount of exposed fasteners. Fabric and color shall be selected by the Library from vendor's offerings.

3.2.6   Cork type fabric-covered bulletin boards shall be installed wherever possible in the vehicle, including, but not limited to, all overhead cabinet doors. Number and size of bulletin boards furnished shall be determined by the exact configuration of interior. Bulletin boards shall be as large as possible and installed where space is available inside the coach. Smaller spaces and trim areas shall be finished in complementing materials. All upholstery used within the vehicle shall meet provisions of FMVSS-302.

3.2.7   Three (3) staff workstations shall be furnished as depicted in the preliminary drawings. Workstations shall be constructed of furniture-grade plywood with the same finish as that of the bookshelves. Desktop shall be constructed of minimum 3/4″ thick furniture-grade plywood with a high-impact laminated plastic bonded to the plywood and installed to allow easy removal and replacement as these surfaces are subject to excessive wear and tear. Desks shall be appropriately configured for installation of technologies by the Library, including cable pass-through grommets and defined wire paths from desktop to other locations as designated.

  3.2.7.1   Desk faces (modesty panels) shall be set 8″–10″ off the floor to allow heat circulation beneath the work surface.

  3.2.7.2   Desks shall include one (1) three-drawer cabinet below the work surface on the outboard side. Drawers shall include a positive latching mechanism.

  3.2.7.3   Rear desk shall include a 12″ lift-up extension with heavy duty hardware.

  3.2.7.4   Front desks shall have a finished height of 36″ (stand-up) and include a lower, 30″ high (sit down) positive latching sliding work surface beneath the main work surface for use while seated. Desks shall also include a 24″ lift-up bridge between them with heavy duty hardware and latching mechanism.

3.2.8   Four (4) overhead storage cabinets shall be provided; one (1) each above the three (3) staff workstations and one (1) above the rear wall window, as depicted in the preliminary drawings.

  3.2.8.1   Cabinets shall include lockable, top hinged bulletin board type doors, with mechanical stays, per final design.

3.2.9   One (1) storage closet shall be furnished as depicted in the concept drawing. Closet shall be constructed of furniture-grade plywood with the same finish as that of the bookshelves. Closet shall contain three (3) interior shelves within the corner section to maximize storage in this area and a dedicated cavity aligned with the top of the engine davenport for reserved item crate storage.

  3.2.9.1   Door shall be a lockable bulletin board.

  3.2.9.2   Closet door shall include key locks that are keyed alike to the other storage cabinets.

3.2.10 Four (4) aluminum reserve item crates shall be fabricated and provided. Crates shall be as light as possible; approximately 20.5"L x 20"W x 10"T, interlocking and stackable with hand-holds, and powder coated a complementary color. *Final design of reserve item crates shall be approved by the Library prior to fabrication.*

3.2.11 All bookshelves shall be constructed from superior grade materials and be built to withstand the unique stresses imposed by a mobile environment. The shelving layout shall be designed to accommodate approximately 4,000 items, which includes but is not limited to: books of various sizes, DVDs, CDs, videos, books on CD, oversized materials of odd shapes, magazines, etc. Shelving shall allow for easy access to body wiring and concealed components. All shelving running along the sidewalls of the coach shall slope back 15 degrees. All shelving running along the rear wall of the coach shall slope back 20 degrees. All shelves shall be a minimum 7.5 inches deep and be constructed of minimum 3/4" thick wood.

    3.2.11.1 The wood used in all vertical uprights shall be a minimum 1-inch thick. With the exception of the shelves located in the wheel well areas, all shelves shall be a maximum of 36 inches wide. With the exception of the lowest (bottom) shelves, all shelves shall be adjustable. Vertical spacing between shelves shall be on 10-1/2" centers and vertically adjustable up or down continuously on maximum 1.5" centers. The hardware used to allow adjustability shall positively secure the shelving in the selected location to prevent accidental dislodging of the shelf in transit. All wood shall be finished to "high-end" furniture quality with wood finish color chosen by the Library. Exact sizes and locations shall be authorized by the Library prior to installation.

    3.2.11.2 It is anticipated that there be a combination of standard and oversize shelves included in certain shelving sections. The oversize shelves shall include removable dividers to aid in the storage of odd size books and magazines.

    3.2.11.3 One (1) "puzzle shelf" shall be fabricated and installed as depicted in the conceptual drawings. Shelf shall be 11" deep with a 3" lip on the face to retain puzzles while in transit.

    3.2.11.4 Five (5) extra shelves shall be provided and shipped loose with the completed Bookmobile. The size of these shelves shall be determined by the Library.

3.2.11.5   One (1) hanging bag rod shall be included. Location shall be determined by the Library per finalized plans.

3.2.12   One (1) set of two (2) paperback bookcase doors shall be provided as depicted in the preliminary drawings. Doors shall conceal the ADA access doorway when not in use, but easily expose this entrance when needed, without having to remove any materials.

3.2.12.1   Doors shall have heavy-duty hardware to latch the doors in either position.

3.2.13   Three (3) paperback carousels shall be provided as depicted in the preliminary drawings. Carousels shall mount and swivel using heavy duty hardware suitable for this application. Carousels shall utilize 1/4" clear lexan on the title side of each shelf and have the ability to swivel regardless of the position of adjacent carousel.

3.2.14   One (1) CD cabinet shall be constructed as depicted in the preliminary drawings. Cabinet shall contain nine (9) pull-out trays that have been suitably constructed to hold CDROM and DVD cases.

3.2.15   Finish cabinetry and component mounting shall allow an approximate 58" aisle width.

3.2.15.1   *Final configuration of the interior shelving and cabinetry shall be subject to approval of the Library prior to installation.*

3.2.16   Two (2) display racks for flyers and brochures shall be provided and located as depicted in the concept drawing. Racks shall be capable of displaying a variety of materials and include removable dividers. Exact size shall be determined by the Library.

3.2.17   Two (2) magazine racks shall be provided as depicted in the preliminary drawings. Racks shall be of a "tiered" design with 1/4" lexan faces, allowing display of 25-35 titles each (50-70 total), and stacked one above the other within the same bookshelf section. Final design of this rack shall be subject to approval by the Library prior to construction.

3.2.18   Two (2) Bostrom high-back air-suspension seats or equivalent shall be installed for the driver and front passenger.

3.2.18.1   Seats shall have an air suspension with 6" ride zone, 9.5" of fore and aft adjustment, 2 chamber air lumbar, adjustable dampening, armrests, and 180° swivel capabilities.

3.2.18.2   Seats shall be covered in a durable fabric complementing the vehicle interior. Color shall be selected by the Library from vendor's offerings.

3.2.18.3   Seats shall be installed and include 3-point detachable seatbelt systems per FMVSS 207.

3.2.19   One (1) Bostrom high-back seat or equivalent shall be installed at the rear staff workstation per preliminary drawings.

3.2.19.1   Seat shall be fix-mounted on the engine davenport and include 9.5″ of fore and aft adjustment.

3.2.19.2   Seat shall be covered to match the front driver and passenger seats.

3.2.19.3   Seat shall be installed and include a 3-point seatbelt system per FMVSS 207.

3.3   Electrical System—AC

3.3.1   System shall be a 120/240-volt rated, single-phase type system designed to provide and distribute electrical power at a level of performance that meets the requirements of all components and/or accessories utilizing such power throughout the vehicle.

3.3.1.1   System furnished shall be designed and installed to meet all requirements of the National Electrical Code (NEC), with all system components, accessories, plugs, receptacles, switches and circuit breakers being Underwriter's Laboratories (UL) listed and approved.

3.3.1.2   System furnished shall also meet any and all applicable state code requirements and regulations pertaining to the design and installation of AC electrical systems.

3.3.2   All AC wiring shall be installed using multi-stranded, multi-conductor flexible armored or boat rated cable; 600 volt rated, UL approved or equivalent. All wire shall be color-coded and grounded throughout the system. Aluminum wire is not acceptable due to its history of involvement in electrical system fires. Since the body and chassis of a motor vehicle is constantly flexing in torsion when in use, fixed type conduit is not acceptable due to the long-term potential electrical shorting and the resulting potential of fire hazard.

3.3.2.1   Wiring and harnesses shall be installed in easily accessible locations to aid long-term serviceability and maintain a minimum 2″ air-insulated clearance from parallel low-voltage wiring harnesses per NEMA standards.

3.3.2.2   All wiring shall be sized using NEMA ratings to 125% of anticipated load.

3.3.3   One (1) Onan 12.0 HDKCD-2209, 12KW quiet diesel generator set shall be installed. Unit shall certified by the Environmental Protection Agency (EPA) to conform to Tier 2 emissions regulations, and feature Advanced Control.

3.3.3.1   Unit shall be rated for a mobile continuous 12kW per ISO 3046, ISO 8528-1, with a voltage regulation at no load/full load of +/- 0.1% and a frequency regulation at no load/full load of +/- 2.0 %.

3.3.3.2   Unit shall contain integral shut-down protection system to protect against high engine temperature, low oil pressure, loss of coolant, overcrank safety, overspeed, over/under voltage, over/under frequency and auxiliary fault.

3.3.3.3   Unit shall be controlled by the Energy Command system (*reference 3.4.11*).

3.3.3.4   Unit shall draw its fuel from the main vehicle fuel tank through a separate tap that does not allow the generator to draw the fuel level below 1/8 tank.

    3.3.3.4.1   *Engine shall be capable of running on #2 diesel or ultra low sulfur diesel, or bio-diesel fuel (B20) at user's discretion with no modifications.*

3.3.3.5   Unit shall utilize the auxiliary battery bank (*reference 3.4.14*) for starting/re-charging.

3.3.3.6   *Unit exhaust shall be merged with the vehicle's engine exhaust stack.*

3.3.3.7   Unit shall be mounted in an underbody compartment with an exterior access, ventilated aluminum door. Generator mounting compartment shall maintain a minimum 12" ground clearance.

3.3.4   One (1) 125/250VAC, 15-foot, 50A rated, 3-pole 4-wire waterproof shore cord shall be provided.

3.3.4.1   One (1) NEMA CS6364/65, twist-lock, 3 pole 4 wire weather resistant grounding inlet shall be on the street side of the vehicle for attachment of shore cord.

    3.3.4.1.1   Inlet shall include a waterproof cover for use when the cord is not attached.

3.3.4.2   One (1) NEMA CS6364/65, twist-lock, 3 pole 4 wire weather resistant grounding plug (female) shall be provided on the female end of the cord to attach to the vehicle.

3.3.4.3   One (1) NEMA 14-50P, right-angle, straight-blade, 3 pole 4 wire weather resistant grounding plug (male) shall be provided on the male end of the cord to plug the vehicle into an external source.

3.3.4.4   Shore cord shall be shipped loose with completed vehicle.

3.3.5   One (1) ATS3W50 or equivalent automatic transfer switch shall be installed to provide automatic switching between generator and shoreline power sources. Unit shall have a 24kW maximum rating and mechanical interlock to prevent any possibility of electrical feedback.

3.3.6   One (1) 100A rated distribution panel shall be installed flush-mounted in the console over the windshield.

3.3.6.1   All AC electrical circuits shall be safety-protected from short circuits and current overloading by UL-approved resetting type circuit breakers, each properly capacity-sized to the circuit they serve. A master circuit breaker that controls all AC electrical system circuits shall also be furnished.

3.3.6.2   Panel(s) shall be readily accessible, yet out of view of the general public.

3.3.7   A minimum of six (6) 15A-rated, UL listed, NEMA 5-15, three-hole grounded duplex receptacles shall be furnished inside the vehicle for general and specific uses. These receptacles shall be powered directly from the generator/shore power system and white in color.

3.3.8   A minimum of six (6) 15A-rated, UL listed, NEMA 5-15, three-hole *isolated ground* duplex receptacles shall be furnished inside the vehicle for technology use. *These receptacles shall be orange in color and backed by the inverter system.*

3.3.9   Twelve (12) 48" low-energy, electronic ballast, double-tube fluorescent light fixtures shall be mounted on the interior ceiling in two (2) continuous rows set approximately 14" off-center.

3.3.9.1   Lights shall be controlled by a 3-way circuit, with one (1) switch by the front entry door, and one (1) switch near the driver's seat.

3.3.9.2   These lights shall be *inverter backed.*

3.3.10   Three (3) Duo Therm Penguin or equivalent, 13,500 BTU low-profile air conditioners shall be installed per drawings.

3.3.10.1   Units shall provide 13,500 BTUs of cooling and 5,600 BTUs of heat.

3.3.10.2   Units shall include self-contained, low-profile ceiling assembly with remote controls.

3.3.10.3   Units shall be controlled by central thermostat in the front workstation area (*reference 3.4.19*).

3.3.10.4   Units' power consumption shall be monitored by the Energy Command 30 system (*reference 3.4.13*).

3.3.11   Three (3) Broan 114, or equivalent, 1,500 watt kick space heaters shall be installed in locations depicted on the preliminary drawings.

3.3.11.1   Units' power consumption shall be monitored by the Energy Command 30 system (*reference 3.4.13*).

3.3.11.2   Units shall be flush-mounted and controlled by the central thermostat (*reference 3.4.19*).

3.3.12   One (1) Onan 3HJBAA-3202D or equivalent, 3,000 watt inverter shall be installed.

3.3.12.1   Unit shall back the 120VAC power for the fluorescent interior lights (*reference 3.3.9*) and all isolated ground receptacles (*reference 3.3.8*).

3.3.12.2   Unit shall provide extensive diagnostic information and fault history.

3.3.12.3   Unit shall provide full AC and DC metering.

3.3.12.4   Unit shall provide 140 amps of DC charging capability for the auxiliary battery bank (*reference 3.4.14*).

3.3.12.5   Unit shall utilize and monitor the auxiliary battery bank (*reference 3.4.14*).

3.3.12.6   Unit shall be controlled by an Onan 541-1183 remote panel and installed with *ALL* available options per manufacturer specification.

3.3.12.7   Unit shall be installed within the vehicle interior, with proper ventilation, per finalized design.

3.3.13   Two (2) Elmech Q-scan Uniplex, or equivalent, people counters shall be installed; one each at each entry door.

3.3.13.1   Systems shall include magnetically activated, 4-digit 12mm high LED displays.

3.3.13.2   System shall count each person crossing the beam, regardless of the direction of approach.

3.3.13.3   Systems shall include non-volatile memories to protect against power failure.

3.3.13.4   Reference: http://www.q-scan.co.uk/uniplex.htm

3.4   Electrical System—DC/Other

3.4.1   Shall be a 12-volt, negative ground type system designed to provide and distribute electrical power at a level of performance that meets the requirements of all components and/or accessories utilizing such power throughout the vehicle.

3.4.2   Design emphasis of system furnished shall be on both reliability and serviceability. System furnished shall be a modular type design, modular being defined as a system where major power train, chassis, body component assemblies, including lighting, wiring and switch harnesses, and heater harnesses are easily separable for purposes of repair or replacement, using either simple hand tools or automotive type plug-in connectors. Special emphasis shall be made on accessibility to all wiring harnesses in all locations. Wiring shall not be rendered inaccessible behind permanently installed panels or appointments.

3.4.3   The power source for all body electrical equipment furnished shall be taken from a single point on the power train specifically designed for this purpose.

3.4.4   The main ground wire grounding the body to the chassis shall be minimum 8-gauge size; all ground wires furnished for insulated-return type systems shall be equal in size to the feed wire in the respective circuit. Redundant grounds shall be used if required to attain a satisfactory level of system performance desired. For maximum system reliability, all serrated eyelets and screws or bolts utilized at points of ground shall be either coated or plated with an electrical conductive type material to improve their resistance to corrosion.

3.4.5   All electromagnetic type switches, relays and solenoids furnished shall be suppressed to protect the entire electrical system from major damage from the large negative voltage spikes these devices can produce.

3.4.6   All auxiliary electrical circuits shall be safety-protected from current overloading by automatic resetting type heavy-duty automotive circuit breakers, each properly capacity-sized to the circuit they serve. A master circuit breaker, minimum 150-amp, shall also be furnished.

3.4.7   All terminals and connectors furnished shall be designed and approved by their manufacturer for heavy-duty automotive vocational application; material shall be a corrosion-resistant type. To eliminate disconnects, all terminals furnished shall incorporate a positive locking, seated type design to assure terminal position. Socket (female) side of connectors shall be wired to electrical source side of circuit and plug (male) side of connector shall be wired to electrical load side of the circuit to help prevent a short circuit when disconnected. All connections made on the vehicle underbody shall be adequately protected against moisture and corrosion with dielectric grease, heat shrink tubing, or other similar techniques.

3.4.8   All insulated cable furnished shall comply with SAE Standards J1127 and J1128. All wiring furnished in the engine compartment area, where extreme heat and fire are of concern, shall be multi-stranded, low-voltage insulated automotive type cross-linked polyethylene fire-retardant SAE approved SXL type. All wiring furnished in the body portion of the coach shall be multi-stranded, low-voltage insulated automotive type; either SAE approved SXL or GXL types are acceptable. All wiring in each circuit shall be of sufficient size, and with 125% capacity rating of anticipated load to transmit the electrical current load of the circuit. Sizing shall take into account the length of the circuit and the voltage drop occurring in the circuit. Voltage at the load shall be +/- 5% of rated voltage when measured in a normal operating state.

3.4.9   All wiring shall be routed meeting the following minimum requirements:

    3.4.9.1   No contact with sharp or puncturing edges.

    3.4.9.2   No tension or strain between fixed points.

    3.4.9.3   Adequate and safe clearance of moving parts.

    3.4.9.4   5" clearance from radiant heat sources.

    3.4.9.5   Adequately secured to prevent pinching.

    3.4.9.6   Wiring to be color-coded and numbered, grease-, oil- and moisture-resistant and securely fastened.

3.4.10   All wiring furnished shall be routed in protective harnesses, either woven vinyl or corrugated vinyl or nylon types acceptable. When harnesses go through metal structure, rubber grommets shall be used to further protect the integrity of the harnesses.

3.4.11   One (1) Ricon Mirage or equivalent, underbody wheelchair lift shall be installed to serve the ADA access door (*reference 3.1.2*).

    3.4.11.1   Lift shall be FMVSS and ADA compliant, with a manual back-up system.

3.4.11.2   Lift shall have a rated load capacity of 660 lbs.

3.4.11.3   Lift shall have a usable platform 48"L x 31.7"W.

3.4.12   One (1) AM/FM radio with CD player shall be installed.

3.4.12.1   Radio shall include eight (8) total deluxe *commercial quality* coaxial radio speakers; six (6) interior and two (2) weatherproof speakers mounted on exterior curbside. Speaker systems shall be switchable in the cab.

3.4.12.2   Radio shall include a public address (PA) with cab-mounted microphone and configured to allow staff to speak *over or with* music source.

3.4.12.3   Shall include exterior mounted AM/FM antenna.

3.4.13   One (1) Onan Energy Command 30 power management system shall be installed.

3.4.13.1   System shall provide main and auxiliary battery monitoring.

3.4.13.2   System shall provide generator monitoring including: digital hour meter, manual start/stop switch with digital readout, service reminders, and diagnostic text messages.

3.4.13.3   System shall provide automatic generator starting functions including: programmable "quiet time", look-ahead battery top-off feature prior to the "quiet time", auto start/stop on low/full battery, auto start/stop for up to three air conditioning systems, and built-in memory for all programmable settings.

3.4.13.4   System shall feature a safety start inhibit feature.

3.4.13.5   *System shall be installed with **ALL** options per manufacturer specification and fully tested prior to delivery.*

3.4.14   Four (4) Interstate USRM8D, or equivalent, group 8D, 12V *deep-cycle*, multi-purpose batteries shall be provided as an auxiliary battery bank for stationary 12VDC component power.

3.4.14.1   Both the vehicle alternator and the inverter/charger shall charge these batteries.

3.4.14.2   A heavy-duty battery isolation system shall be installed to allow charging of both the main and auxiliary battery banks from the vehicle alternator only when the engine is running.

3.4.14.3   A battery merge system including dash-mounted momentary switch shall be incorporated to allow jumping of one battery system to the other without the use of external cables.

3.4.14.4   Batteries shall be installed within the underbody battery compartment with a positive hold-down system.

3.4.15   One (1) Audiovox 1600056 or equivalent, LCD color observation system shall be installed. It shall have a vibration and shock resistant mounting, waterproof, and a minimum viewing angle of 114 degrees horizontal and 90 degrees vertical. Monitor's controls shall include instant on, day/night sensitivity switch, camera selection and a standby position, which automatically changes to on when vehicle is shifted into reverse.

3.4.15.1   A 5-1/2 inch (minimum) LCD color monitor shall be mounted on the dash or in the dash for easy view of the driver.

3.4.15.2   Shall include one (1) video camera with sun shield and built-in microphones mounted to rear exterior.

3.4.16   Four (4) 12VDC fluorescent dome lamps shall be installed on ceiling to assist with nighttime entry/egress.

3.4.16.1   Lights shall be switched at both the driver's area and patron entry door on a two-way circuit.

3.4.17   Two (2) ThinLite 162 or equivalent weatherproof fluorescent outdoor area lights shall be installed; one (1) over each patron entry door.

3.4.17.1   Units shall be switched in the driver's area.

3.4.18   Eight (8) Whelen 97 series or equivalent, 8-32°, 12VDC weatherproof "scene" lights shall be installed on the exterior; 3 street side, 3 curbside, and 2 rear. Lights shall be switched in the driver's area.

3.4.18.1   Rear-mounted scene lights shall be activated by the vehicle back-up lights in addition to the driver's area switch.

3.4.19   One (1) Duo Therm Comfort Control Center thermostat shall be installed in the rear area. Unit shall utilize a series of advanced heat sensing devices to track temperatures in each of two (2) zones (front and rear) and activate heat or air conditioning as needed to maintain selected temperatures.

3.4.19.1   Unit shall be a full digital system creating up to four (4) zones from one centralized location.

3.4.19.2   Unit shall utilize a LCD readout and Intelliset technology to allow easy setting changes.

3.4.20   One (1) Aiphone AT-406, or equivalent, handset intercom system shall be installed to allow communication between the passenger side front workstation and the rear workstation.

3.4.21   One (1) Wilson Electronics 301133, 806-894MHz/1850-1990MHz spring-mount cellular antenna shall be installed as high as practical on the driver's side front, with cable run to the driver's side front desk, for connection of a customer provided Novatel Merlin S720 laptop wireless card.

> 3.4.21.1   Antenna installation shall include a Wilson 3-way mount with spade stud (#901104) and a 15' low loss cable extension (#951103). Boulevard.

3.5   Miscellaneous Components

3.5.1   One (1) SkyScan or equivalent atomic LCD clock shall be furnished, with a minimum 2-inch main character size. Unit shall include readouts for interior and exterior temperature (via wireless remote sensor), day and date, and receive its synchronization signal from NIST.

> 3.5.1.1   Clock shall be firmly and securely attached to a wall in an easy-to-see location.

> 3.5.1.2   Clock shall include a long-life premium alkaline battery, installed and running when coach is delivered.

3.5.2   High-quality pleated shades shall be provided for the two (2) rear windows, as well as the windshield(s) and side cockpit windows. Shades shall include side-mounted guide tracks and be infinitely adjustable. Shade color shall be chosen by the Library from vendor's offerings.

3.5.3   One (1) battery-operated carbon monoxide (CO) detector shall be installed on the interior ceiling.

3.5.4   One (1) battery-operated smoke detector shall be installed on the interior ceiling.

3.5.5   Two (2) 5 lb. ABC fire extinguishers shall be installed in the interior, one front and one rear.

3.5.6   One (1) IL State DOT approved first aid kit shall be supplied and installed within the completed vehicle.

3.5.7   One (1) set of three (3) red emergency reflective triangles with dedicated ABS plastic enclosure shall be provided and installed.

_____END OF SPECIFICATIONS_____

Appendix C

Sample Bookmobile Pre-Construction Questionnaire

Organization: _____ Contact: _____

Project: _____ Date: _____

Patrons:

- ❑ Elderly
- ❑ Children
- ❑ Preschoolers
- ❑ ADA accessible
- ❑ Lift (non-ADA) accessible

Notes: _____

_____

_____

Environment

- ❑ Basically flat
- ❑ Hilly
- ❑ Mountainous
- ❑ Primarily paved roads
- ❑ Primarily nonpaved, dirt roads
- ❑ Off-road
- ❑ House-to-house, very poor road conditions
- ❑ Temperature range (typical) _____
- ❑ Unit housing _____

Notes: _____

_____

_____

Hours of Operation:

- ❑ Daytime
- ❑ Night stops
- ❑ Weekend stops
- ❑ Approximate distance traveled per day, round-trip
- ❑ Approximate weekly hours in service _____

Notes: _____

_____

_____

Type of Service:

- ❏ Provide books and other media
- ❏ Provide programming (story-telling, puppets, etc)
- ❏ Provide refreshments
- ❏ Provide reference literature/brochures
- ❏ Neighborhood block parties
- ❏ Fairs

Notes: _____

_____

_____

Staff:

- ❏ Driver
- ❏ Second staff person
- ❏ Third staff person—regular
- ❏ Third staff person—occasional
- ❏ Fourth staff person—occasional

Notes: _____

_____

_____

Financial:

- ❏ Bid process
- ❏ Low bid requirement
- ❏ Lease option?
- ❏ Payment terms
- ❏ Budget _____

Notes: _____

_____

_____

Chassis & Body Issues:

- ❏ Brand concerns
- ❏ Service issues
- ❏ Body style desired
- ❏ Construction material concerns
- ❏ Diesel
- ❏ Gas

- ❑ CNG
- ❑ Brakes: Air
- ❑ Brakes: Hydraulic
- ❑ Entry doors:_____
- ❑ Front engine
- ❑ Rear engine
- ❑ Transit style—flat-nose
- ❑ Conventional style—traditional school bus (cowl-nose)
- ❑ Stepvan style
- ❑ Cutaway style
- ❑ Low floor style
- ❑ Air suspension
- ❑ Vehicle length restrictions
  - ❑ Parking garage length restriction (describe):_____
  - ❑ Due to terrain of route (describe):_____
- ❑ Vehicle height restrictions
  - ❑ Parking garage height restriction (describe):_____
- ❑ Vehicle weight restriction (describe):_____
  - ❑ No C.D.L. (Commercial Driver's License)

  Notes: _____

  _____

  _____

Interior Amenities:

- ❑ Seating—premium
- ❑ Seating—midline
- ❑ Seating—baseline
- ❑ Bench seating
- ❑ Wheel hump seating
- ❑ Storage desired:_____
- ❑ Side window(s) at desk
- ❑ Desks across front (driver's and passenger's seats swivel to desks)
- ❑ Rear desk
- ❑ People counter(s) at entrance(s)
- ❑ Bulletin boards
- ❑ Refrigerator
- ❑ Microwave
- ❑ Coffeemaker

- ❏ Provisions for file folders
  - ❏ 1 drawer
  - ❏ 2 drawers
  - ❏ Legal
  - ❏ Letter
- ❏ Audio:
  - ❏ AM/FM/Stereo
  - ❏ AM/FM/Stereo/Cassette
  - ❏ CD Player
  - ❏ PA System
  - ❏ Intercom System
- ❏ Carpeting
- ❏ Commercial vinyl flooring
- ❏ Window covering:
  - ❏ Miniblinds
  - ❏ Shades

Notes: _____

_____

_____

Exterior Amenities:

- ❏ Color scheme:_____
- ❏ Simple graphics
- ❏ Full-wrap "traveling billboard" graphics
- ❏ Moderate graphics (somewhere in between simple & wild)
- ❏ Advertising "card yarder" on side exterior
- ❏ Wheelchair lift—underbody
- ❏ Wheelchair lift—interior
- ❏ Leveling system—manual
- ❏ Leveling system—semiautomatic
- ❏ Leveling system—fully automatic
- ❏ Awning—manual
- ❏ Awning—powered
- ❏ Wheel liners—SS

Notes: _____

_____

_____

From *On the Road with Outreach: Mobile Library Services* by Jeannie Dilger-Hill and Erica MacCreaigh, Editors. Santa Barbara, CA: Libraries Unlimited. Copyright © 2010.

Exterior Compartments:

- ❑ Generator
- ❑ Batteries
- ❑ Shoreline
    - ❑ 25' standard
    - ❑ Other: _____
- ❑ Storage (describe):_____
- ❑ Compartment with 4' table with 4 folding chairs

    Notes: _____

    _____

    _____

Air Conditioning and Heat:

- ❑ Cab air conditioning
- ❑ Roof-mounted A/Cs
- ❑ Basement-mounted, ducted A/C system (for overall height restrictions)
- ❑ Wall-mounted thermostats—A/C
- ❑ Heat—electric
- ❑ Heat—propane
- ❑ Heat—hot water
- ❑ Wall-mounted thermostats—heat

    Notes: _____

    _____

    _____

Electrical

- ❑ Shore power at stops (voltage)?_____
- ❑ Generator preference?_____
- ❑ Wiring preference?_____
- ❑ Voltage preference?_____
- ❑ "Generator Off" (inverter) requirements?_____

    Notes: _____

    _____

    _____

Computers:

- ❑ Staff computers (indicate qty.):_____
- ❑ Patron computers (indicate qty.):_____
- ❑ Permanent patron computer station(s)—sit-down, standard desk height

- ❑ Permanent patron computer station(s)—stand-up, counter height
- ❑ Removable patron computer station(s)—adjustable height
- ❑ Each workstation to be equipped with:
    - ❑ Pull-out keyboard tray
    - ❑ Pencil drawer
    - ❑ Chair with tie-downs
    - ❑ Stool with tie-downs
    - ❑ Permanent stool (base-mounted in floor)
    - ❑ Printer mounted above
    - ❑ Networking to central printer
    - ❑ Networking to central server
- ❑ Using laptop computers
- ❑ Back-up requirements:
    - ❑ Back-up of entire computer system for ____ minutes
    - ❑ Back-up of each computer individually
    - ❑ Back-up just long enough to turn off all computers
    - ❑ Power surge protection only
- ❑ Each computer workstation to be equipped with:
    - ❑ Quad electrical outlet below desktop (grommet in desktop)
    - ❑ Cellular antenna and wiring
    - ❑ Hardwired for telephone/data/fax hookup
- ❑ Local Area Network (CAT6)
    - ❑ Include hub

    Notes: _____

    _____

    _____

Lighting:

- ❑ Fluorescent ceiling lights
    - ❑ Powered by inverter/batteries
- ❑ 12-volt fluorescent ceiling lights (run off battery)
- ❑ Porch lights
- ❑ Graphics lighting
- ❑ Exterior perimeter lighting
- ❑ Skylight(s)

    Notes: _____

    _____

    _____

Safety Items:

- ❑ Fire extinguisher(s)
- ❑ Triangle reflector kit
- ❑ Backing alarm
- ❑ Backing camera and monitor
- ❑ First aid kit
- ❑ Egress windows
- ❑ Roof hatch/ventilator/emergency escape
  - ❑ Power
  - ❑ Non-power
- ❑ First aid kit
- ❑ Alarm system

Notes: _____

_____

_____

Shelving:

- ❑ Luan plywood or laminated hardwood
- ❑ Solid hardwoods
- ❑ Aluminum shelving
- ❑ 5" paperback shelving
- ❑ 7"
- ❑ 9" oversized
- ❑ 11" double oversized
- ❑ Magazines
- ❑ Hanging bag rods

Notes: _____

_____

_____

Generator:

- ❑ Size desired:_____
- ❑ Slide-out tray
- ❑ Exhaust routing:_____
- ❑ Gauge/monitoring desired:_____

Notes: _____

_____

_____

Delivery/Inspection of Bookmobile:

- ❑ Training at library
- ❑ Video required
- ❑ Pick-up and training at vendor plant
- ❑ Inspection visit to plant
    - ❑ Indicate number of staff required to visit:_____
    - ❑ Indicate number of visits required:_____
    - ❑ Staff will visit at library's expense—do not include

Notes: _____

_____

_____

Warranty:

- ❑ Extended warranties

Suggested Readings and Resources

OUTREACH SERVICES (GENERAL)

Association of Bookmobile and Outreach Services. Available at: http://abos-outreach.org.

Office for Literacy and Outreach Services. American Library Association. Available at: http://www.ala.org/ala/olos/aboutolos/aboutolos1.cfm.

Osborne, Robin, ed. 2004. *From Outreach to Equity: Innovative Models of Library Policy and Practice.* Chicago: American Library Association.

BOOKMOBILES

Association of Bookmobile and Outreach Services. "Guidelines." Available at: http://www.abos-outreach.org/2008BookmobileGuidelines.pdf.

Meadows, Jan. 2001. "United States Rural Bookmobile Service in the Year 2000." *Bookmobile and Outreach Services* 4 (1) : 47–63.

Titcomb, Mary L. 1951. *The Washington County Free Library: 1901–1951.* Hagerstown, MD: Press of Hagerstown Bookbinding & Printing.

Utah State Library. 2006. "Collection Management Policy Draft, Utah State Library Bookmobile Program." State of Utah. Available at: http://library.utah.gov/about/board/documents/Collection%20Management%20Policy%209-27-06%20Draft.doc.

Writing Specifications

American National Standards Institute. Available at: http://www.ansi.org.

Federal Motor Vehicle Safety Standards. Available at: http://www.fmvss.com.

National Association of Fleet Administrators. Available at: http://www.nafa.org.

National Electrical Code. Available at: http://www.nfpa.org/freecodes/free_access_document.asp.

National Fire Protection Association. Available at: http://www.nfpa.org.

National Highway Traffic Safety Administration. Available at: http://www.nhtsa.dot.gov.

Occupational Safety and Health Administration (OSHA). Available at: http://www.osha.gov.

Society of Automotive Engineers. Available at: http://www.sae.org/servlets/index.

U.S. Department of Transportation. Available at: http://www.dot.gov.

Bookmobile Manufacturers and Consultants

Farber Specialty Vehicles. Available at: http://www.farberspecialty.com.

Matthews Specialty Vehicles, Inc. Available at: http://www.msvehicles.com.

Moroney Bookmobiles. Available at: http://www.moroneybookmobiles.com.

OBS, Inc. Available at: http://www.obsinc.net.

Specialty Vehicle Services, LLC. Available at: http://www.vehiclesuccess.com.

OUTREACH TO IMMIGRANTS AND ENGLISH LANGUAGE LEARNERS

Denver Coalition for Integration. Available at: http://www.denvergov.org/DCI.

Eitner, Mike. 2006. "The Vietnamese Collection at the Denver Public Library: Evolving Needs and Preferences." Colorado Libraries, 32 (4).

Flores, Edward, and Harry Pachon. 2008. "Latinos and Public Library Perceptions." Dublin, OH: OCLC Online Computer Library Center. Available at: http://www.trpi.org/PDFs/Latinos__Public_Library_Perceptions_Final.pdf.

"How to Serve the World @ Your Library." American Library Association, Available at: http://www.ala.org/ala/aboutala/offices/olos/toolkits/LI_toolkit.pdf.

"Mango in Your Library." Mango Languages. Available at: http://www.mangolanguages.com/main/libraries.

Rosetta Stone. Available at: http://www.rosettastone.com.

"Serving Non-English Speakers in U.S. Public Libraries: 2007 Analysis of Library Demographics, Services and Programs." . Chicago, IL: American Library Association Office of Research and Statistics, 2008. Available at: http://www.ala.org/ala/aboutala/offices/olos/nonenglishspeakers/docs/Linguistic_Isolation_Report-2007.pdf.

Spring Institute for Intercultural Learning. Available at: http://www.spring-institute.org.

"U.S.A. Learns." Sacramento County Office of Education. Available at: http://www.usalearns.org.

OUTREACH TO CHILDREN

Fox, Mem. 2008. *Reading Magic.* New York: Harcourt.

Lima, Carolyn W. 2008. *A to Zoo: Subject Access to Children's Picture Books.* Westport: CT: Libraries Unlimited.

Neuman, Susan B., Donna C. Celano, Albert N. Greco, and Pamela Shue, eds. 2001. *Access for All: Closing the Book Gap for Children in Early Education.* Newark, DE: International Reading Association.

OUTREACH TO SENIORS

BookPage—America's Book Review. Available at: http://www.bookpage.com.

Honnold, RoseMary and Saralyn A. Mesaros. 2004. *Serving Seniors*. New York: Neal-Schuman Publishers.

Mates, Barbara T. 2003. *5-Star Programming and Services for Your 55+ Library Customers*. Chicago: American Library Association.

OUTREACH TO PRISONERS

Lehmann, V. 2003. *Planning and Implementing Prison Libraries: Strategies and Resources*. Paper presented at the 69th IFLA Council and General Conference held in Berlin, Germany.

De la Peña McCook, Kathleen. 2004. "Public Libraries and People in Jail." *Reference and User Services Quarterly*, 44 (1), 26–30.

Dowling, B. 2007. "Public Libraries and the Ex-Offender." *Public Libraries* (November/December), 11–18.

Clark, S. and E. MacCreaigh. 2006. *Library Services to the Incarcerated: Applying the Public Library Model in Correctional Facility Libraries*. Westport: Libraries Unlimited.

"Resolution on Prisoners' Right to Read." American Library Association. Available at: http://www.ala.org/ala/mgrps/divs/ascla/asclaissues/prisonrights.cfm.

Rubin, Rhea Joyce and Daniel S. Suvak. 1995. *Libraries Inside: A Practical Guide for Prison Librarians*. Jefferson, NC: McFarland & Company.

Vogel, Brenda. 2002. *Down for the Count: A Prison Library Handbook*. Lanham, MD: Scarecrow Press.

Gilman, I. "Beyond Books: Restorative Librarianship in Juvenile Detention Centers." *Public Libraries* (January/February 2007), 58–66.

LIBRARY PLANNING AND MANAGEMENT

Alire, Camila and Orlando Archibeque. 1998. *Serving Latino Communities*, New York: Neal-Schuman Publishers.

Giesecke, Joan, ed. 1997. *Practical Help for New Supervisors*. Chicago: American Library Association.

Management Help. Available at: http://www.managementhelp.org.

Matthews, Joseph R. 2005. *Strategic Planning and Management for Library Managers*. Westport: Libraries Unlimited.

McNamara, Carter. 2003. *Field Guide to Nonprofit Program Design, Marketing and Evaluation*. Minneapolis: Authenticity Consulting.

Montgomery, Jack G. 2005. *Conflict Management for Libraries: Strategies for a Positive, Productive Workplace*. Chicago: American Library Association.

Nelson, Sarah. *Strategic Planning for Results*. ed., rev. 2008. Chicago: American Library Association.

Stanley, Mary J. 2008. *Managing Library Employees: A How-To-Do-It Manual.* New York: Neal-Schuman Publishers.

WebJunction. Available at: http://www.webjunction.org.

COLLECTION DEVELOPMENT

Dilger-Hill, Jeannie. 2000. "Is Separate Really Equal? The Bookmobile Collections Debate." *Bookmobile and Outreach Services* 3 (2): 28–32.

Disher, Wayne. 2007. *Crash Course in Collection Development.* Westport, CT: Libraries Unlimited.

Doll, Carol Ann. 2002. *Managing and Analyzing Your Collection: A Practical Guide for Small Libraries and School Media Centers.* Chicago: American Library Association.

Evans, G. Edward. 2007. *Developing Library and Information Center Collections.* Westport, CT: Libraries Unlimited.

Hoffmann, Frank. 2005. *Library Collection Development Policies: Academic, Public, and Special Libraries.* Lanham, MD: Scarecrow Press.

Johnson, Peggy. 2009. *Fundamentals of Collection Development and Management.* Chicago: American Library Association.

Index

About the Editors

JEANNIE DILGER-HILL is Director of the La Grange (IL) Public Library, a suburban library serving 15,000 residents. She began her career as a Youth Services Librarian for the St. Louis (MO) Public Library, later worked for the Salem (IN) Public Library, then became Community Outreach Manager for the Monroe County (IN) Public Library for six years, and Outreach Services Manager for King County Library (WA) System for three years, where she oversaw eight outreach vehicles and three jail/juvenile detention libraries. Most recently, she was a Library Consultant for the Metropolitan Library System, consulting for over 500 public, school, academic, and special libraries in the Chicago metropolitan area. A 2006 *Library Journal* "Mover and Shaker," Ms. Dilger-Hill holds an MSLS from University of North Carolina-Chapel Hill, has long been active in various state library associations, and is a past-president of the Association of Bookmobile and Outreach Services.

ERICA MAcCREAIGH holds an MLIS from the University of Wisconsin-Milwaukee and has 19 years of experience in Colorado libraries, including 6 years in public library outreach and 5 years in correctional libraries. She served as Arapahoe Library District's Bookmobile Librarian for three years, then as Outreach Coordinator for two-and-a-half years, during which time she supervised early childhood literacy services, homebound delivery, bookmobile, foreign language services, and the county jail library. In 2007, she became a Senior Consultant with the Colorado State Library where she oversees operations at nine state prison libraries serving nearly 5,000 inmate patrons. Ms. MacCreaigh co-chairs the Colorado Association of Libraries Continuing Education Committee and is a frequent workshop presenter at local, state, and national conferences. She coauthored *Library Services to the Incarcerated: Applying the Public Library Model in Correctional Facility Libraries*, published by Libraries Unlimited in 2006.

About the Contributors

Julie Abbott ("Mobile Library Collections" and "Bookmobile Services to Urban and Suburban Communities") is a 1989 graduate of the University of Michigan School of Information and Library Science. She has 18 years of experience on the road, first as Bookmobile Librarian at South Brunswick Public Library in New Jersey, 1990–1992, and as Outreach Services Manager at Cook Memorial Library in northern Illinois, 1992–present.

Jeremy Andrykowski ("Vehicle Maintenance") is the Circulation Services Supervisor at Arlington Heights Memorial Library in Illinois and has several years' experience supervising bookmobile services. A self-professed automotive enthusiast who loves the art of technology, he has devoted himself to studying the machinations of vehicles of all types, including bookmobiles.

Candice Brown ("Planning and Marketing Outreach Services") began her library career as Homebound Librarian at the Aurora Public Library in Colorado. She then moved to the Arapahoe Library District, where she was Extension Services Manager for 10 years, managing homebound services, mobile library services, and the jail library. She also established the library's early literacy program, Begin with Books. After serving as Adult Services Manager and then Manager of the main library, she moved east, where she served as Director of the New Britain Public Library in New Britain, Connecticut before assuming her current position as Director of the Clifton Public Library in Clifton, New Jersey.

Pilar Castro-Reino ("Library Services to Immigrants and English Language Learners") has lived in the United States for 24 years. In 1984, she earned her GED and proceeded to study for her Associate's Degree, Bachelor's and then MLS degree. She received her MLS from the University of Arizona in 1993. In 1994, she joined the Denver Public Library in Colorado, providing customer services and programming in Spanish and English, and is now the Learning and Language Cluster Manager.

For 19 years, **Bernie Garrison** ("Lobby Stop Service to Nursing Homes and Retirement Facilities") managed the Outreach Services Division of the Columbus Metropolitan Library in Ohio. During his tenure, programming expanded to include lobby stop service, books-by-mail, preschooler bookmobiles, and the establishment of the Raising

Reader's program. He also contributed to a turnkey customer service packet entitled *CLASS: Customers Leaving Appreciative, Satisfied and Sold.* Semi-retired, Mr. Garrison recently returned to the Willoughby-Eastlake Public Library where his career began in 1976.

Theresa Gemmer ("Serving Preschool Children and Childcare Providers"), a veteran bookmobile patron from childhood, holds an MLIS from the University of Washington. After working five years as Assistant Director/Youth Services Librarian at San Juan Island Library, she came to Everett Public Library in Washington state, where she has served as Outreach Services manager and Bookmobile Librarian for the past 12 years.

Emily Klopstein ("Library Services to Immigrants and English Language Learners") is the Senior Librarian at Denver Public Library's Hadley branch in Colorado, having joined the Library's Language and Learning team in 2007. A graduate of UCLA, Klopstein worked for five years with the diverse populations of public library customers in Los Angeles, so hearing English, Vietnamese, and Spanish at the public service desk makes her feel right at home.

Mary Anne Marjamaa ("Serving School-Age Children") is a librarian and has been the manager of Outreach Services for the St. Louis County Library in Missouri for 10 years. The County Library has 10 mobile units that serve school children, preschoolers, seniors, and the homebound. She is an active member and on the board of the Association of Bookmobile and Outreach Services. She has spoken at American Library Association conferences on Outreach Services.

Kathleen Mayo ("Books-by-Mail") has over 35 years of experience in library outreach. She directed library programs at a large mental health treatment facility and was a consultant at the State Library of Florida. Since 1989 she has been the Outreach Services Manager for the Lee County Library System in Fort Myers, Florida, where she directs Assistive Technology, Bookmobile, Books-by-Mail, Literacy, Senior Outreach, and Talking Book programs.

A long-time prisoner rights activist, **Maggie McFalls-Picher's** ("Library Services to Incarcerated Adults") first post-college job was as a paralegal for a death penalty defense firm in Oregon. Realizing she wanted to work more directly with inmates, she decided that prison libraries offered the perfect balance of activism and service. After receiving her MLS from the University of Pittsburgh and working for a few years in public libraries, she is now a librarian at the Ontario Correctional Institute (OCI), a medium security men's prison outside of Toronto, Ontario.

Jan Meadows ("Rural Bookmobile Services") is Mobile Library Services Coordinator at the Pikes Peak Library District in Colorado, where she has worked for 22 years. She has spoken at Association of Bookmobile and Outreach Services (ABOS) and American Libraries Association (ALA) conferences as well as the Mobile Libraries Conference in Taupo, New Zealand. She writes the ALA "21st Century Bookmobiles" column and is published in several books and journals.

Lisa Murillo ("Library Services to Immigrants and English Language Learners"), Senior Librarian for the Woodbury Branch, has worked for the Denver Public Library in Colorado for more than 10 years. She holds an MLIS and a BA in Journalism from Florida State University. She has presented workshops for the Colorado Association of Libraries and the Public Library Association and served as the president of Colorado's REFORMA chapter in 2004.

Lou Petterchak ("Library Services to Immigrants and English Language Learners") is the Senior Librarian at the Ross-Barnum branch of the Denver Public Library in Colorado. He graduated from the University of Illinois Graduate School of Library and Information Science in 1989. He has been employed at the Denver Public Library since 1991 in the Government Publications & Business Reference and General Reference Departments prior to his assignment to the Ross-Barnum branch in 2003.

Before working in Outreach, **Ruth Pettibone** ("Serving Preschool Children and Childcare Providers") served as the Assistant Manager/Youth Services Librarian at the Hilltonia Branch of the Columbus Metropolitan Library in Ohio for seven years. She is now the Assistant Manager of the Outreach Services Division at the Columbus Metropolitan Library where she has served seniors and youth for 14 years.

Scott Pointon ("Designing Your New Bookmobile") is Director of the Des Plaines Valley Public Library District in Illinois. He has worked in public libraries since 1992 and spent many of those years directly managing outreach services. He presents frequently at the annual Association of Bookmobile and Outreach Services (ABOS) conference as well as the American Library Association (ALA), Indiana Library Federation (ILF), and Illinois Library Association (ILA) conferences. He recently published an article in *Public Libraries* magazine, entitled, "Library Outreach is the Future."

Becky Russell ("Library Services to Immigrants and English Language Learners") is Senior Librarian at the Hampden Branch of the Denver Public Library in Colorado; she also has experience in children's services and with the Burnham Hoyt Department for popular materials. Previously, she worked in the Colorado State Library's Library Research Service department.

Amy Varner Stephens ("Managing Outreach Staff") began her professional career as a Children's librarian at the Broken Arrow branch of the Tulsa City County Library System in Oklahoma. She managed two branches before becoming Outreach Services Department Manager for 12 years. Today, she is the manager of the Martin Regional Library of the Tulsa City-County Library System, a large branch serving a multicultural community.

Michael Swendrowski ("Writing Vehicle Specifications") is founder and president of Specialty Vehicle Services, LLC., a professional consultation firm with high focus on library outreach vehicles. After nearly 20 years on the manufacturing side, he now serves on the American Library Association's Subcommittee on Bookmobiles and independently assists libraries worldwide in determining their vehicle needs, developing vehicle specifications, and managing and inspecting the construction of outreach vehicles.

Teresa Valenti ("Library Services to Incarcerated Youth") has worked in just about every department in all types of libraries. Her work experience includes three years as supervising librarian for the Youthful Offender System in Pueblo, Colorado. She also supervised correctional libraries for adult female offenders and mentally-ill male offenders. Currently, she is Technical Services Manager for the Pueblo City-County Library District.

As manager of the Community Services department of the Arlington Heights Memorial Library in Illinois, **Joyce Voss** ("Homebound Delivery Service") is responsible for the Bookmobile, ESL/Literacy, School Services, Senior Services, Institutional Services and other outreach in the community including homebound. She is a speaker and workshop presenter on outreach topics.

Previous to undertaking the position of Systems Manager for the Charleston County Library in Charleston, South Carolina, **Tom Walker** ("Automating Your Bookmobile with Communications Technologies") was the Field Product Support Manager for Geac Computers in Markham, Ontario. Since 2000, he has served the Charleston County Library bookmobile users and staff by managing online circulation and Internet connectivity via satellite, cellular, SIP2, and WiFi technologies.